the
social documentary
photography
of
milton rogovin

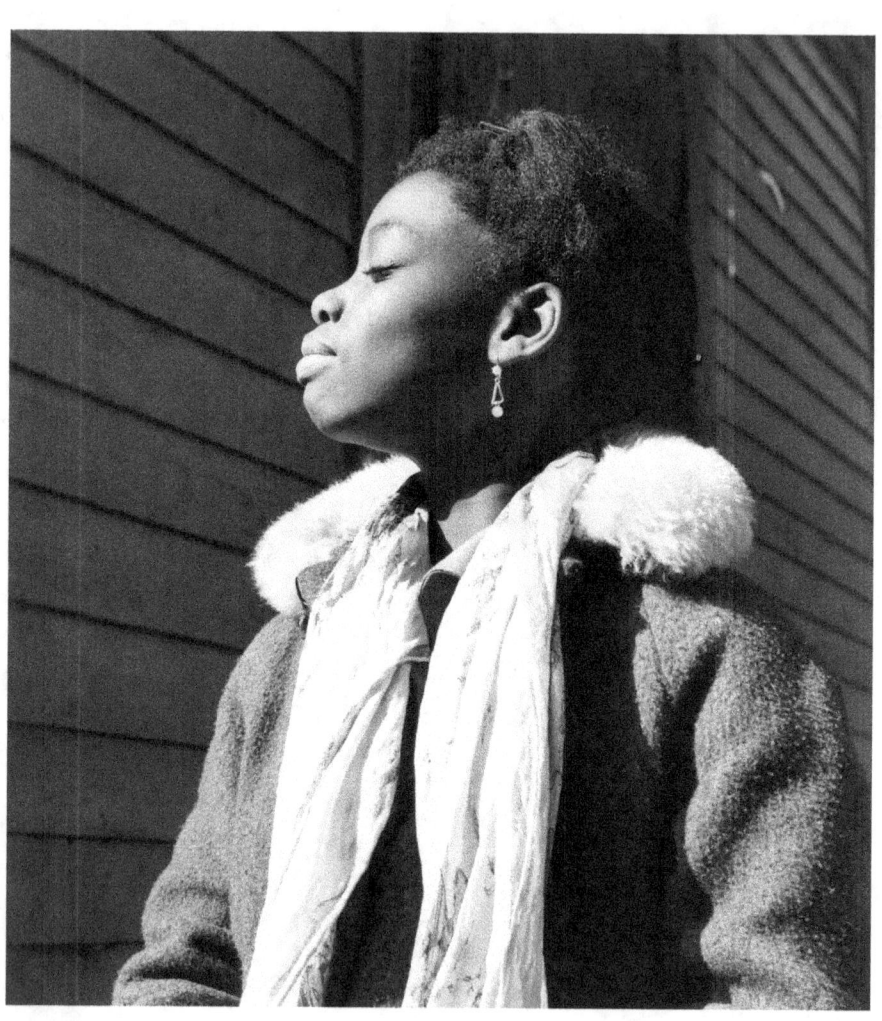

the social documentary photography of milton rogovin

EDITED BY **CHRISTOPHER FULTON**

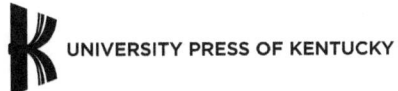 UNIVERSITY PRESS OF KENTUCKY

Scholarly publisher for the Commonwealth,
serving Bellarmine University, Berea College, Centre
College of Kentucky, Eastern Kentucky University,
The Filson Historical Society, Georgetown College,
Kentucky Historical Society, Kentucky State University,
Morehead State University, Murray State University,
Northern Kentucky University, Transylvania University,
University of Kentucky, University of Louisville,
and Western Kentucky University.
All rights reserved.

Editorial and Sales Offices: The University Press of Kentucky
663 South Limestone Street, Lexington, Kentucky 40508-4008
www.kentuckypress.com

Untitled, *East Side—Home,* 1961–1963. The Rogovin Collection,
Chicago. Copyright © Milton Rogovin. Courtesy, Center for
Creative Photography, University of Arizona Foundation.

Library of Congress Cataloging-in-Publication Data

Names: Fulton, Christopher B., editor.
Title: The social documentary photography of Milton Rogovin / edited by
    Christopher Fulton.
Description: Lexington, Kentucky : University Press of Kentucky, [2019] |
    Includes bibliographical references and index.
Identifiers: LCCN 2019014994| ISBN 9780813177489 (pbk. : alk. paper) | ISBN
    9780813177496 (pdf) | ISBN 9780813177502 (epub)
Subjects: LCSH: Working class—Portraits. | Documentary photography. |
    Rogovin, Milton, 1909-2011.
Classification: LCC TR681.W65 S63 2019 | DDC 770.92—dc23

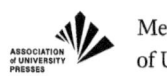

Member of the Association
of University Presses

Contents

Contents

Photo gallery appears after page 60

Preface

SOMETIME IN 1986, I RECEIVED a phone call from Milton Rogovin at my home in Buffalo, New York. Milton was already recognized far beyond Buffalo as an eminent documentary photographer. But I had come to know him through the American studies program at State University of New York at Buffalo, in which I was a faculty member. Already in his seventies, Rogovin had become a graduate student, earning an American studies master's degree and teaching documentary photography and darkroom technique. My friend and faculty colleague Dick Blau had come to Buffalo from Yale to help launch a radically different American studies program and create the Buffalo Theater Workshop; he went on to be the longtime head of the Film Department at the University of Wisconsin at Milwaukee. But he was then just becoming a photographer and grabbed the opportunity in our program to work under Rogovin. Dick has always said that although everyone could see Milton was a great photographer, few appreciated his consummate skill as a photographic printmaker and how much that skill had to do with his art. From hours together in the darkroom, Dick had come to marvel at how Milton intensified the textures and sharpened the contrasts so essential to the impact of his distinct photographic portrait style—as can be seen in so many of the images in the book you are holding.

Milton was calling me to explore an idea for a collaboration. In the late 1970s, he had produced a well-known series of portraits of workers in Buffalo's steel mills and shops, pairing a portrait at work with one taken at the worker's home. But every single facility in which he had taken these photographs, he told me, had closed by 1986. Every single worker in those photographs had lost his or her job in steel. And so, he mused, the subjects of his photos were a kind of "leading human indicators" of a profound transformation in American industry, in our city, and in our society. What had happened to them? What might their stories have to say about these changes?

He had already begun rephotographing earlier photographic subjects, including some of the steelworkers. How about my developing a text about Buffalo's steelworkers to accompany his then-and-now portraits? he proposed. You know, like *Let Us Now Praise Famous Men,* he joked (or maybe it wasn't a joke)—he would play Walker Evans, and I could play James Agee.

Well, I certainly thought of Milton as a photographer in the same league as Walker Evans, but I had to tell him I was a very far cry from James Agee and that in any event their book had been a flop upon publication and for many years afterward, due mainly to Agee's over-the-top prose. I was, however, getting pretty involved in oral history at that point: How about instead of James Agee, I played Studs Terkel? I could interview the workers in his photographs from the 1970s, asking about the impact of the plant closings on their lives and what they thought about it all. We framed a proposal to link photographs and extensive oral histories and shopped it to what turned out to be some ten publishers. They all rejected it, either because of the daunting costs of the high-quality duotone photographic reproduction Rogovin insisted on or because of my insistence on long life-review interviews without the usual academic commentary standing in between interview subjects and readers. Finally, we found Peter Agree, then an editor at Cornell University Press, who really got it. *Portraits in Steel* appeared in 1993 as a general trade book in a beautiful large-scale format designed by Cornell.

Some details in this personal story provide framing clues to Rogovin's broader work, to the Hite Art Institute exhibition of 2016, titled *Milton Rogovin and the Photography of Conscience,* and to the sparkling essays responding to the donation of Rogovin photographs to the Photographic Archives of University of Louisville—all brought together by Christopher Fulton in this powerful book.

Milton was a proud, exacting artisan concerning his photography, determined that it should be presented at the highest professional level in any exhibit or publications. But as he emerged into prominence, he also came to feel limited by the professional photography venues and museum catalogs for which such presentation was natural. He was a radical activist and a labor and political organizer long before he was a photographer and remained so throughout his life; he was a fixture at weekly peace demonstrations in Buffalo pretty much up until his death at 101. He was driven to have his art serve a social purpose and to speak to audiences beyond the orbit of photography as such. His proposal for a book grounded in social issues was part of a broader determination to move beyond the reach of "coffee table" art books in which he feared he might be imprisoned.

He would have been proud of the exhibition *Photography of Conscience* and of the essays exploring this defining dimension of his work from many different vantages. The essays here also evoke a more complex biographical dimension. Milton turned to photography only after he had become a victim of McCarthyite purges of radicals. These purges made him and his family pariahs in Buffalo in the 1950s and destroyed his optometric practice. Out of this pain came his turn to documentary photography as well as a drive and determination that propelled his work very powerfully—a drive not only for social justice but also for personal redemption and recognition. Aspiring to *Let Us Now Praise Famous Men* was part of that. But it was deeper—and led him to the full completion of more ambitious projects conducted all around the world. It made his eighties and even his nineties perhaps the most powerful and creative period of his long life. This explosive range of work was well represented in the unique *Photography of Conscience* show and is explored thoughtfully in the following essays.

One other dimension central to our *Portraits in Steel* collaboration involved Rogovin's increasing focus on direct engagement—people presenting themselves directly to the camera. A rich personal connection to human subjects is not always (or even often) associated with activist photographers driven by a social vision. But it has been definitional in Rogovin's work: a modest, respectful commitment to recording the full humanity of the people he photographed and to encouraging their self-presentation, which he understood it to be his responsibility to receive. As has often been observed, he did not "take" pictures—his subjects gave them to him.

This commitment characterized not just the photography but in fact every interaction with his subjects, based on equality and reciprocity—and friendship. It is palpable in the photos he took in the field, where he was usually accompanied by his wife, Anne. She was a full and active partner in building the field relationships animating his photography, whether in mines in China or Cuba or in the neighborhood of Buffalo that became his remarkable *Lower West Side* series. As I pursued the interviews for *Portraits in Steel*, I found all I needed to mention was my partnership with Milton, and every door would open with the warmest of greetings.

The quality of the photographic work provided a template for the interviews themselves: literally, in that I basically asked people to talk about some photographs and let the story of their work and life spiral out from that. But also more deeply in that I modeled my interviews on the respectful receipt of each person's self-presentation that I find at the core of Rogovin's photography—perhaps the greatest expression of the photography of conscience explored in this book.

As I release the reader to explore the riches that follow, let me offer an intriguing accompaniment in an appropriately contemporary digital mode.

In recent years, I have been working with new digital tools for direct-media (not transcript) indexing of oral history and other large audio-video collections. As an experiment, I applied these tools to the original interviews in *Portraits in Steel*. My colleagues and I produced a video presentation combining interview audio clips with Rogovin's portraits of some people in our book. This is not a finished or "produced" work, but simply a first attempt at presenting powerful portraits that engage and hold attention while the viewer listens to the voice of the actual subject. It's a simple and obvious idea, but surprisingly—or maybe not so surprisingly—one for which there are very few sustained examples in the long history of documentary photography.

It was a great privilege to have this experiment presented in the *Photography of Conscience* exhibit at the Hite Institute, shown in a multimedia stream on a large screen in an adjacent gallery. To hear voices of some of the people in the photographs actually seemed, in a wonderfully paradoxical way, to heighten the impact of the silent photographs in the main gallery, confirming in a deeper way the imaginative power of Rogovin's portraiture.

Hoping the installation may provide something similar for readers of this book, the University Press of Kentucky and I have made it available through the press's website (www.kentuckypress.com). There are four subjects and about six to eight minutes of clips per subject.

Michael Frisch
Buffalo, New York
February 2018

Introduction

Christopher Fulton

THIS BOOK IS DEDICATED TO the photography of ordinary working- and lower-class people, men and women from the bottom rungs of society who construct their personal and communal identity in subcultures that are underappreciated and seldom seen. It concerns visual material that describes this stratum's way of life and articulates the self-awareness of people who are consistently neglected by the mass media and other vehicles of public representation.

The pictures filling this volume were taken by the social documentary photographer Milton Rogovin (1909–2011), who lived and worked in Buffalo, New York, and traveled widely to record communities around the world. The book is inspired by a recent gift of his photographs to the University of Louisville, which was graciously arranged by the collector and photo critic David Knaus and facilitated by the photographer's son, Mark Rogovin. In the autumn of 2015, this donation was celebrated with an exhibition at the university's Hite Art Institute and a symposium on the artist and his work.

Previous publications about Rogovin's photography tend to focus on his personal biography and seek to validate his artistic project in laudatory prose. The present anthology takes a different approach. By attending more closely to the images themselves and delving into the social issues they raise, it broadens the range of discussion and elucidates the photographs through multiple analytical frames. The major essay, "Photography with a Conscience," begins this program of inquiry by describing Rogovin's creative process and questioning the ways in which the pictures are received by viewers and convey the experiences of the portrayed subjects. This essay is followed by a series of shorter pieces examining the photographs from the various disciplinary perspectives of the authors, most of whom are faculty members at the University of Louisville. These contributions take up a diversity of issues and concerns and show the photographs' potential to generate new meaning in response to new questions.

The photo historian John Szarkowski liked to discriminate between a photograph's "subject matter" and its "subject." The former refers to that which is plainly visible and identifiable in a photograph: the pictorial content that is explicitly shown. The latter is the underlying or justifying idea a photograph alludes to: the essential theme addressed by the image but not overtly manifest in it. In the case of the Rogovin pictures, one might say that the *subject matter* is individual blue-collar workers and members of the underclass, along with their family members, whereas the ultimate *subject* is the vibrant and variegated life of the lower class as a whole, a population kept down by rigid social systems and exploited by global forces of economic production. Taken singly, the separate photographs offer portraits of individuals or small groups set in their native environment and surrounded by material articles that reflect their social position and style of life. Taken as a whole, the entire corpus of photographs describes the common experience of the lower classes—their daily work, avocations and interests, modes of interaction, material culture, and sense of self and community.

Rogovin affiliated with the political Left and was motivated by an abiding concern for social justice. His photographs were conceived as tools to effect a deeper understanding of lower-class life, both for members of that social stratum and for people from other class positions. By transmitting knowledge of subaltern populations, the pictures are educative, and Rogovin hoped they might inspire the struggle for social and political change. Several of the essays from this anthology address the political function of the photographs by setting them in relationship to Marxist thought, the culture of Popular Frontism, and the political orientation of academic social history.

What is perhaps most unusual and striking about the photographs is their elegant simplicity and calmness. They are unpretentious and unsensational images, mainly showing figures posed in balanced compositions, illuminated under clarifying light, and picked out in sharp, high-resolution, black-and-white prints. These modest, straightforward pictures diverge from epic representations of working-class subjects by photographers such as Lewis Hine and Sebastião Salgado as well as from images of utter decrepitude by operators such as Jacob Riis and Kevin Carter. Nor do they resemble the objectivizing pictures taken by August Sander, who employed portrait photography to produce a taxonomic survey of his society. They are instead sympathetic portrayals of individuals in their homes, neighborhoods, and places of work, filled with detailed information from which their personal stories can be (partly and imperfectly) gleaned.

Rogovin worked alone, although occasionally accompanied on photo shoots by his wife, and enjoyed neither institutional support nor gallery representation. He operated on a shoestring and practiced optometry to support his family during much of his photographic career. His effort and persistence are truly astonishing, and his large body of work testifies to his extraordinary dedication to his subject and solidarity with those whose lives he so sensitively recorded. Sustaining this herculean labor was a steadfast commitment to social justice, arising from his experience of the Great Depression and informed by Marxist philosophy.

In taking pictures, Rogovin adopted an uncomplicated, workmanlike procedure, relying on a no-frills Rolleiflex camera fitted to a portable tripod. He didn't want to spy on his subjects by stealthily taking their picture unawares, and he didn't want to usurp their self-presentation by closely managing the photographic situation or by asserting his presence as the creative agent behind the camera. He wanted his sitters to exercise their own agency and become cocreators of their photographic image. In most of the photographs, they look directly into the camera with full awareness that their picture is being taken; they assume poses of their own choosing and are frequently invited to select the specific location where the portrait is to be made. Even candid shots find subjects in their daily haunts, be it a neighborhood bar, dance studio, or social club, and for the most part they appear completely at home in these settings and ultimately in control of the photographic situation.

Like everybody else, the people appearing in the photographs must live within the particular social conditions of their time and place. Whatever

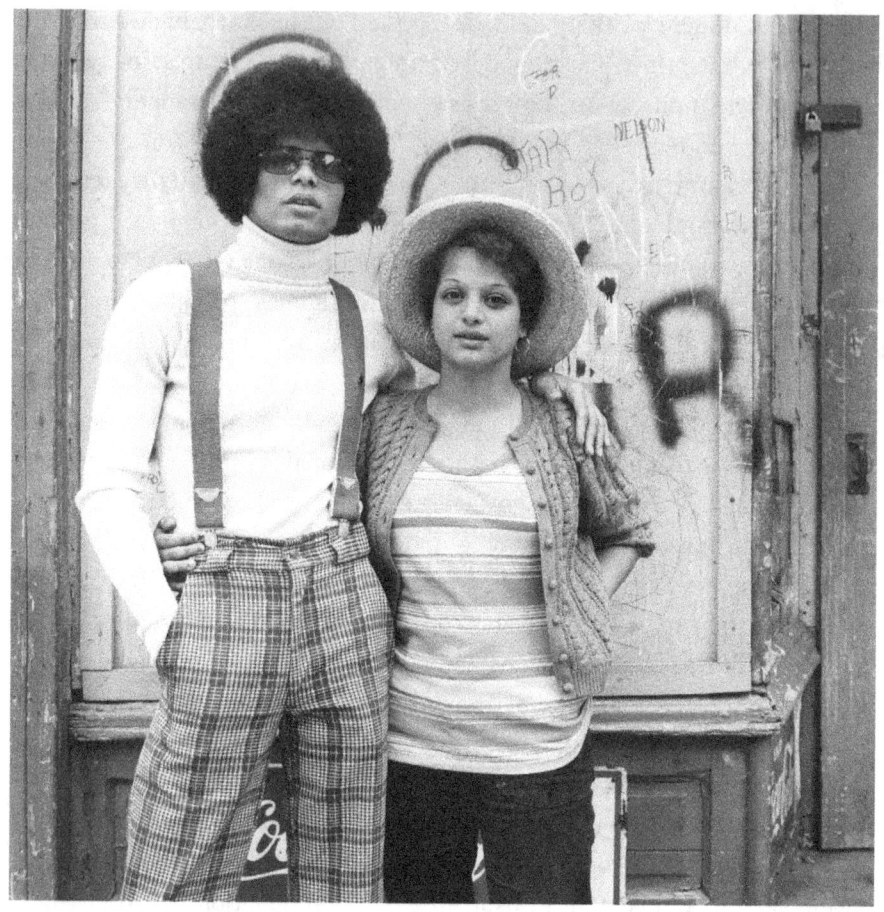

Untitled, *Lower West Side—Quartets,* 1992. The Rogovin Collection, Chicago. Copyright © Milton Rogovin. Courtesy, Center for Creative Photography, University of Arizona Foundation.

privilege is granted to them in constructing their self-image, they are inevitably subordinated to the social and economic structures and hegemonic culture of late-twentieth-century modernity. We thus find them in domestic spaces filled with mass-produced commercial goods, accompanied by images drawn from popular culture; they don the latest fashions, mimic the airs of public idols, and gravitate toward pastimes commonly shared within their social group. These elements form the language in which they constitute their personal identity and project their self-image in daily life and in the photographs. In addition, these elements are often blended and organized into templates that a person puts on to emulate one of many socially recognized types—for example, the carefree hipster, the man of cultivated taste, the dutiful working mother. The photographs define and objectify these templates and present to the sitters a specular image of themselves in their assumed identities. Subjects can see in their portraits the degree to which they have embodied their chosen templates and approximated their ego ideals. Of course, the clear danger here is that they might grow satisfied in conforming to the prescribed templates, thus limiting their range of self-expression, and they might become complacent in obeying the standards and expectations associated with their adopted roles and thus not seek to challenge them through transgressive gestures or political action. Similarly, other viewers of the photographs may be tempted to regard the portrayed figures as essentially content in their social position and may indiscriminately set them into narrow categories of subalternity without concern for their complex subjectivities or achievements as social actors.

However, the photographs also show evidence of individuals selecting and combining elements from the general culture in a creative process of self-fashioning that is not confined by specular templates; for instance, a person will be seen to decorate her home with miscellaneous items freely selected from the marketplace or to choose to wear certain articles of dress in novel combinations or to embrace unexpected hobbies and leisure activities, and so forth. The photographs illustrate the outcome of this self-fashioning as individuals present themselves knowingly to the camera with appropriated objects, images, and gestures. One witnesses a high level of inventiveness and combinatory skill in their taking from the culture, and one sometimes discerns a proud individualism and even rebelliousness against social norms.

The rhetoric of documentary photography commonly avers that the photographic process affords a direct reflection of the visible world and is uniquely more truthful than other representational mediums. But the Rogovin photographs make no such claim. They are not snapshots that pretend to capture a pregiven, found reality, nor are they unbiased sources of data suitable for scientific or classifying analysis. To a greater or lesser extent, depending on the specific circumstances in which they were made, the photographs are formally composed, and their representational content is purposively constructed; the creative process also frequently involves a measure of precogitation and artifice on the part of both sitters and cameraman. Moreover, the willful production of the images remains quite transparent and may be easily detected in the self-conscious posing of figures as well as in the tight framing, artificial lighting, selective cropping and dodging, and other manipulations by the photographer. Unlike purer or "straighter" forms of documentary photography, the Rogovin pictures are cast as dignified representations that grant their subjects authorial agency and elevate them as persons worthy of formal portraiture.

Within the history of photography, socially conscious operators have constantly struggled with the problem of how best to represent poverty and social disadvantage. How do you show the face of privation without shaming the people you portray? How do you avoid condescension and the voyeurism that puts the privileged viewer on a higher plane than the photographed subject? The complexities of this issue are thoughtfully explored in *Stranger with a Camera* (2000), a documentary film by Elizabeth Barret that investigates the tragic death of Canadian television journalist Hugh O'Connor. Working in poor districts of eastern Kentucky in 1967, O'Connor unintentionally stirred up hostility among local residents, who felt their dignity was being violated. One angry landowner decided to take matters in his own hands by murdering the journalist while he was filming on the man's property. More recently, resentment greeted the national airing of Diane Sawyer's televised documentary *A Hidden America: Children of the Mountains* (2009) for the ABC news magazine 20/20. A native of Kentucky, Sawyer wished to publicize the toxic mix of poverty and drug addiction in her home state, but in the process she provoked virulent protest from locals, who felt the program turned them into objects of scorn and derision.

Rogovin hoped to avoid these traps by recording another kind of truth: the truth seen through the eyes of the subjects themselves and in the light in which they wished to have themselves portrayed. This strategy is at the heart of his achievement in documentary photography. It involves a method of image making in which the photographer intentionally dials down his rhetorical and artistic skill to avoid speaking for his subjects or otherwise imposing his ideas on them. By restraining his artistry, he allows his subjects to tell their own stories and define their own identities. The completed photographs aspire to a knowledge and intelligence, a self-conception, a view of the world that arise from below, among the lower classes, rather than from above through the personal views of the photographer or in terms of official discourses on poverty and social class.

It is necessary, of course, to distinguish between a photographer's declared aspirations and the actual effect his pictures have. In exploring this disjuncture in Rogovin's work, one may initially observe that his attempt to represent the "truth" of subaltern subjects involves a decisive editing out of information that might confuse or contradict that truth. For example, nearly all the photographs portray figures in relaxed and self-possessed states and avoid showing disagreeable aspects of their character or the abject circumstances in which some of them live, even though these things are also determinative of their identity and outlook on the world. Before accepting the photographs as reliable sources of evidence about lower-class life, one must recognize that they give partial and slanted views of the sitters in accordance with Rogovin's expressed desire to render the better side of their nature.

There is, furthermore, the issue of Rogovin's creative intervention and manipulation of the images. While he did forgo some popular techniques of artistic photography, such as dramatic lighting and oblique camera angles, in the interest of suppressing his own voice in favor of his subjects', he nevertheless closely controlled the taking of photographs and development of prints in the darkroom. At each stage of the creative process, he exercised much artistic skill and discrimination to produce images that seem to disclose the independent truth of the lower classes but are in fact profoundly touched by his personal aesthetic sensibility and ideas about his subject. And so we are led back to the classic problem of photographic objectivity and the truth-value of documentary photography. Although Rogovin explored a realm of truth that few operators in the history of the medium have tried to capture, its representation was filtered through his artistic technique and taste as well as bound to his socialist vision and political objectives.

Rogovin's discursive practice—from his selection of subject matter, shooting of scenes, and development of prints to the dissemination of photographs in illustrated books and public exhibitions and their reception by diverse audiences—emerges as the major concern of the essays in the present volume. These studies connect his work with intellectual and political currents of his time and explore the situational and historically specified character of his photographic activity. They further show that the meaning of the pictures is predicated on the many contexts of their circulation and use. Though the pictures appear at first glance to be rather simple, unambiguous representations, they in fact possess a discursive content that is complex, flexible, and multivalent, and their meaning is not stable but must be negotiated by each audience and in each interpretive context.

The major essay of the book, "Photography with a Conscience," investigates Rogovin's creative process and representational strategy. It considers the execution of the photographs in separate and well-defined series, each dedicated to a single theme or geographical region, and it queries the documentary value of these targeted projects. Finally, the essay contends with the reception of the photographs by diverse audiences as well as with the possibilities and difficulties of interpreting the pictures on the basis of viewers' prior knowledge.

The broad sweep of this essay is followed by seven shorter pieces on narrower issues related to the authors' fields of study. The variety of topics and approaches does not in any measure exhaust the scope of inquiry into the photographs but rather illustrate their value in inspiring new lines of investigation.

The first of these pieces, by Elizabeth E. Reilly, discusses the recent donation of Rogovin photographs to the University of Louisville Photographic Archives. Reilly relates the gift to the university's prior holdings, especially the work of photographers employed in the mid-1930s by the Farm Security Administration, whose head, Roy Stryker, chose the University of Louisville as the repository for his personal papers and more than nineteen hundred vintage prints. She further connects the gift to the university's collections of photographs commissioned by Standard Oil Company of New Jersey and the Jones and Laughlin Steel Company. Reilly describes the shared interests between Rogovin and the photographers working for these corporations as well as other socially conscious operators represented in the archive. The main strength of the university's collection lies in the area of social documentary photography, and the recent donation significantly augments and enriches this concentration.

The second essay, by Thomas B. Byers, focuses on the *Family of Miners* series. Byers discusses the series in terms of Marxist revolutionary rhetoric, exemplified above all by the *Communist Manifesto* of 1848, and connects the photographs with the radical political tradition to which Rogovin belonged. Byers criticizes the prevailing opinion that celebrates Rogovin as a liberal humanist, arguing that he should instead be understood as a politically committed, socialist photographer (albeit with strong humanistic proclivities). With regard to these divergent positions, one may recall Hilton Kramer's mixed review of an exhibition of Rogovin photographs at the International Center of Photography in New York. Writing for the *New York Times* on February 21, 1976, Kramer admired the "patient and affectionate exchange between the photographer and his subjects" but went on to say that the pictures contain no radical spark and are constrained by "the limit of a sweet, old-fashioned liberalism." Rogovin recoiled from these condescending remarks, and in rebuttal he defended his photography as a tool for consciousness raising and as a viable weapon in the struggle for social reform. Nevertheless, it is certainly true, as Byers states, that Rogovin did not often identify himself as a faithful Communist and rarely invoked the names of Marx, Lenin, or other socialist thinkers when discussing his photography. Byers looks into this evasion, too, and places it in the context of the chronic failure of the Communist Party USA to unify the working class into a cohesive force of revolutionary change.

Cynthia Negrey attends to another group of photographs from the *Working People* series, which includes portraits of Buffalo factory workers before and after the steel industry collapse of the early 1980s. Whereas Byers examines the rhetorical function of the pictures within Marxist discourse, Negrey moves from the *Working People* series to meditate on the rise and fall of Buffalo's industrial economy, which at its peak comprised a dozen or more steel-production facilities and manufacturing plants. She further contemplates the human cost of the downturn and finds it poignantly revealed in Rogovin's portraits of workers and their families, which are sometimes set into diptychs, with images of subjects before the economic slump paired with images of the same persons after the catastrophe.

It is notable that the *Working People* series was made during a phase of history when industrial capitalism was in a process of transformation through globalized systems of manufacture, trade, and finance. Tellingly, the steel crisis was one of the first shocks to American heavy industry as it confronted the new, integrated world economy. It made dramatically apparent the disruptive force of globalization, which weighed most heavily on the backs of blue-collar workers. Rogovin's photographs of men and women thrown out of their jobs or in other ways coping with the regional malaise are directly tied to global currents that shifted steel production from the titanic mills of Buffalo, Cleveland, and Pittsburgh to new centers in Japan, India, and China. Rogovin knew full well he was recording an industrial sector in decline and modes of labor that were fast disappearing. To document this passing era, when he ventured into steel mills, coal mines, or manufacturing plants, he sought out older, more traditional facilities where the use of raw muscle power was still prominent. And he generally photographed workers tasked with the toughest, most physically demanding jobs, such as chiseling smooth the interiors of great ingot molds or welding steel plates with large torches. In a similar vein, when he photographed people in private homes or communal spaces, he was depicting a working-class culture before it became transformed by the homogenizing influence of the Internet and cable television and the wide availability of mass-communication technologies. These changes affecting cultural practice, like those in heavy industry, altered working-class life forever. And when we encounter the photographs today, we see them as historical documents, records of a bygone era rather than reflections of current reality.

In an essay that considers her own professional activity as a social and oral historian, Tracy E. K'Meyer contends with the documentary value of Rogovin's photography and the difference between visual and verbal sources of historical information. She comments on the problem of neutrality in the gathering of this information and the reliability of personal testimony after it has been processed and filtered by a photographer or oral interviewer. Although fraught with such methodological problems, both social documentary photography and oral history bring to light material that is otherwise difficult to access and open up new areas for historical study. K'Meyer's essay further questions whether documentary photography and oral history effectively promote social reform by uncovering the harsh conditions of lower-class life or whether these practices serve only to elicit passive sympathy for their subjects and unwittingly mask oppressive social processes and systems of power. Implicit in this discussion is a critique of Rogovin's photographic project, which does not seek to document mechanisms of domination and exploitation. Their existence can only be inferred from the photographs, and it requires an astute viewer to trace the personal misfortune represented in the pictures to its ultimate source in social structures and processes. Nevertheless, K'Meyer recognizes the photographs' contribution to bringing the experience of lower-class people out of the shadows, and she concludes her essay by contemplating their potential use in reform movements.

An essay coauthored by Catherine Fosl and Peter S. Fosl places Rogovin's work within the context of the Popular Front, a political movement of the late 1930s that was guided by the International Communist Party and charged with unifying liberal and socialist groups in the struggle against fascism and for universal social justice. As the Fosls point out, Rogovin experienced his political awakening in this period, and his photographic work can be seen as a later manifestation of the cultural program inspired by Popular Frontism. It may be added here that the documentary project itself appears to be rooted in the 1930s, although it was executed at a much later date, and is roughly comparable with photographic initiatives of that decade, such as the survey of American rural poverty under the auspices of the Farm Security Administration. The 1930s also saw the radicalization of photography throughout the Western world as leftists strove to take back artistic representation from the bourgeoisie and apply it to an emancipatory politics. These aims were wholeheartedly shared by Rogovin and lay behind his effort to restore the independent voice of the common person. Even the look of his photographs, with their precise and matter-of-fact portrayal of ordinary people, has analogies in the work of Depression-era photographers, including Minor White and Paul Strand, each of whom lent Rogovin technical advice when he was starting out in the late 1950s.

Next, Karen Christopher zeros in on images of women, particularly from the *Working People* series, and elucidates the acting out of gender roles that she detects in the photographs. Drawing on the work of the social historians Candace West and Don Zimmerman, Christopher conceptualizes gender as a performative activity in which individuals may vary their behavior to negotiate the demands of different situations, such as the factory floor and the private home. She scrutinizes specific photographs and the verbal testimonies of their subjects to discover how the portrayed women freely put on or take off gender identities, and she is led to conclude that for these persons gender definitions are not as fixed or restrictive as might be supposed. Although other essays in this collection highlight the adaptability of working-class people in contending with economic and social pressures, Christopher leads us to marvel at the freedom and intelligence of working women in managing gender bias and formulating new gender identities.

The final essay in this book is written by Joy Gleason Carew. It considers the potential of the photographs to erase or at least to mitigate the psychological divisions between people of disparate social classes, nations, races, and genders. Whereas Byers and the Fosls stress Rogovin's political convictions and associate him with leftist politics, Carew gives precedence to his capacious humanism. She affirms the inherent value of his tender and sympathetic photographs and emphasizes their special relevance in the present time, when people appear ever more distant from each other and isolated in self-centered shells. In a final word, she notes that the photographs cannot compel a change of thought and that viewers must be willing to go inside the worlds the photographs depict and open themselves to their gentle influence.

Carew also admits the essential impenetrability of the photographs and the impossibility of entirely knowing the people depicted in them. Not only do these subjects inhabit a world that is utterly distant from our own both in time and place as well as in social and economic conditions, but as much as they allow us into their homes and lift their gaze to meet ours, they also seem to withhold their deepest secrets and warily protect the buried treasure of their selfhood. They peer intently into the camera and through it to the cameraman and to the photograph's eventual viewers, from a subject position that is equally well defined as his or ours and with a self-knowledge that brooks no prying inquisition or patronizing sympathy. Yet this very secretiveness is another human quality brought forth in the photographs that we learn to value and accept. We more deeply appreciate these persons because they are in possession of their subjectivity and do not yield to our intrusive gaze. And we more greatly respect their individuality, which is fundamentally unknowable but also an intrinsic property of our common humanity, for, as the author Charles Dickens observed in *A Tale of Two Cities*, it is "a wonderful fact to reflect upon, that every human creature is constituted to be that profound secret and mystery to every other."

Photography with a Conscience

Christopher Fulton

HOW DID A MIDDLE-AGED OPTOMETRIST from Buffalo change direc-
tions and become an internationally renowned documentary photographer?
Milton Rogovin (1909–2011) was not born into the world of art, much less
into the lap of privilege. The youngest of three sons of Russian Jewish immigrants who ran a small dry-goods store, he was raised in humble conditions
on New York City's Upper West Side and later in the Bay Ridge neighborhood of Brooklyn. His parents struggled to make ends meet, and shortly
after the start of the Depression Milton's father went bankrupt and then died
suddenly of a heart attack a couple of years later. But this precarious life in
the ethnic boroughs of New York laid the groundwork for Milton's photographic career. It put him in contact with people of different backgrounds
and economic standing, leading him in later years to point his camera on the
poor and underprivileged, blue-collar workers, people of color, and members
of ethnic groups. A childhood spent in the colorful districts of New York
further instilled in him an affection for the expressive character of common
folk. And this fascination for the brilliant and bright, intimate lives of ordinary people became the most distinctive element in his unique brand of
social documentary photography.

Milton followed his elder brother into the optometry profession because
it seemed a good way of making a living. He received his professional degree
from Columbia University in 1931 and settled in Buffalo in 1938, where he
opened a private office. Before leaving New York, however, he joined the
Communist Party USA in search of answers for the social and economic

disruption brought on by the Great Depression. With his brother Sam, the optometrist, he engaged in political work and agitated for a variety of leftist causes, including the struggle against fascism in the Spanish Civil War. He became involved in the American League against War and Fascism, a Communist front organization, and helped organize a union of optometrists and opticians. After relocating to Buffalo, he continued to work for the Communist Party by taking charge of the local branch's literature department. Inducted into the army during the Second World War, he resumed political activity once his term of service ended.

A decisive turning point came in 1957, when Rogovin was subpoenaed by the House Subcommittee on Un-American Activities (HUAC), which had sent agents to Buffalo to uncover radical groups operating there. Rogovin refused to cooperate with the investigators and divulged only his name and professional title. Although hardly a major figure in the Communist Party, he was excoriated by the local press, whose headlines identified him as "Buffalo's Number-One Red," and he soon found himself a man condemned in the court of public opinion. Many of his optometry patients left him, and the labor union that had sent him business withdrew its support. His earnings were nearly halved overnight, and the Rogovin family was put under severe financial pressure. Still worse was the social stigmatization suffered by Milton, his wife, Anne, and their three young children, as neighbors, schoolmates, and former friends shunned the family for fear they too might be labeled Communist sympathizers.

Up until this time, Rogovin had showed only a passing fancy for photography. He had purchased his first camera in 1942 and while in military service had begun taking pictures of scenes he encountered at home and abroad. On vacation in Mexico in the winter of 1953–1954, he had explored the medium with special concern and took a set of arresting images of popular markets and street life.[1] However, only after his agitational work had been effectively ended with the HUAC investigation did he seriously take up the camera as an instrument of personal expression. A political motive thus animated his work from the start and would continue to guide him throughout a long and productive career in photography. His primary objective, he later said, was to use photography to expose injustice and bring to light the hidden problems of society while inspiring the fight for social justice. He dismissed the label of artist because, he reasoned, "it's not a question of my having come to documentary through art, I came to art through documentary";[2] and elsewhere he said he cared not a jot how people categorized his work or judged him in aesthetic terms since his overarching goal was to produce something socially meaningful and politically effective.

This is not to say that he was unconcerned with aesthetic issues or disregardful of artistic processes. On the contrary, he was a scrupulous technician who took enormous pains setting up photographic situations to achieve desired effects of composition, lighting, focus, tonality, and framing and spending countless hours in the darkroom processing negatives and hand making prints to satisfy exceedingly high standards.

He was furthermore aware of artistic traditions and placed himself within an extended lineage of socially concerned artists. He admired the art of Honoré Daumier, Käthe Kollwitz, Francisco Goya, and David Alfaro Siqueiros and was an avid reader of socially minded authors such as Bertolt Brecht, Carl Sandburg, and Kurt Tucholsky. He collaborated with poets of his own era and on three occasions arranged for the publication of books that brought together his photographs and others' poems—namely, work by the Chilean Pablo Neruda, the Cuban Nancy Morejón, and the Native American Eric Gansworth.[3] A volume issued after his death paired a selection of his photographs with poetry he wrote in old age.[4]

The curator and photo historian Robert Doherty points out that Rogovin's formative years coincided with the period in which the United States was inundated by new pictorial communication media, marked above all by the appearance of *Life* and *Look* magazines in 1936 and 1937, respectively.[5] In a certain sense, Rogovin took the lucid, direct, and informative style of photojournalism and applied it to a high-minded photography with political intent. Yet while his work shared with photojournalism a dedication to objectivity and close observation, it ran against the mainstream media's naïveté and neglect of social problems as well as against their crude stereotyping of industrial workers and the underprivileged. A truer and more faithful representation of these groups could be found in the work of socially concerned photographers who also emerged in the 1930s and willfully employed photography as an instrument of political dissent. Rogovin encountered this brand of documentary work in leftist publications such as the *Daily Worker* and *Masses* and became aware of photographers working for the Farm Security Administration, such as Walker Evans, Dorothea Lange, Carl Mydans, and Russell Lee. The first photography book he ever bought was *You Have Seen Their Faces* by photographer Margaret Bourke-White and novelist Erskine Caldwell, which treated the underclass of the rural South. And he knew as well the images emitted from the Photo League in New York City, an organization that had ties to the Communist Party and whose members documented the urban scene in the postwar period. When he turned to photography, he was influenced by the methods of these forerunners and sought to emulate their honest and unadorned portrayal of ordinary people.

More directly, when starting out, Rogovin received guidance in photographic technique from more experienced friends and acquaintances. Especially helpful were the photographers Minor White and Paul Strand and photography critics Beaumont Newhall, Weston Naef, Cornell Capa, and Robert Doherty. Yet, despite the debt owed to these persons, Rogovin remained very much his own man. He did not affiliate with any photography group, movement, or doctrine and was content to pursue his solitary projects and operate with his own creative process.

What was this process, and how was it developed? Rogovin engaged in his first serious photographic effort soon after the HUAC investigation, when in 1958 William H. Tallmadge, a professor of music at Buffalo State University College, invited him to collaborate on a study of religious services at the Holiness Church, a small African American congregation housed in a disused movie theater in downtown Buffalo. As Tallmadge made audio recordings of the music and sermons, Rogovin photographed the services and ecstatic prayer of worshippers. After three months of working collaboratively, Tallmadge finished his recordings and quit the project, but Rogovin continued to photograph for another three years at the Holiness Church and at four other African American sanctuaries located on Buffalo's East Side, with special attention to a facility run by the charismatic minister Mother Tokio. He titled the completed series *Storefront Churches* to indicate that these places of worship were found mainly in abandoned commercial stores, which could be rented cheaply.

Week after week Rogovin visited the same five churches, observing the services and prayers, the boisterous singing and music making, the worshippers' lurid trances and tremors. Most of the pictures were action shots taken with a hand-held, 35-mm camera, though Rogovin also experimented with a tripod and longer exposures. The series was intended to give a sympathetic portrayal of religious practices. It was the product of the belief that the lives of all people, no matter what their social class, ethnicity, or color, are significant and ought to be celebrated through photography. The documentary value of the project was recognized by Minor White, who had previously given Rogovin technical advice and now agreed to publish forty-eight images from the series in *Aperture* magazine, which he directed.[6] Yet when some of the pictures were shown to members of Buffalo's African American community, they were criticized as representations of backward, regressive habits born out of slavery and the weariness of the rural South (many members of the congregations had taken part in the Great Migration to northern industrial cities or were sons and daughters of those who had joined the exodus). Seeking confirmation of his work, Rogovin took the photographs to New York City and shared them with the eminent civil rights leader W. E. B. Du Bois, whose book *The Soul of Black Folk* (1903) had shaped Rogovin's thinking about his project. Du Bois declared the photographs important documents of African American experience and volunteered to write a brief statement for the *Aperture* magazine spread. There he affirmed that the photographs "show how little the church of America and the other institutions of our culture have reached these people, and yet how alone and segregated they live and worship."[7]

Moving forward, Rogovin resolved always to work in series. He would choose a specific subject matter and throw himself into it for a period of time before turning to other material. Over the years, he rarely took photographs on the fly, rarely captured stray incidents that chanced his way. His process of selecting subjects and taking pictures was instead methodical and premeditated. He thought long and hard before initiating a project, as he knew he would be committing himself to a large effort. To better prepare, he researched the environment he was about to enter and studied its history and social background. He corresponded with individuals who knew the lay of the land and could assist him with travel plans or locating subjects. Having done this advance work, he could be more efficient in pursuing his photography once he arrived on site and more cognizant of his human subjects and their circumstances.

In July 1962, after three years of working in Buffalo's urban churches and photographing in the homes of church members, Rogovin and his wife, Anne, decided to venture into Appalachia, where Rogovin would take pictures of the mining communities. The poverty and destitution in this area had recently become a matter of public interest, with attention brought to it by a number of illuminating academic and political writings. In the same year Rogovin chose to enter the mountain landscape, the socialist writer Michael Harrington published *The Other America: Poverty in the United States,* which dealt significantly with Appalachia and its miners, and in the following year Harry M. Caudill issued *Night Comes to the Cumberlands: A Biography of a Depressed Area,* which drew heavily on personal experience to describe daily life in the region (Caudill's later publication, *My Land Is Dying,* of 1971, would be illustrated with pictures taken by Rogovin, among other photographers).[8] Rogovin's work in Appalachia was therefore current with new awareness of rural poverty in the area, and, like the authors who approached this topic, he wished to shine light on the face of hardship that was invisible to most Americans.

Over the succeeding nine years, the Rogovins spent about a month each summer in the hills of West Virginia and Kentucky, and years later they returned to the area to carry out additional photography, with a concentration on women miners in 1981 and African American miners of northern Alabama in 1987. Each season of work revealed new facets of the local scene, and the photographic images changed from year to year as Milton's techniques evolved and his points of interest shifted. As he later recalled:

> Each trip brought new observations, new approaches. For example: the first trip resulted mostly in distant shots of villages and an occasional close-up of a miner near his little truck or mine. For the second trip, I was fortunate in having as a guide a woman who was well known in the area. Her husband suffered

from "Black Lung disease"—[my portraits of] the four remaining daughters [of this family] create the atmosphere of despair. She introduced us to families and now I could photograph groups sitting on porches as well as recording scenes in homes. . . . On the third trip I had as guides a retired black miner and a black social worker—and I photographed scenes at the mines as well as homes.[9]

Despite the variety of subjects that caught Rogovin's eye, the Appalachia photographs usually concern families and their domestic habitats rather than industrial processes or the labor of mineworkers. Unlike the storefront-church pictures, which capture the excited actions of worshippers, those from Appalachia are mostly individual or group portraits, sometimes taken at the mine but more often set in or around a private home. The figures assume static, frontal poses, look straight into the camera lens, and appear conscious of being photographed and playing a part in the documentary project. They enter into a compact with the photographer with the intention of having their story told, and in this collusion there is a shared trust. Yet one also senses that their attitude is generally formal and self-aware rather than relaxed and familiar. In most photographs, the figures stand rigid and aloof and maintain a psychological distance from the cameraman. They seem to greet him as a stranger to the hills and hollows, a welcomed guest but an outsider and interloper nonetheless. One is left with a sharp sense of the independence of these mountain people, who have admitted Rogovin into their midst to record and publicize their way of life but remain fundamentally reticent and unyielding.

Rogovin confessed that "going to Appalachia . . . was a physically difficult and emotionally exhausting experience."[10] During the first summer, he and his wife slept on the floor of a union office in Beckley, West Virginia, and spent other nights in the back of their Volvo station wagon at outlying hollows and small villages. Much effort went into planning the trips. Rogovin studied relevant publications and corresponded with individuals who could connect him with local residents. The sociologist Robert Coles provided contacts in Kentucky, and Dr. Donald Rasmussen, a physician from West Virginia who treated black lung disease, introduced him to afflicted miners. He

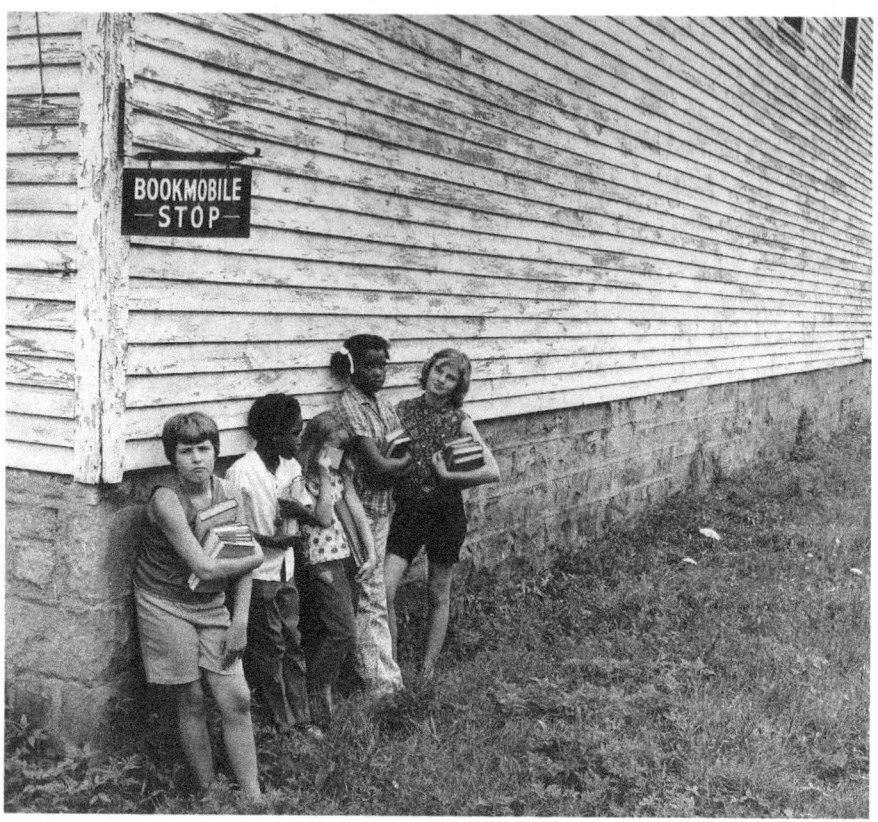

Untitled, *Appalachia*, 1962–1970. The Rogovin Collection, Chicago. Copyright ©
Milton Rogovin. Courtesy, Center for Creative Photography, University of Arizona
Foundation.

received further assistance from the United Mine Workers of America and
coordinated his movements with leaders of the union's districts in Beckley,
West Virginia, and Pikeville, Kentucky. In 1981, when he returned to the area
to document women miners, who had only recently entered the coal industry,
he operated through June Rostan of the Coal Employment Project, a pub-
lic-interest group helping women obtain and hold coal-mining jobs.

Rogovin's next photographic project was deliberately chosen to be
different from the *Appalachia* series. Wishing to make a more direct connection with his subjects, he picked out a district on Buffalo's Lower West

Side, bounded by South Elmwood Avenue, Hudson Street, Cottage Street, and Trenton Avenue and located just around the corner from his optometry office. For four years, from 1972 to 1975, he documented this compact area of about six square blocks.[11] Usually in the company of Anne, he walked the streets, became acquainted with residents, and photographed people as he encountered them outdoors or found them in their homes.[12] Whereas the *Appalachia* series documented the rural poverty of mountain people, this project, titled *Lower West Side*, revealed dimensions of life in an urban slum. Nevertheless, the two series have in common the disclosure of "hidden" realities. Both in the mountains of Appalachia and on the streets of inner-city Buffalo, Rogovin found populations that were largely unknown to the American public and woefully neglected by policy makers. And whereas the photographs in the two series offer highly particularized views of two different local conditions, their underlying message is generalizable and point to a more extensive social reality. The final goal in venturing into Appalachia was not to record this or that instance of personal hardship but to give a compendiated image of the entire coal-mining region or of rural poverty in a still wider sense. Similarly, the import of the Lower West Side photographs is not the depiction of isolated incidents appearing in this single poor area of Buffalo, but the documentation of lower-class life as it may be found in any North American metropolis—hence, Rogovin settled on the generic title *Lower West Side*, without reference to Buffalo.[13]

Most of the Lower West Side photographs (the series contained around 150 prints at its inaugural exhibition in 1975) are arranged in formal compositions, as are the Appalachia pictures, and they likewise usually represent individuals standing directly in front of the camera and leveling their gaze directly into its lens. As much as possible, Rogovin refrained from posing figures or asking people to act out something they would not ordinarily do. He sought a cross between a formal portrait and candid snapshot, and he wanted a natural image that did not betray his artistic intervention. Speaking of the relaxed and noninvasive approach, he said, "As I'm walking along I usually see them in a position in which I'd like to photograph them, so I just tell them to stand the way they are and that I would like to photograph them just the way they are. Now, if I'm in a home, and I see something photographically interesting on the wall I'll ask them to sit down near the wall. But I'd never tell them how to pose or what to do. They seat themselves the way they want to and that's the way I like it."[14]

He further stated in a personal notebook, "Essentially what I've tried to do is to make a portrait of a neighborhood in transition."[15] As much as the *Lower West Side* photographs capture individual personalities and their unique ways of being, the series as a whole provides a documentary record of the entire neighborhood and its resident population and reflects demographic and social changes affecting urban communities throughout the United States at a specific phase of history. Before the outbreak of the Second World War, Buffalo's Lower West Side had been occupied by a mostly white, middle-class population with a large number of Italian Americans. By the early 1970s, when Rogovin photographed there, the neighborhood had fallen on hard economic times. Its businesses had declined, its streets and infrastructure had fallen into disrepair, and its middle-class residents had fled to the suburbs to be replaced by a mixed population of blacks, Latinos, Native Americans, and lower-income whites, alongside some holdovers from the Italian American group. The area became plagued with social ills—unemployment, prostitution, drug addiction and alcoholism, crime and violence, family discord, delinquency, and other issues. This pattern of urban decay and social erosion endemic to inner-city neighborhoods of the period forms the historical and sociological backdrop for the photographs, which represent individuals struggling to live in difficult conditions and bearing scars from a range of personal adversities.

The content of the photographs can be regarded in two distinct yet interrelated ways. On the one hand, they can be seen chiefly as portraits of human subjects, either an individual or a small group of intimates (friends, family members, etc.). The placement of figures in the middle of the pictorial field magnifies the sense of their physical presence, and each subject's frontal gaze toward the spectator accentuates his or her unique personality. On the other hand, the portrayed figures repose in determinable settings—a street corner or store entrance, a bar or playground, the front stoop of a house, a private living room or bedroom—such that they are paired with their immediate environments. As the surroundings supplement the portraits by giving information about the conditions in which the individuals live, they also describe the neighborhood itself and in a sense subordinate the human subjects to that geographical and social context. Rogovin was uncomfortable with the characterization of his photographs as mere portraits because they offer more than natural likenesses, being equally representations of physical habitats and social formations.

The Lower West Side photographs tell many stories. They tell the story of poverty and urban decay and their corrosive effects on people's lives. They tell of persons contending with economic hardship and striving to maintain a sense of dignity and self-worth. They tell the story of a subculture emergent from this milieu, a style of expression, a rhythm of life and mode of being that evolve in pockets of urban space.[16] They tell of a neighborhood in physical ruination, with its dilapidated buildings, graffitied walls and rundown streets, its businesses teetering on bankruptcy, and its economic vitality bled dry. They tell the story of social injustice delivered to the urban poor, who have been sloughed off by the productive economy and left to their own devices. By telling these and other stories, the series bears witness to the vicissitudes of life in a declining and neglected neighborhood and presents this local reality as a single incidence of a widespread phenomenon.

Eight years after completing the series, Rogovin revisited the same district of Buffalo to rephotograph the individuals who continued to live there. He titled this second set of photographs, taken from 1983 to 1985, *Lower West Side—Revisited* and exhibited the new images alongside the older ones. Later still, in 1992, he returned once again and produced a third set of pictures, documenting the same persons at a further stage in their lives.[17] By combining this new set with the earlier images, he formed the *Lower West Side—Triptychs* series; and with the addition of photographs from 2001–2002, this series was enlarged into the *Lower West Side—Quartets* series.

The *Triptychs* and *Quartets* series introduce a narrative element as subjects are seen to mature into new physical states and become involved in new or changed relationships across a span of time. In one triptych, for example, we first meet a young Puerto Rican woman in halter top, lingering with a cigarette outside a clubhouse and accompanied by her distracted four-year-old, who is carelessly left to drift from her mother's side. From Rogovin's personal

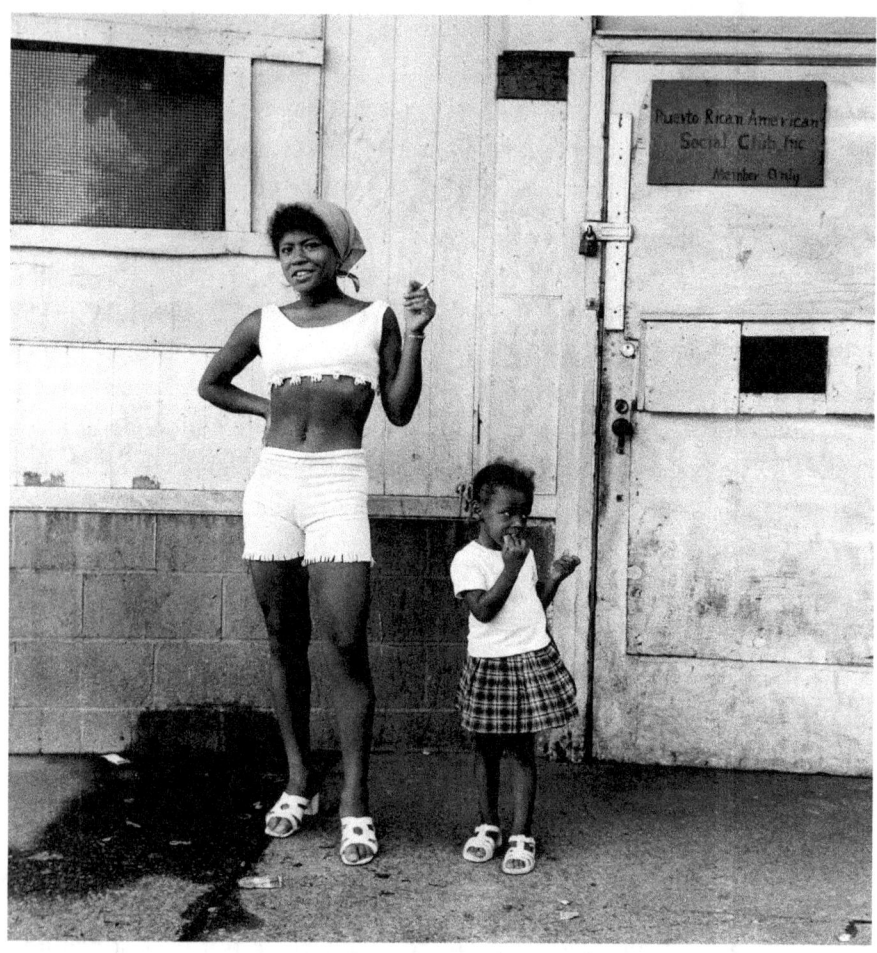

Untitled, *Lower West Side*, 1974. The Rogovin Collection, Chicago. Copyright ©
Milton Rogovin. Courtesy, Center for Creative Photography, University of Arizona
Foundation.

notes, we learn that the woman's name is Yvonne, that she is a prostitute,
and that the daughter is Sonya, then living with her grandmother. Eleven
years ahead, a second photograph shows Yvonne in a changed state. She
assumes a modest pose and is conservatively dressed, clean, and tidy. She
draws close to Sonya, now a teenager, who mimics mom's spotless wardrobe
and reserved manner. In the third photograph of the sequence, Yvonne is
middle-aged, and Sonya an aspiring white-collar worker in pressed shirt and

jacket, with her own little child standing at her knee and under her protective shadow—she has clearly made choices different from her mother's. All three photographs were taken out of doors in unsightly settings: the banged-up and padlocked door of the Puerto Rican American Social Club forms the backdrop of the first image; the mother and daughter sit on a concrete table of a corner park in the second; and the figures in the third image are posed in front of a graffitied wall. The triptych shows a family that has risen above its destitute surroundings—morally if not also financially—and remains united despite the trials they have endured.

The reader will note that this reading of the Yvonne–Sonya triptych is supported with information gleaned from one of Rogovin's notebooks.[18] For several of his projects, he kept written records of subjects' names and addresses and basic facts about their lives; for the *Lower West Side–Revisited* series, he went a step further and conducted oral interviews with some persons. When speaking about his photographs, he would often draw on information from these sources. But he also felt uneasy about relying on texts as interpretive tools. First, he did not want to seal up a photograph's narrative and abbreviate its meaning with an authoritative account. He instead hoped that viewers would enter into an extended encounter with the images, plunging intently into them and drawing out their own observations. And for this reason he typically developed his finished prints in a small, 8-by-10-inch format, which pulls you nearer to the image and forces you to study it up close.

The other reason he hesitated before leaning on his notebooks and other verbal records is that he conceived the photographs as emblems of broad social phenomena and common varieties of human experience, not simply as likenesses of solitary subjects. They document social groups and habitats and raise questions about the systems of power that engender poverty and exploitation. For this documentary and educational function, what does it really matter that the mother in a certain triptych is named Yvonne and her daughter Sonya? Or that the specific facts of their lives are this and that? Ordinary viewers will never actually meet them and get to know them on a personal level. The mother and daughter are rather of general interest because they tell about the social world from which they come and about the human experience in that environment. To spoon out biographical facts about them would have the adverse effect of overparticularizing the images and narrowing their reference.

For these reasons, Rogovin withheld external information whenever he exhibited original photographs at museums and galleries, where the detail-laden prints were made available for close study. However, when he published photographs in books or articles, he freely provided textual information, as print mediums imply a different mode of reception and convey meaning through the interplay of image and text. Thus, the posthumous book *The Lens & the Pen* pairs photographs with poems that give facts and impressions about the sitters, and the book *Portraits in Steel* includes transcripts of interviews with workers who are depicted in accompanying images.

Given that Rogovin was a white, Jewish professional stepping into the urban ghetto of the Lower West Side, the degree of naturalness and ease about his photographed subjects is all the more remarkable. The sitters neither greet the camera with hostility nor retreat warily from it. They instead assume a relaxed attitude and project an implicit trust and familiarity with the man behind the camera. This feeling of ease and trust did not come automatically—Rogovin remarked that the residents at first eyed him with much suspicion.[19] Trust was built up only after the photographer became a known presence in the neighborhood, the result of his spending innumerable hours walking the streets in the company of his wife, chatting informally with residents and making friends. He always showed respect for those he met, no matter what their present circumstance or past history. While later reminiscing on his years in the area, he said he was moved by the kindness he found there and noted he was never once molested or threatened even in that rough part of town.[20] James Wood, who curated the inaugural exhibition of the *Lower West Side* series at the Albright-Knox Art Gallery in 1975, commented on the relationship Rogovin formed with his subjects: "This elimination of distance [that is apparent in the photographs] begins with Rogovin's involvement with the life of the community. Over a period of years he has become a familiar presence on the street, in the churches and shops and in people's homes, where he is not only an observer but a guest. We sense immediately in the photographs that they are not the work of a casual visitor, but the result of a mutual trust and shared respect."[21] The role of Milton's wife, Anne, in building trust and enabling the photography is described by a woman named Dee Dee, an area resident and one of the sitters: "His taking the pictures and him looking around. She does this . . . yeah, she convinces you, she's the mind, she's the manipulator, he takes the pictures, she talks you into it."[22]

Yet Rogovin also felt a need to set limits on his friendships with residents of the neighborhood. He refused to lend money or write letters of recommendation or invite people to his home because he believed these actions might complicate his relationships and affect his neutral standing. While always friendly, he was careful not to be drawn too deeply into residents' personal lives. As he said, "You have to put a little distance between you and your subject if you want to continue photographing in an area. In some cases you can understand the people, but there is no longer any possibility of photographing them. The relationship, even the very way they look at you, is different from the way it was before, and especially in an area like the Lower West Side you have to be careful not to get too deeply involved because then you will inherit some of their problems while you're doing the work."[23] Moreover, from a strictly photographic point of view, too much familiarity could spoil the naturalness that he sought in the images. Once a close relationship is formed with a photographic subject, a different kind of dialogue emerges, in which the subject constantly attempts to elicit certain responses from the photographer and stops presenting himself or herself in a wholly natural and self-possessing manner. Rogovin observed that this problem is most acute with children, who start to act up once they get to know the photographer, though the hazard pertains to adults as well. He wanted his subjects to appear and act as they ordinarily do, without looking either suspicious and ill at ease or obsequious and overly expressive. To this end, he moderated his relationships and maintained a degree of separation.

Rogovin's photographic equipment and procedure had further bearing on the final images. Rather than slip into an area with a hand-held camera and take dozens of shots of curiosities he might stumble upon, he resolved on a more deliberate, less-intrusive, and slower-working system. Whenever possible, he employed a twin-lens, 80-mm Rolleiflex camera mounted on a stabilizing tripod, which gave him the sharp focus and high resolution he desired. With this basic, no-frills apparatus, he worked efficiently and with purpose—setting up the tripod, composing the image, and taking only three or four pictures before moving on. To his sitters, he did not seem like a spy or prowler sneaking into their private space, but just a kind, elderly man doing his business with a gentle smile and easy-going manner. He noted that a 35-mm camera is brought up to the operator's eye and aimed at subjects like a gun, whereas the Rolleiflex is kept on its tripod or held at waist level, and the operator looks down into the viewfinder, which is less threatening.[24] He further put his subjects at ease by keeping a comfortable physical distance from them. He made little fuss, set up quickly and quietly, told his subjects to assume a pose or relax in the pose they were already holding, and then took his pictures with little ceremony, little hoopla, so simply and effortlessly that sitters were often unaware their photograph had been taken. The procedure mirrored his work at the optometry office, where he treated patients respectfully, worked calmly and efficiently, and showed care and concern for their well-being.

Although the photographs have the superficial appearance of casual snapshots, they are in fact contrived and manipulated images, and the end product of Rogovin's art is not the untreated negative but the final print that is processed with fastidious care and to exacting standards. His method involved spending a relatively short time taking pictures and a great deal of time laboring over prints in the darkroom, and the effect of this exertion was decisive on the finished work. For example, the centrality and balance that distinguish the compositions were achieved as much through darkroom editing as through decisions taken in the field. The cropping of negatives defines and demarcates pictorial space, with everything off frame decisively cut away. The pictures are normally composed with a grid of horizontal and vertical lines in the background, which provides a stable architecture locking figures in place (this use of a grid is more frequently seen in Rogovin's photographs from the 1980s, such as those from the *Lower West Side–Revisited* and *Triptychs* series). By enclosing and centering figures in a bounded space, Rogovin gives the impression that the persons are comfortably nestled in their immediate surroundings rather than cut adrift in a world extending infinitely beyond. Although they are not immune from outside pressures—which can

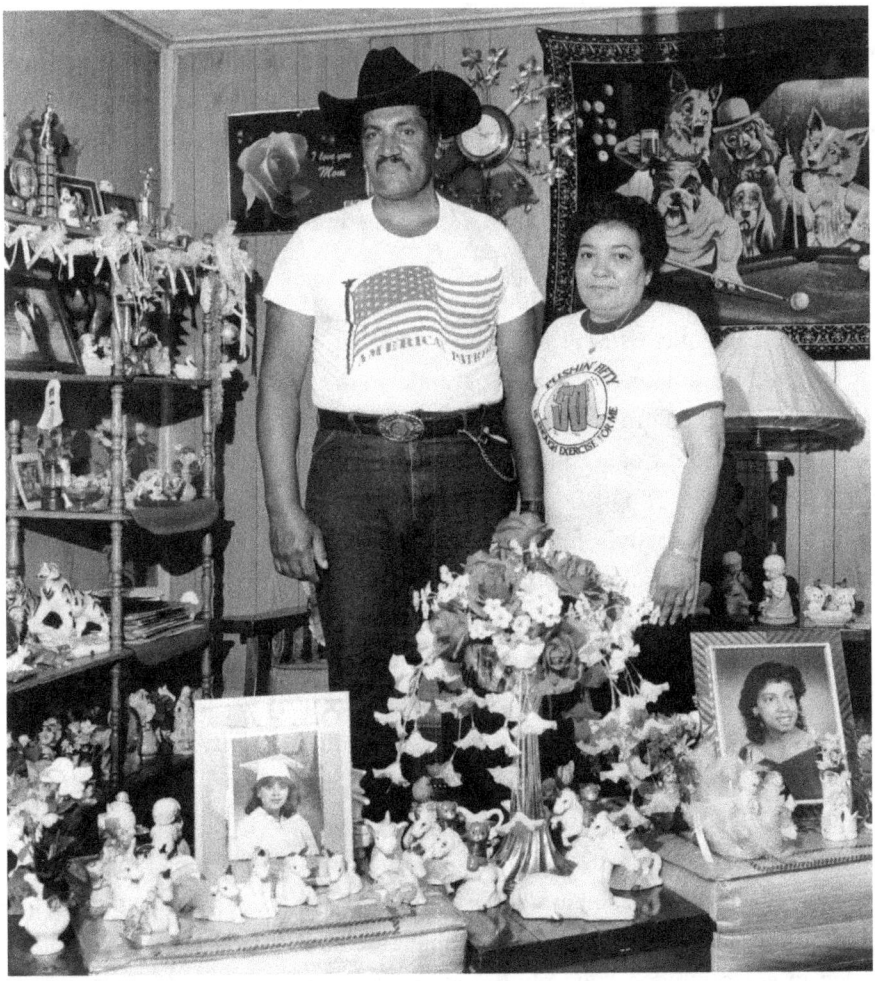

Untitled, *Lower West Side—Triptychs,* 1992. Photographic Archives, University of Louisville. Copyright © Milton Rogovin. Courtesy, Center for Creative Photography, University of Arizona Foundation.

be inferred from their expressions and from the conditions in which they are compelled to live—these pressures are not specifically indicated in the photographs, and there is an implied insulation from the dangers and disintegrative forces that lie outside this place and this present moment. Similarly unrepresented are the abjection, the suffering and bitter toil, the moments of confrontation, grief, and despair, and a host of other degradations. This omission was conscious and intentional, warranted by the overriding interest of lending dignity to the figures. Rogovin created placid images in the tradition of formal portraiture, and in that tradition he depicted subjects in the manner they would like to be seen. Whatever disintegration we observe pertains more to the environment, less to the individual, even when we look directly into the face of human tragedy.

Further darkroom manipulations were made possible by the choice of film stock. Rogovin usually shot with Kodak Tri-X film, which had been widely adopted by documentary photographers since its introduction in 1954. It is a versatile medium with a wide-exposure latitude and can be effectively used in either dark or well-lit areas. In development, it can be overexposed or pushed by one or more stops, and its wide tonal range yields a rich palette of grays, which Rogovin fine-tuned by dodging and burning and adding filters.[25] In combination with camera work, the use of Tri-X film rendered pictorial detail supremely legible and gave an artistic allure to the images that elevated them above your everyday family photograph.

The technical proficiency and artistry evident in the portrait photographs bestows dignity on the sitters. Like other socially minded photographers, Rogovin regretted the denigrating representation of the underclass that pervades the history of photography and persists in contemporary popular media. He hoped to avoid class stereotypes and the depiction of laboring men and women as characterless drones of the industrial system. At the same time, he wished to avoid the objectification that is commonly found even in socially concerned photography and sometimes turns human subjects into objects of pity or romanticizes their abject conditions. This kind of well-meaning but misdirected sentimentalization may in fact be detected in some of Rogovin's early Appalachia photographs. Even though he averred that his concern in that project was not to illustrate the exotic character of mountain people or the picturesque quality of the villages and landscape, some photographs, by conforming to conventions of Depression-era photography, nevertheless do seem to aestheticize these rural communities' primitive style of life. By profoundly altering his process and inventing an essentially new mode of documentary photography, Rogovin was able to overcome this voyeuristic tendency in the Lower West Side photographs.

The cultural critic bell hooks reminds us that historically within the black community, particularly in the era of Jim Crow, the taking of family photographs and their display in the home provided an alternative to the degrading images of black people by white photographers and thus countered segregation and dehumanization.[26] For people of color, home-made portrait photographs carried social and political significance. These pictures were generally of mediocre quality, however, crude Instamatic snapshots taken by amateurs and shown only within private domiciles. With Rogovin's *Lower West Side* series, the representation of minority subjects is treated professionally, and these persons become sitters for formal artistic portraiture. The images are furthermore brought into the public realm by being shown in museums and galleries or reproduced in glossy art books. This simple fact—that sympathetic and ennobling portraits would be made by a professional photographer and presented at distinguished venues—was deeply moving. Many of the sitters were able to attend the exhibition at Buffalo's Albright-Knox Art Gallery and felt enormous pride at the sight of their image on display. At the opening reception, one black man spent most of the evening standing next to his framed picture, as if to let everyone know, "It is I who am the subject of this work of art." That event reminds us of the hope expressed by Langston Hughes, when the poet cried:

> But some day somebody'll
> Stand up and talk about me,
> And write about me—
> Black and beautiful—
> And sing about me,
> And put on plays about me!
> I reckon it'll be
> me myself.

> Yes, it'll be me.[27]

Over his long career in photography, Rogovin pursued a dozen or more projects, some of great ambition and others of more limited range and duration. The latter sort includes a series taken on Isla Chiloé, Chile (1966), and published in a book with poems and introductory remarks by Nobel laureate Pablo Neruda; a series on Native Americans in the Buffalo area, built up over a forty-year period; another on the Yemeni enclave in the Lackawanna neighborhood of Buffalo (1974); *Punks* (1991), a project on young punk rockers; and *Children Having Children* (1991), on the theme of unwed teenage mothers. However, five projects stand out for their large scope and extraordinary level of effort: *Storefront Churches* (1958–1961); *Appalachia* (1962–1970, 1981, 1987); *Lower West Side,* inclusive of *Lower West Side–Revisited* and *Triptychs* (1972–1975, 1983–1985, 1990); *Working People* (1975–1978, 1987); and *Family of Miners* (1981–1990). With the exception of the earliest, the *Storefront Churches* series, these projects share key features that define Rogovin's documentary method: they depict indigent or working-class people at their job, at home, or in their neighborhood; they are generally portraits, often posed and static in character; they are taken in high resolution and sharp focus, with a wide tonal scale, and under a clarifying and inclusive light that picks out details and provides a density of visual information; the finished prints are meticulously developed and altered in the darkroom, giving them an aura of original works of art.

The series titled *Working People* was begun shortly after the exhibition of the Lower West Side photographs at the Albright-Knox Art Gallery and occupied Rogovin for a period of three years. To find time for the project, he began taking off Wednesday afternoons and Saturdays from his optometry practice and closed the office completely in 1978. The theme of the series was inspired by Bertolt Brecht, one of Rogovin's favorite authors, whose poem "Questions from a Worker Who Reads" extolls those who actually build the world as we know it—that is, the ordinary workers engaged in heavy industry rather than the inventors, planners, and money men who ordinarily attract recognition and honor. Rogovin explained in a letter to Alfred Neumann, editor of the journal *Fotografie,* published in Leipzig, (East) Germany: "When we talk about an auto all we hear is that it's built by Ford or GM. I want to show that it is built by Joe and Mary, Michael and Linda etc etc— men and women of all shades and origins."[28] In keeping with this statement and in accord with Brecht's poem, the series salutes those whose lives and labor are yet unsung, lifting them up to inherit a seat of honor.

The human subjects of the series were picked out from a dozen steel-producing and manufacturing plants in the Buffalo area after Rogovin had secured permission from management to bring his camera into the factories.[29] Each figure was photographed resting at his workplace near his tools or machines, and if time allowed, another shot was taken of the same individual performing his job. Rogovin concentrated on workers who had the most physically demanding tasks and were lowest on the ladder, just as he had earlier photographed the poorest settlements in Appalachia. "I wanted to show who did the toughest work in industry," he explained. "I wanted to show them because nobody does. I wanted to show the people who are slugging it out at the bottom, especially the women, because women are just coming into the steel mills."[30] The mention here of female workers refers to beneficiaries of a ruling by the Equal Opportunity Commission in 1973 granting equal rights in the steel mills to women and minorities and through which many women secured positions in the factories soon before Rogovin began his series.

Before 1975, Rogovin had never set foot inside an industrial facility, and he immediately faced new technical challenges from the dim light, cramped spaces, and distracting noise and activity as well as by the fact that he was photographing people at their work and did not want to interrupt them for very long. "For me, it was like entering a new world," he said. "Everything was so unusual. I had to learn to adapt my photography to these situations."[31] He brought with him the same Rolleiflex camera and tripod he had used for the *Lower West Side* series. By this time, he had refined his picture-taking method and become more expert at darkroom processing. As always, he stuck with a simple, direct approach. His lighting system was no more than a single bare-bulb strobe fixed to a stick and connected to a power pack. With one hand he controlled the light, and with the other he snapped the picture. He moved nimbly through the workplace with this unwieldy equipment, identified a promising subject, took a few shots, and went immediately to another area for more photography. In the cavernous plants, the strobe cast a sharp light on human figures and objects in their vicinity while leaving deeper recesses in near total darkness. This had the effect of isolating the workers rather than placing them in the larger context of the factory operation. The photographs are not descriptions of industrial processes or facilities as much as they are renderings of people at work. They focus in on independent figures, their tools and physical labor, singling them out from the plant's anonymous expanse.

In truth, the photographic activity at the factories represented only half the effort that went into the series. To complement the pictures of men and women at work, Rogovin made appointments with the same persons to photograph them and their families at home. The two sets of photographs were then exhibited and published in pairs or triplets (in the combination of a worker at rest, at labor, and at home), documenting each subject in the twin spheres of life.

For both factory and home pictures, Rogovin employed the same photographic equipment, but the results were not the same. At private residences, he could afford more time setting up and composing shots. The camera lens could be set at a longer exposure, which increased the depth of field and made details more distinct, while the strobe directed overhead rather than directly on the subjects permeated interior spaces with an even cast of light, filling in shadows and illuminating all objects in the pictorial field. Rather than sharply isolating figures against an opaque background, as in the factory pictures, the photographs taken in private homes gave equal emphasis to human subjects and domestic spaces and articles and brought sitters into close association with their personal possessions.

The series represents individuals in two spheres of life. In the factories, the subjects are usually clad in overalls and T-shirts, their faces soiled by industrial grit, and they are seen either immersed in their work or posing momentarily for the camera. They leap out from the shadows and announce themselves as the persons behind the industrial process, the ones responsible for the products society enjoys. By contrast, the home photographs allude to the subjects' hobbies and pastimes, their aspirations and ideals, and the quality of their domestic relations. These aspects of private life can be read from the figures' clothes and accouterments, their physical deportment, facial expressions and gestures, and their interaction with family members and loved ones. Further inferences can be drawn from the household decor, the collectibles and knickknacks and cherished possessions—we find in various photographs subjects posing with a prized boat, a motorcycle, a horde of Elvis memorabilia, a gilded mirror, a television and lounge chair. These domestic articles contrast with the standardized hand tools and machines associated with figures in the factory photographs. But whether in the home or at work, people are shown in tandem with objects that represent their activities and in no small way define their mode of life.

In some pairings, the disparity between an individual's appearance at the workplace and private home can be striking. For example, in one factory picture we discover a man in a grease- and sweat-stained T-shirt resting in front of a bare and scrubby wall, but the corresponding home portrait catches him in a dapper floral shirt, lounging beside a gilded baroque-style mirror and flaunting a flamboyant taste for splendor. At first, it is hard to recognize him in the two photographs as the same person. Yet closer inspection finds that he brings his personal style into the workplace as well, where his *contrapposto* stance takes on a eurythmic flair and his intense gaze expresses an inner zeal. The art historian Fred Licht commented on this man's avid quest for beauty: "The grace with which the mirror's owner tries to live up to the beauty of the only rococo available to him [that is, a store-bought, F. W. Woolworth rococo] is more moving than the grace with which the original patrons of the Amalienburg filled its mirrored ballroom. His recognition of the consolations that beauty affords, his *need* for beauty is far greater and far more sincere than most collectors of real rococo decorations find in themselves."[32]

As the name implies, the *Working People* series portrays laboring men and women as individuals, each with his or her own personal story, emotional life, private avocations, thoughts and dreams. At first, one may be tempted to regard the work and home pictures in starkly contrasting terms, a black-and-white opposition between the monotonous moil of the factory and the personal freedom and joy of the home environment.[33] But the two sets of images are complementary, and the pairings in fact deny the clear separation of work and home by showing that it is real human beings, not mindless drudges, who make up the workforce. Moreover, throughout the series, individuals seem to bring a sense of dignity and self-worth to their jobs as well as to their domestic lives. Even those shouldered with the hardest menial tasks perform

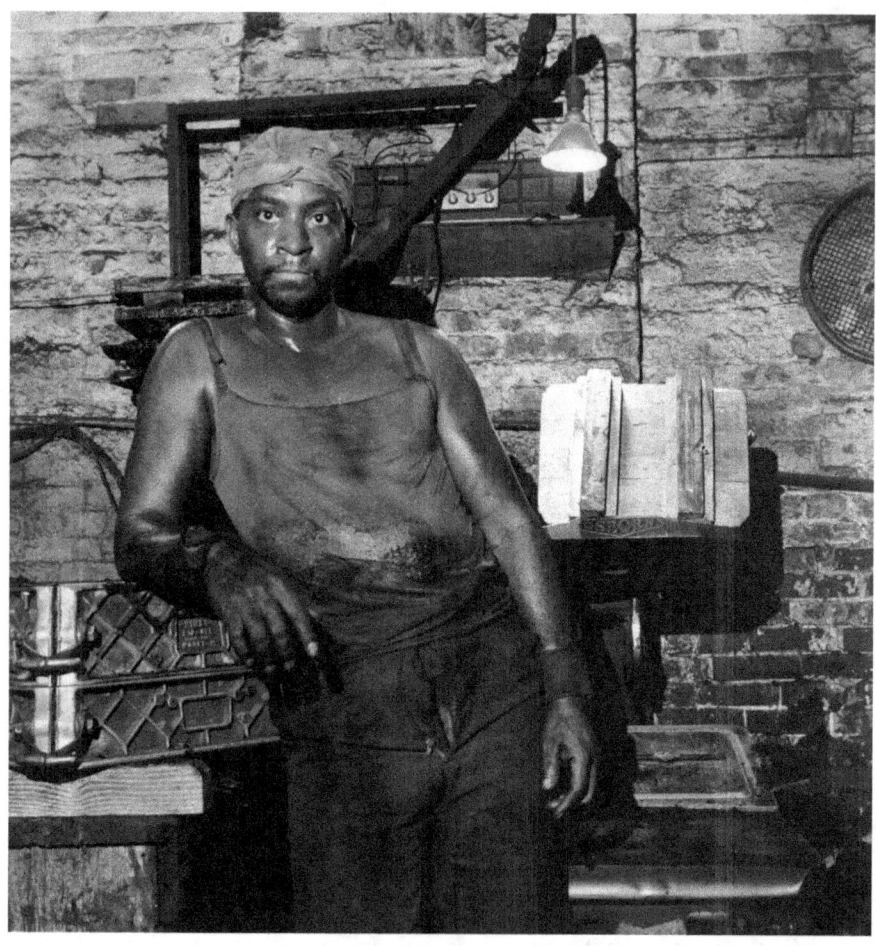

Untitled, *Working People,* 1979. Photographic Archives, University of Louisville. Copyright © Milton Rogovin. Courtesy, Center for Creative Photography, University of Arizona Foundation.

their labor conscientiously and with self-respect; one then finds these same persons leading full lives outside of work in a multitude of private pastimes and relationships.

With this series, Rogovin added an important element to his photography. Earlier, when composing the *Appalachia* and *Lower West Side* series, he photographed people as he encountered them on the street or in their moun-

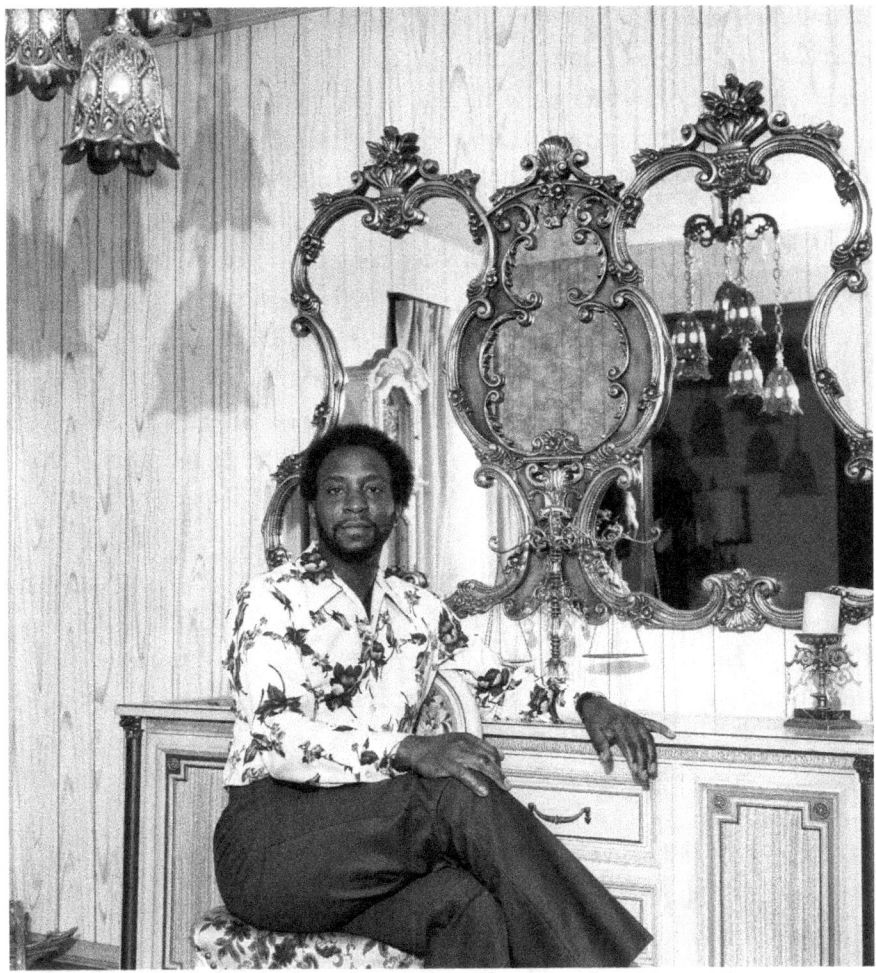

Untitled, *Working People,* 1979. The Rogovin Collection, Chicago. Copyright ©
Milton Rogovin. Courtesy, Center for Creative Photography, University of Arizona
Foundation.

tain hamlets or more rarely in their private homes, having arrived unan-
nounced or with little forewarning. But for the *Working People* series, he made
appointments with workers to visit their residences for photo shoots, which
gave his subjects ample time to prepare. They could dress as they wanted,
choose places in the home where photographs might be taken, tidy up the
house, and set out favorite objects. Rogovin repeated this procedure in pre-

paring the *Lower West Side—Revisited* and *Triptychs* series, and one therefore sees a clear divergence between the more candid photographs of the 1960s and 1970s and the more formally arranged pictures of the subsequent decade.

The domestic portraits in the *Working People* series are as much self-representations of sitters as they are the photographer's original creations—as Michael Frisch stated, Rogovin "does not 'take' photographs; rather, his subject 'gives' them to him."[34] Indeed, this coresponsibility for the image is something Rogovin specifically strove for. As much as possible, he removed from the photographs any sign of his presence at the scene. The images are simple, straightforward, and unassuming. More assertively than in earlier series, figures peer head-on into the lens to engage the viewer directly, and the level camera angle eliminates any sense of an artistically invented point of view. The figures are normally shown full-length and placed squarely in a nook of space, which makes the photograph appear as a natural and self-sufficient image rather than the result of the cameraman's creative choices. The even lighting and uniformly high focus further obscure the photographic process. By thus masking his own responsibility for the image and surrendering a measure of control over the photographic situation, Rogovin grants his sitters an authorial role in the making of their visual representation. Indeed, in some cases they appear conscious of this fact as they look knowingly at us. They are our interlocutors, speaking their own mind and telling their own story.

Little did Rogovin realize at the time he began the *Working People* series that he would be recording the end of an era of steel production in the Buffalo area. But only a few years after he completed the project, the industry sunk into a deep and irreversible crisis, and soon the full brunt of the downturn came to be felt in the workers' communities. As the plants closed down, thousands were left without jobs, families were thrown into financial crisis, and entire neighborhoods began to fall apart. Having witnessed this calamity and wishing to document its effects on workers' lives, in 1987 Rogovin decided to rephotograph the same persons he had portrayed earlier, in the same way he had rephotographed the Appalachian mining communities in 1981 and the residents of the Lower West Side in 1983–1985. Indeed, much of his photographic activity from the 1980s consisted of returning to subjects he had previously treated, and this material, combined with the earlier work, offers an extensive record of working-class life over a period of three decades.

In the second campaign of photographing steelworkers, Rogovin took pictures only at private homes and did not attempt to enter the beleaguered factories. The goal of this labor was a book, eventually published in 1993 under the title *Portraits in Steel* and produced in collaboration with the urban historian Michael Frisch of the University of Buffalo.[35] As Rogovin tracked down and rephotographed workers and their families—many of whom were now jobless and in financial ruin—Frisch conducted a total of twenty interviews, twelve of which were published in the book. The volume is a masterpiece of social history, with a consistency in approach, as both Frisch and Rogovin chose to restrain their own interventions and let the subjects speak for themselves, either by relating their own stories or presenting themselves in a self-determined way for their photographic portraits.[36]

The human toll of big steel's sudden decline is written on the faces of Rogovin's sitters. In many instances, a dramatic change is registered in the pre-and postcrisis pictures. For example, in a photograph from the first series we find a bearded man jauntily chewing on a pipe and joined by his gleeful wife and children behind the basement bar he has built. Nine years later, the same family is gathered in shabbier quarters heated by a pot-belly stove; their care-worn faces express a severe loss of confidence and hope. Other images, however, indicate more resilient responses to the economic catastrophe. For example, from the earlier suite of photographs is a portrait of Doris McKinney with her two boys: one holds the family puppy, while she wraps her arms affectionately and supportively around their waists. Later on, the boys have grown into young men, dressed in fresh, James Brown–inspired, urban fashion. The mother sits on a chair between them. She no longer envelopes them in a protective embrace but lays her hands on her lap, and it is the boys who gently touch the back of her chair with endearing gestures. Yet, however much Doris is reduced in physical presence, she remains the adored sovereign of the home and the family's stabilizing ballast—an unshaken fact duly recognized by her sons. What is remarkable about the many sets of photographs is that there is not a single narrative adequate for all subjects. There exist instead multiple story lines attached to an individual or family and their particular response to the common crisis.

Rogovin's return trip to Appalachia in 1981 became the catalyst for the most ambitious project of his career as it stirred up the idea of documenting

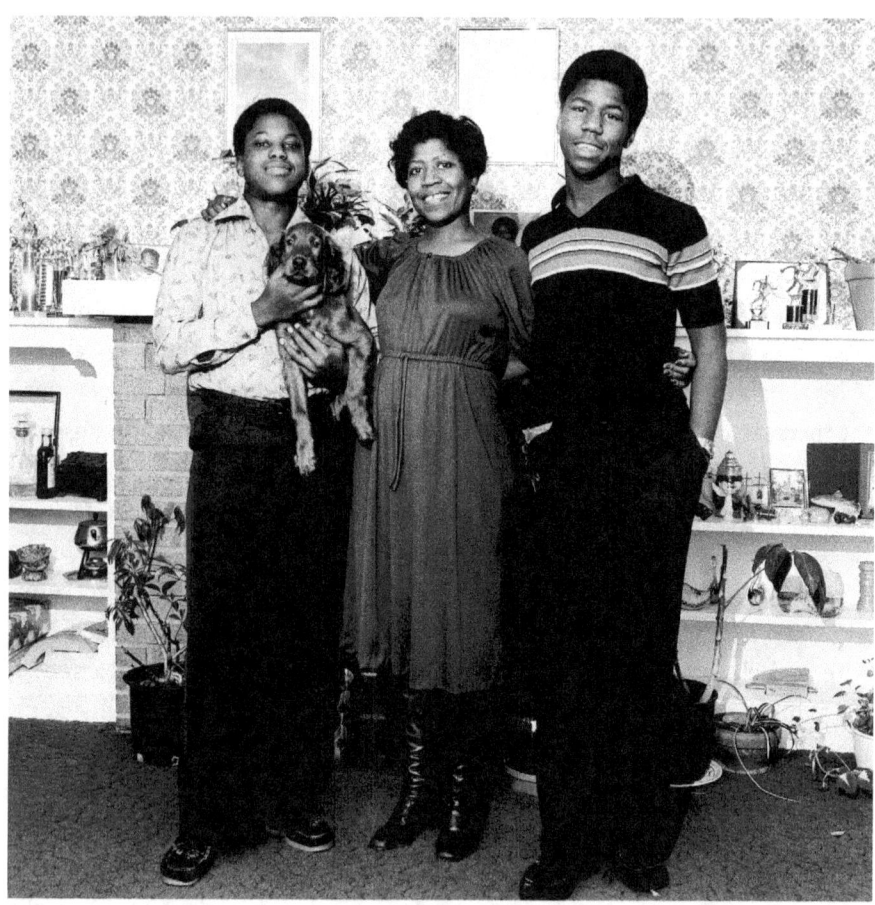

Untitled (Republic Steel), *Working People*, 1978–1979. The Rogovin Collection, Chicago. Copyright © Milton Rogovin. Courtesy, Center for Creative Photography, University of Arizona Foundation.

mining communities from distant parts of the world and thereby producing a global portrait of workers in this sector of industry. The project, which he titled *Family of Miners*—echoing the name of Edward Steichen's landmark exhibition of 1955, *The Family of Man*—included selected images previously taken in Appalachia and new images from photographic campaigns conducted in nine different countries: France, 1981; Scotland, 1982; Spain, 1983; Germany, 1984; Cuba, 1984, 1986, and 1989; China, 1986; Mexico, 1988; Zimbabwe, 1989; and Czechoslovakia (today's Czechia and Slovakia), 1990. The project

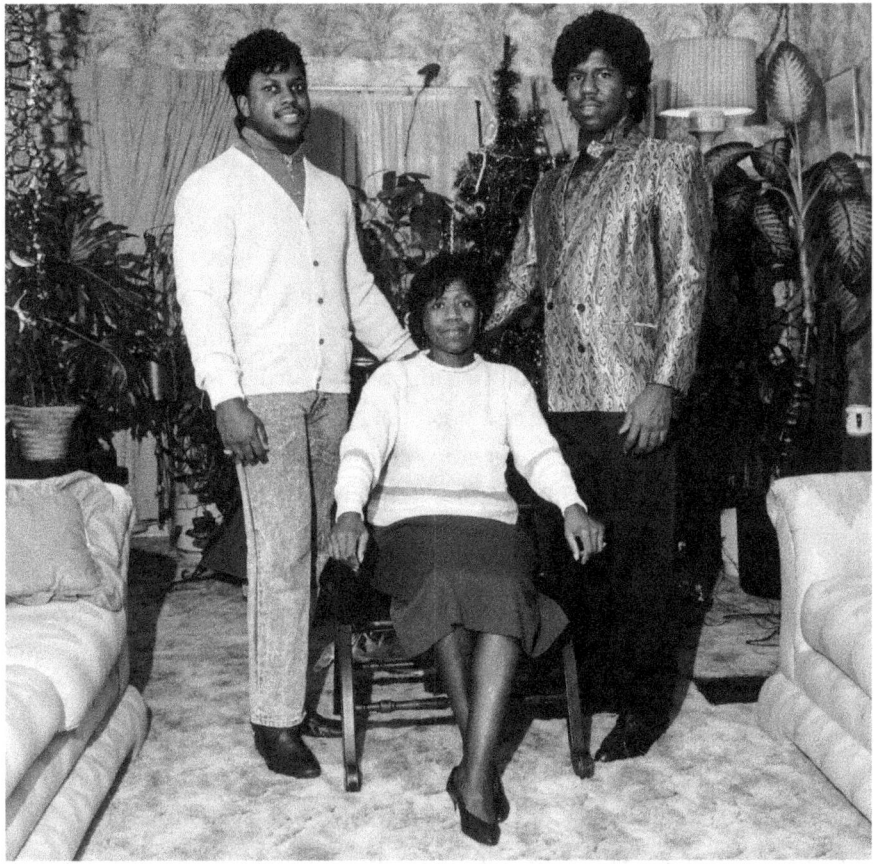

Untitled (Republic Steel), *Working People*, 1987. Photographic Archives, University of Louisville. Copyright © Milton Rogovin. Courtesy, Center for Creative Photography, University of Arizona Foundation.

was enormously taxing and required tremendous persistence in planning, organization, and execution. Rogovin carried out the work on a shoestring, drawing heavily on personal savings, though the receipt of $15,000 from a W. Eugene Smith Memorial Fund Award for Documentary Photography in 1983 allowed the project's scope to be widened.

In conducting the new photography, Rogovin preferred to work at deep mines rather than surface mines and at older facilities rather than newer, more automated operations. He wanted to show the hard labor of hands on shovels in the belly of the earth—though in actuality doing so would prove impossible because he was rarely allowed to go underground where the mining work was being done. He mainly visited coal mines, though the series included silver and copper mines in Mexico, gold mines in Zimbabwe, and nickel mines in Cuba. He was also keen to photograph members of minority groups and people of color; for example, he homed in on Turkish workers at the German mines of the Ruhr district, Gypsy workers in France and Spain, and miners of African descent in Cuba.[37]

Circumstances beyond his control often dictated what Rogovin could and could not observe. At several sites, official handlers limited his access to certain areas, and constraints of time and money further restricted the work. His personal correspondence and notebooks describe the many difficulties he encountered in scheduling visits to mines and mining communities and sometimes betray his deep frustration in not being able to accomplish what he had set out to do.

The most successful trip was the one to Scotland, where he was warmly received by the National Union of Miners and admitted into private homes, social clubs, and bars.[38] He also felt welcomed at the Mexican mines and towns. There, as in Scotland, he enjoyed the cooperation of the local union and management and was able to observe miners at work and in their homes.

By contrast, the trips to France and Spain were less fulfilling. In France, his escorts had few contacts in the mining district, and time was wasted trying to locate miners willing to be photographed. In Spain, the miners' union had offered to escort Rogovin to various locations over a period of two full weeks but actually provided assistance for only four days. Further hindering his work in Spain was the entourage of officials forced upon him. At each site, he was accompanied by a union liaison, two or three representatives of the bosses, a safety man, and other hangers-on, up to eight or ten people, which encumbered his movement, confused the miners, and defeated any attempt to achieve naturalness and authenticity in the photographs.[39]

However, Rogovin's activity was most frustrated in Communist bloc countries. In letters to party officials and comments in private notebooks, he complained bitterly about obstacles placed in his way. Despite his impeccable leftist credentials and much prior planning, once he arrived in these countries, his retainers steered him away from industrial subjects and restricted his movement in the mining areas, apparently because they did not welcome unadulterated images of socialist workers and the prospect of their circulation among Western audiences. Impediments were therefore thrown up in every Communist country he entered, with the exception of Czechoslovakia, which he visited in 1990, near the end of the Soviet era. Of his three trips to Cuba, for example, only the third resulted in an acceptable set of pictures. In China, he fared slightly better and inveigled his way into the Shaugang Steel Complex outside Beijing to photograph at the workers' barracks there (most of the men had come from other areas without their families). He was also given limited access to mines and miners' homes in Shanxi Province. But he later characterized the China trip as a failure and complained he had lost precious time due to countless delays and cancellations and was unable to work in the mining zones he had planned to visit. These doleful dealings with Communist officialdom were epitomized by the abortive trip to Russia in July 1972. Rogovin had hoped to photograph in the Donetsk mining district and had been given a preliminary indication that this area would be open to him, but, after arriving, he was kept away from the mines and communities, and after several weeks of utter frustration he and his wife decided to leave the country without carrying out any substantive work.

A good leftist and faithful observer of party discipline, Rogovin spoke little of these difficulties. In published statements and correspondence with third parties, he normally pasted over his unhappy experiences and spoke only positively about his travels, lauding the Communist system and the health and prosperity of its mining towns. When interviewed about his trip to Russia, for instance, he swallowed his disappointment and said he had been given complete liberty to photograph as he liked.[40]

The *Family of Miners* series is the largest suite of photographs Rogovin ever made. However, in certain respects it is less satisfying than the earlier work. As described earlier, circumstances often prevented him from carrying out the photography as planned, and even when access to mines and communities was obtained, Rogovin had less time to interact with his subjects than he did in Appalachia or Buffalo. Also, when communicating with people in non-English speaking countries, he had to rely on translators. He was further unable to revisit his subjects after an interval of time and document changes in their lives, as he had done on the streets of the Lower West Side and in the Buffalo factories. As a result, most of the photography in the *Family of Miners* series lacks the intimacy and depth that one observes elsewhere.

Rarely do Rogovin photographs deliver a knock-out punch in the manner of Lewis Hine's brawny images of industrial workers or Walker Evans's rhetorical heights.[41] The small, finely crafted prints are decidedly noniconic, unmonumental, and artistically unostentatious. They convey the simple facts of life without fanfare or pretense. The Rogovin photograph is an intimate image putting the viewer directly at the scene and offering a wealth of descriptive detail. But this immediacy brings with it an unexpected complexity and a difficulty in interpretation. Standing in front of a Rogovin photograph, viewers are supplied an abundance of detail and visual data but are left to make sense of this information quite on their own. They must grapple with the expressions and gestures of portrayed subjects as well as with the many items in the subjects' surroundings. Among these objects are some that have been consciously set out to serve a symbolic function—for example, a porcelain figure, religious token, or item of sports memorabilia. Other things, however, may not be intended to carry an explicit message—for example, an ordinary cigarette lighter, a can of beer, an article of furniture—but nonetheless impart meaning metonymically as evidence of the conditions of life or their owner's character and status. These things, too, the viewer must contend with, both as individual signifiers and in association with other objects appearing in the pictorial field. Viewers may even seek to amplify their understanding by reading photographs against one another; for example, by comparing the dress and deportment of an individual in factory and home pictures or by examining the content within a sequence of images from the *Triptychs* series in the effort to derive a plausible narrative about the human subjects.

A certain level of cultural literacy is required to decipher the pictures, and there will be much variability in viewers' interpretive skill. Some are better equipped to read the photographs by dint of their familiarity with relevant cultural lexicons: perhaps one viewer is better acquainted with working-class life; perhaps another has wider knowledge of material culture. By employing multiple lexicons and drawing on deep stores of knowledge, the viewer can expand and enrich the meaning of the photographs. This interpretive task may be demanding, but it rewards the viewer with a more complete understanding of the images and their pictorial content.

The photographs further induce self-reflection as viewers become aware of the limits of their knowledge and of their own social position vis-à-vis the photographed figures. For privileged viewers looking at images of lower- and working-class people, a temptation may arise to draw invidious comparisons and to disparage, ridicule, or feel an aversion toward the persons pictured and their style of life. Yet Rogovin's humane and respectful treatment of subjects works against such invidious judgment and awakens in viewers a sense of shared humanity. While viewing the images, viewers feel a growing bond of sympathy and begin to confront the stereotypes and biases that may have at first informed their reading. The mind flips from attention on the figures within the photographs to attention on ourselves as viewers, and we become conscious of our own class position and the class-based nature of our thinking. Through this self-reflexive process, we draw a portrait of ourselves that is connected by sympathy and difference with the others in the photographs.

The fostering of mutual understanding is one favorable outcome that Rogovin hoped to realize with his photography. Other outcomes were equally desired. The very choice of lower- and working-class people as subject matter was politically guided, Rogovin said. It was an attempt to humanize those persons who are often scorned and neglected and to draw attention to their plight:

> It should be obvious to everyone that when we go into an area
> we do not do so with a "clean slate." On the contrary we come,
> like a turtle, carrying our prejudices, our racism, our politi-
> cal orientations. It is these things which usually go to shape
> our likes and dislikes. I go into the Lower West Side and look
> at things from a Marxist perspective. I try to understand the
> underlying causes of the idleness, the drugs, the prostitution, the
> graffiti etc. The selection of the Lower West Side or the mining
> villages of Appalachia is a political choice based on my desire
> not only to bring to the surface the conditions which exist but
> also to show that we are dealing with human beings.[42]

The same could be said of the steelworkers and the miners of other countries whom Rogovin portrayed. As a Marxist, he was especially interested in the industrial proletariat rather than in agricultural or white-collar workers. Hence, his major series were devoted to the urban poor, industrial workers, and miners and constitute in aggregate a record of late industrial capitalism as it touched three populations.

Rogovin wanted his photography to foment and support the struggle for social justice. In addition to publishing images in local and national newspapers and art journals and books, he placed them in publications of organized labor, such as the United Auto Workers magazine *Solidarity*; in publications that represented disenfranchised groups, such as the magazine of mountain life *Ethos*; and in organs of the Communist Party, such as the propaganda vehicles *Soviet Woman* and *Soviet Foto*, both published in Moscow for international distribution. His photographs also appeared in books by writers of progressive inclination, such as Harry M. Caudill's *My Land Is Dying*, which is a study of Appalachian miners; and on three occasions, as noted earlier, he published photographs alongside poetry by leftist writers, though none of these books was political in an overt sense.

Efforts were made to bring the photography to lower- and working-class audiences. Whenever possible, Rogovin would locate his sitters after their photographs had been taken and give them one of the developed prints. The sitters usually preserved these prints as keepsakes, often matted and framed and set on a dresser or hung on the living-room wall, and occasionally the photographs can be spotted in the background of pictures that Rogovin took of the same people at a later date. He regularly invited the urban community to his exhibitions and endeavored to arrange shows at sites where pictures had been taken. The first major exhibition of his work was the showing of photographs from the *Lower West Side* series, held at Buffalo's Albright-Knox Gallery, where those photographed and their friends and neighbors could come and see the pictures. Rogovin also presented photographs of Scottish miners through a traveling exhibition in that country and shared mining photographs in Cuba, Czechoslovakia (Czechia), South Africa, Germany, and China.[43]

The photographs serve an educational function, especially for the working class. They impart a positive feeling of self-worth and give ordinary

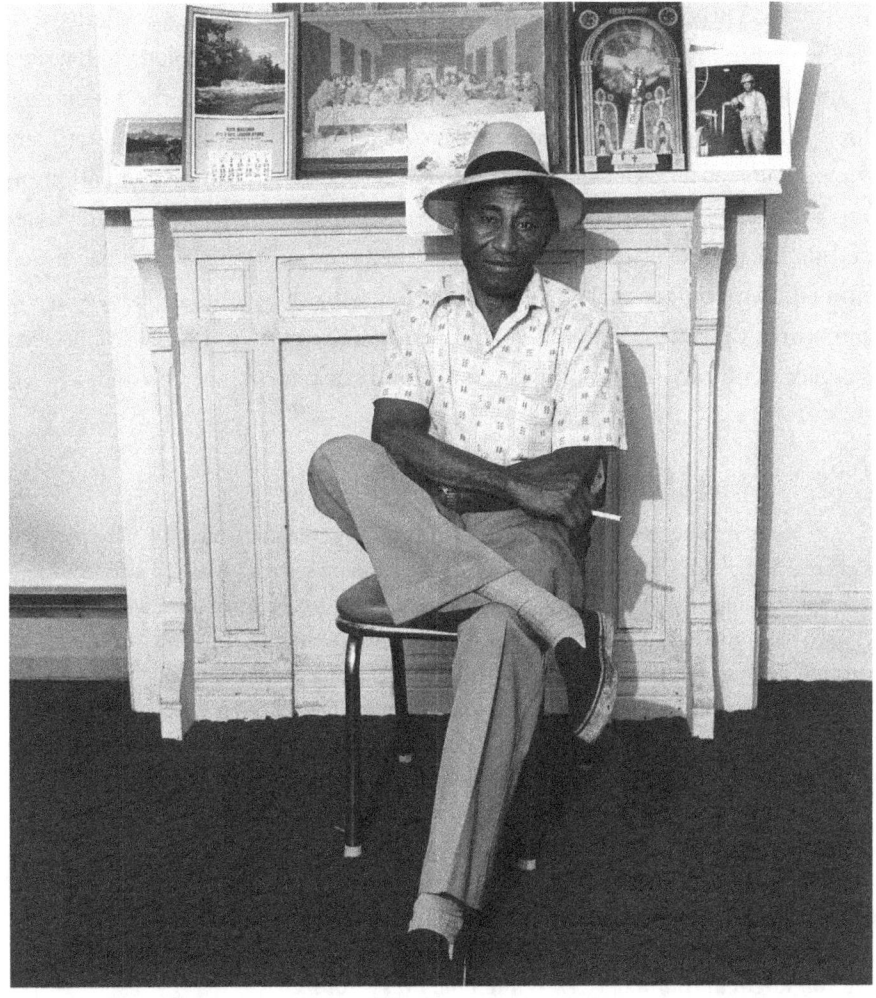

Untitled, *Working People,* 1979. The Rogovin Collection, Chicago. Copyright ©
Milton Rogovin. Courtesy, Center for Creative Photography, University of Arizona
Foundation.

people control over their public representation. The photographs further
bring to light the distinctive culture of underprivileged groups, and as historical documents they provide a record of that culture as it has evolved over
time. Common people learn about their heritage through the images and feel
in consequence a greater pride and allegiance to their social class.

Yet in a different, countervailing way the photographs overcome class divisions. Their individuation and dignification of ordinary people as well as the sympathy they promote in viewers dissolve the psychological barriers standing between the social classes even as they challenge the taxonomic logic that leads to stereotyping and narrow-minded thinking.[44] Although any viewer must as a matter of course employ taxonomic thinking when attempting to make sense of the photographs—placing human figures and material articles into set categories to give them proper definition—the direct, unmediated contact that is so strongly felt with the photographed subjects punctures those very categories and restores the common kinship between peoples of all races, ethnicities, nations, and socioeconomic positions.

Notes

1. Rogovin's journey took him to Mexico City and the states of Chiapas and Oaxaca. He went again to Mexico in the mid-1960s, visiting Mexico City and Cuernavaca, where his son, Mark, was working as an assistant to the painter David Alfaro Siqueiros. On a third trip in 1988, he photographed miners and mining towns around Pachuca and in the states of Guanajuato and Zacatecas.

2. Quoted in Linda Levine, "Milton Rogovin: The Photographer's Poetry (Part 2)," *Buffalo Spree* 17, no. 2 (Summer 1983): 15.3. See Pablo Neruda, *Windows That Open Inward: Images of Chile*, ed. Dennis Maloney, photographs by Milton Rogovin (1984; reprint, Buffalo, N.Y.: White Pine Press, 1999), and *The House at Isla Negra*, photographs by Milton Rogovin (Buffalo, N.Y.: White Pine Press, 1988); Nancy Morejón, *With Eyes and Soul: Images of Cuba*, ed. Dennis Maloney, trans. Pamela Carmell and David Frye, photographs by Milton Rogovin (Buffalo, N.Y.: White Pine Press, 2004); and Eric Gansworth, *From the Western Door to the Lower West Side*, photographs by Milton Rogovin (Buffalo, N.Y.: White Pine Press, 2010).

4. Milton Rogovin, *The Lens & The Pen: Photographs & Poems* (Arroyo Seco, N.M.: Palisade Press, 2009).

5. Robert Doherty, foreword to *Portraits in Steel*, photographs by Milton Rogovin, interviews by Michael Frisch (Ithaca, N.Y.: Cornell University Press, 1993), xv.

6. Milton Rogovin, *Store-Front Churches—Buffalo*, with commentary by W. E. B. Du Bois, *Aperture* 10, no. 2 (1962): 62—85, at http://www.miltonrogovin.com/education.html#resources.

7. Du Bois, commentary in Rogovin, *Store-Front Churches—Buffalo*, 64.

8. Michael Harrington, *The Other America: Poverty in the United States* (New York: Macmillan, 1962); Harry M. Caudill, *Night Comes to the Cumberlands: A Biography of a Depressed Area* (Boston: Little, Brown, 1963), and *My Land Is Dying* (New

York: Dutton, 1971). The relevance of these publications to Rogovin's work is discussed in Judith Keller, *Milton Rogovin: Mining Photographs* (Los Angeles: J. Paul Getty Museum, 2005).

9. Milton Rogovin, "Background Material for Masters' Degree Photo Project," American Studies Department, University of Buffalo, c. 1992, Milton Rogovin Papers, Box 27, Folder 3, Library of Congress, Washington, DC.

10. Milton Rogovin to Robert Doherty, undated, Rogovin Papers, Box 26, Folder 11.

11. Rogovin had worked in Buffalo's inner city a full decade before starting the series, when people he met at the storefront churches invited him to photograph them in their homes. Along with the pictures taken in churches, these early photographs signal the beginning of his life-long interest in portraying people of color. Original prints from the group are dated 1963 to 1965, and the series is titled *East Side, Buffalo, New York*, after the area where the pictures were taken. Although publicly exhibited, the photographs were never published in portfolio.

12. According to a grant proposal in 1975, a letter Rogovin wrote in 1981, and several lectures, the *Lower West Side* series seems to have been started in 1972 rather than in 1970, as claimed in most published sources. The precise dates of Rogovin's projects can be confusing because he often combined photographs from earlier campaigns with photographs from later campaigns or took a number of preliminary photographs of a given subject before commencing a project in earnest.

13. When the photographs were first shown at Buffalo's Albright-Knox Art Gallery in the autumn of 1975, the series was titled *Lower West Side, Buffalo, New York*, which had special meaning for local residents attending the exhibition. However, the following spring, when the photographs traveled to the International Center of Photography in New York City, the series was retitled *Lower West Side, U.S.A.*, to suggest that the depicted conditions are endemic across the country. This title was later shortened to simply *Lower West Side*. In 1976, photographs from the series were sent to Dortmund, Germany, which was Buffalo's sister city, and selected images were published that year in no fewer than nineteen art and photography journals in the United States and abroad. The Albright-Knox show was curated by James N. Wood, who wrote a fine commentary in the slender exhibition catalog, *Milton Rogovin: Lower West Side, Buffalo, New York* (Buffalo, N.Y.: Albright-Knox Art Gallery, 1975), and photographer Paul Strand added a note of appreciation. The exhibition at the International Center for Photography had no independent catalog but was twice reviewed in the *New York Times*, first by Hilton Kramer (February 21, 1976) and then by Gene Thornton (March 21, 1976).

14. Quoted in Bill Magavern, "Rogovin: Interview," press clipping from unidentified source, February 6, 1985, Rogovin Papers, Box 33, Folder 2.

15. Undated notebook, Rogovin Papers, Box 33, Folder 14.

16. The sociologist Pierre Bourdieu developed the concept of "habitus"—the ideational patterns of life—which is dialectically related to the concept of "field"—the objective conditions of social existence; see *Outline of a Theory of Practice*, trans. Richard Nice (Cambridge: Cambridge University Press, 1977).

17. Some photographs of the *Triptychs* series appear to have been taken as early as 1990. The series was shown at the Art Institute of Chicago in 1993, and selected images were published in Milton Rogovin, *Triptychs: Buffalo's Lower West Side Revisited*, essay by JoAnn Wypijewski, foreword by Robert Coles, introduction by Stephen Jay Gould (New York: Norton, 1994). The *Quartets* series was seldom seen in exhibition, though sixteen sets were published in Dave Isay, *Milton Rogovin: The Forgotten Ones* (New York: Quantuck Lane Press, 2003), with oral interviews of some sitters.

18. Undated notes for an interview, Rogovin Papers, Box 26, Folder 12.

19. Quoted in Susan Ortaga, "Look at Their Eyes—They Speak to You," *Daily World*, March 24, 1977.

20. Quoted in Ortega, "Look at Their Eyes."

21. Wood, commentary in *Milton Rogovin*, 92.

22. Dee Dee, resident of the Lower West Side, undated interview, Rogovin Papers, Box 26, Folder 10.

23. Undated notes for an interview, Rogovin Papers, Box 26, Folder 12.

24. Rogovin, typescript with biographical notes, c. 1976, p. 17, Rogovin Papers, Box 21, Folder 2.

25. I thank Professor Mitch Eckert of the Department of Fine Arts at the University of Louisville for information about the Rolleiflex camera and Kodak Tri-X film.

26. bell hooks, "In Our Glory: Photography and Black Life," in *Picturing Us: American Identity in Photography*, ed. Deborah Willis (New York: New Press, 1994), 50.

27. Rogovin typed this quotation on an index card, without line breaks (Rogovin Papers, Box 33, Folder 14). For the complete poem, see Langston Hughes, "Note on Commercial Theatre" (1940), in *The Norton Anthology of American Literature*, 7th ed., vol. D (New York: Norton, 2008), 2032.

28. Milton Rogovin to Alfred Neumann, editor of *Fotografie*, Leipzig, (East) Germany, October 20, 1978, Rogovin Papers, Box 29, Folder 10.

29. The manufacturing companies in which Rogovin took photographs between 1977 and 1980 are Atlas Steel Casting Company; Westinghouse Electric Company, Motor and Industrial Control Division; Ford Motor Company, Buffalo Stamping Plant; Chevrolet Metal Casting Plant; Shenango Inc., Steel Ingot Molds Division; Amherst Foundry; National Steel Corporation, Hanna Furnace Division; Markel Electric Products; Buffalo China Inc.; Republic Steel, Buffalo Works; Bethlehem Steel, Lackawanna Plant; Moog Inc.

30. Milton Rogovin, interviewed by Cheryl A. Brutvan, undated typed transcript, Rogovin Papers, Box 21, Folder 2.

31. Milton Rogovin, interviewed in the documentary *Milton Rogovin: The Forgotten Ones,* directed by David Knaus (ASEITA Film, 1988).

32. Fred Licht, "Photography Class Acts," *Art in America* 72, no. 2 (February 1984): 41.

33. This view is taken in Anthony Bannon, "Duality of Imagery by Rogovin Effective," *Buffalo News,* December 9, 1982: "As the selector of what information to pass along, Rogovin has stacked the cards some, however. The work is dark; the home is light. The work place is an ambiguous space, the home is definite. Rarely at work does one find the relief of a decorative gesture, let alone the visual confidence in recognizing how the workers function there. At home, these factors generally abound." Although Bannon's observation about Rogovin's stacking the deck is well taken, Bannon does not perceive the essential complementarity of the two types of images.

34. Michael Frisch, introduction to *Portraits in Steel,* 3.

35. A year before the publication of *Portraits in Steel,* the show *Working People: Photographs by Milton Rogovin* was held at the Smithsonian Institution's National Museum of American History, with ninety photographs from the *Working People* series. Earlier still, a smaller sample was shown at the Albright-Knox Art Gallery, Buffalo, and at the Brooklyn Museum and published in Cheryl A. Brutvan and Milton Rogovin, *The Forgotten Ones,* with essays by Robert J. Doherty and Fred Licht (Seattle: University of Washington Press, 1985).

36. In his introductory essay to *Portraits in Steel,* Frisch writes: "Milton Rogovin is almost exclusively a portrait photographer: he takes pictures of people who quite deliberately compose, pose, and present themselves to him, generally looking directly into the eye of his camera. Their expression and intention, however implicit, is what he receives, records, and conveys in his photography. I have sought a similar quality in the oral history interviews that provide the text for this book" (2–3).

37. In a letter to Clinton Adlum, Rogovin assured the Cuban representative that the photographs would be a "tribute" to the miners and their families. He added that he would prefer to visit mines where the workers were darker skinned because he had planned on traveling to some African mining areas but was unable to do so (Milton Rogovin to Clinton Adlum, Cuban Interests Section, Republic of Cuba, Washington, DC, September 8, 1988, Rogovin Papers, Box 28, Folder 9). A number of the Cuba pictures are separately published in Morejón, *With Eyes and Soul.*

38. Michael McGahey, president of the Scottish Area for the National Union of Miners and a prominent Communist organizer, put Rogovin in touch with mining families in Scotland.

39. Milton Rogovin to Lupe Vilas, director of international relations, Ministry of Culture, Republic of Cuba, October 22, 1984, Rogovin Papers, Box 28, Folder 8.

40. Rogovin described the many obstructions to his work in Russia in a small notebook he kept on the trip (Rogovin Papers, Box 33, Folder 13).

41. In *Milton Rogovin: The Making of a Social Documentary Photographer* (Seattle: University of Washington Press; Tucson: Center for Creative Photography, University of Arizona, 2006), Melanie Herzog places Rogovin's work within the history of modern photography.

42. Milton Rogovin to Robert Doherty, undated, Rogovin Papers, Box 26, Folder 11.

43. The exhibition traveled for more than a year to Scottish mining villages, and British public television produced a show about the work with commentary from miners: Tariq Ali, series producer, *Images of Atlantis: The Photography of Milton Rogovin* (Oasis Television for Channel Four Television Company, 1992).

44. The philosopher Jacques Derrida warns that the imposition of taxonomic and classificatory systems consigns phenomena and their associated meanings to preexisting codes and synchronic structures (*Archive Fever: A Freudian Impression* [Chicago: University of Chicago Press, 1995]).

Milton Rogovin at Home in the University of Louisville Photographic Archives

Elizabeth E. Reilly

THIS BOOK AND THE EXHIBITION that preceded it were sparked by a series of significant donations of Milton Rogovin prints to the University of Louisville Photographic Archives arranged by collector David Knaus. As curator of the archives, I was thrilled to accept the work of this important photographer. The donated prints are predominantly from his *Appalachia, Working People,* and *Family of Miners* series—images all relating to the archive's mission to collect meaningful social documentary photography and work relating to Louisville and greater Kentucky. Furthermore, Rogovin's legacy as a political activist and his socially conscious photographs are a natural fit in the Photographic Archives; our other collections complement his images and help put his work in historic and artistic context.

The Photographic Archives stand as a preeminent repository of documentary, historical and fine-art photography and is one of the first university-based photographic collections established in this country. Since their founding in 1962, when art faculty member Robert J. Doherty began gathering primary sources to support the university's newly established photography program, the archives have grown to more than two million items employed for teaching, exhibition, and research by students, the public, and scholars alike.

Considered a successor to the greatest social documentary photographers of the twentieth century, such as Lewis Hine, Dorothea Lange, and Walker Evans, Milton Rogovin (1909–2011) used the camera as a tool for social justice. He was a crusader for people he deemed "the forgotten ones"—

the poor, oppressed, working people of the world—and through his photographs he illuminated his subjects with strength and dignity. Rogovin has credited these photographers and especially Roy Stryker's large-scale documentary projects as powerful influences on his own work.

Rogovin is clearly of the lineage of Lewis Hine, one of the first photographers to fully realize and utilize the power of photography for social change. Working between 1904 and 1940, Hine exposed the hazardous working conditions of miners, the exploitation of child laborers, the resolve of new immigrants to America, and the accomplishments of men at work. In a clear example of documentary photography's influence to promote political and social change, Hine's work for the National Child Labor Committee proved vital in transforming child-labor laws in the United States. Like Hine, Rogovin was a concerned photographer; he understood the power of pictures to persuade and strove to create awareness of social inequities. Rogovin's work now joins a study collection of more than 500 posthumous Lewis Hine prints in the University of Louisville Photographic Archives.

Rogovin connects clearly with another major figure in social documentary photography whose work is well represented in the Photographic Archives collections: Roy E. Stryker. After curating and traveling with an exhibition of Farm Security Administration (FSA) photographs titled *USA-FSA*, Robert Doherty met the documentary project's director, Roy Stryker. A friendship was formed, and at Doherty's suggestion Stryker entrusted his personal papers in 1964 to the Photographic Archives. In addition to his personal correspondence with the project photographers, original "shooting scripts," and other documentation is a collection of more than 1,900 vintage prints, including the iconic images *Migrant Mother* by Dorothea Lange and *Fleeing a Dust Storm* by Arthur Rothstein, as well as Walker Evans's photographs of the Fields family that appeared in the book *Let Us Now Praise Famous Men.*[1] Milton Rogovin is quoted as having listed both Dorothea Lange and Walker Evans as great influences to his own artistic vision.

The FSA documentary project operated to record and collect evidence of the plight of farmers struggling through the Depression and Dust Bowl; the images were then disseminated through newspapers and popular magazines to promote President Franklin D. Roosevelt's New Deal assistance policies. Sponsored by the federal government, the project had a clear propagandistic purpose but was nonetheless effective in making citizens aware of the hardships being suffered in poor, rural parts of the country. Furthermore, the outstanding images created by the FSA photographers have since come to define this particular time and place in America because some individuals may know nothing of the Great Depression other than the weathered face of a migrant farm mother surrounded by her children. The project as a whole defined social documentary photography in the twentieth century and solidified a tradition of concerned photography that had been established a few decades earlier by Lewis Hine.

Roy Stryker is credited with launching the careers of the photographers he directed, such as Dorothea Lange and Walker Evans as well as Russell Lee, Marion Post Wolcott, and Gordon Parks, many of whom followed him to his next documentary project for the Standard Oil of New Jersey (SONJ) company. Charged with securing photographs that would improve the general public's very low perception of the monolithic oil corporation, Stryker was again directing a propaganda project. Working with the theme "There's a Drop of Oil in the Life of Everyone," Stryker approached this public-relations mission in much the same way he did for the FSA: to document in the broadest sense.

Some of the other photographers working under Stryker for SONJ included Harold Corsini, Sol Libsohn, Esther Bubley, Todd Webb, and Charlotte Brooks. Sent out to record every aspect of oil production and consumption, the photographers predictably photographed at oil drills and refineries, but more often they focused on the human element within the industry—captains of the tugboats, passengers on the buses, women workers in defense plants, children playing, families eating, everyday life in the small communities across the country and beyond. The SONJ project went outside American borders into South America, Europe, and the Middle East. Stryker emphasized the photo essay or "picture story" type of reporting, thereby allowing the photographers to go in depth with their subjects and spend time shooting a more complete "picture." There may be no better visual document of life between 1943 and 1950 than the images in the SONJ project. Approximately 67,000 photographs were put to use by the company's public-relations

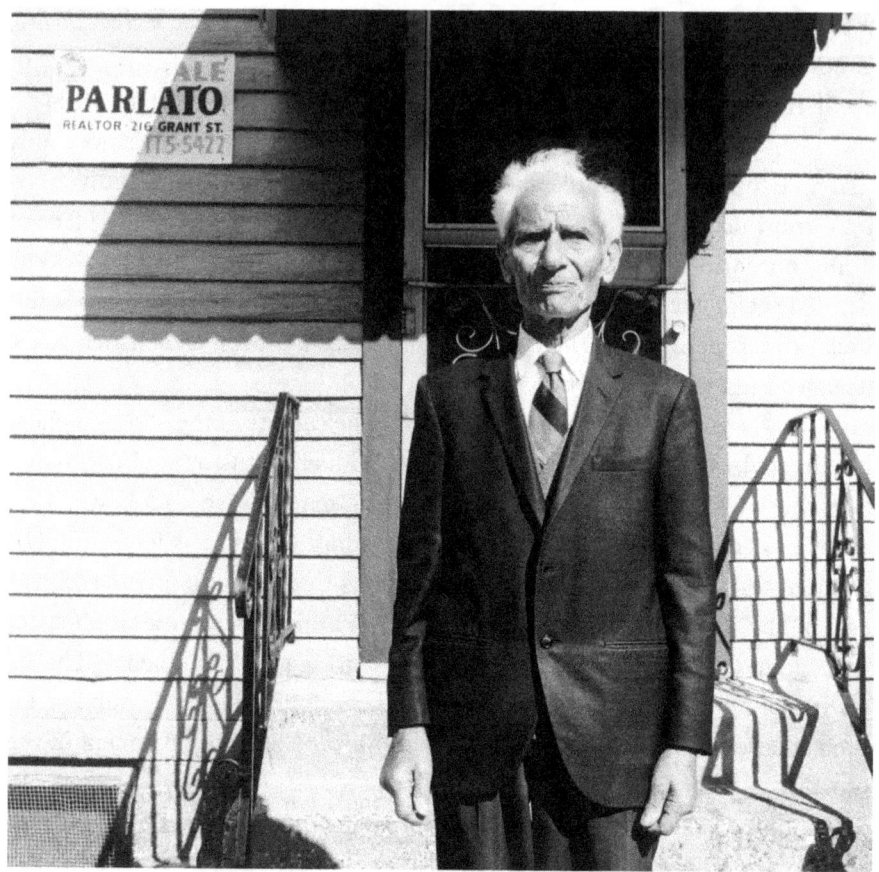

Untitled, *Lower West Side*, 1972–1975. Photographic Archives, University of Louisville. Copyright © Milton Rogovin. Courtesy, Center for Creative Photography, University of Arizona Foundation.

department, all of which now reside at the University of Louisville Photographic Archives along with the 180,000 negatives and associated material.

Milton Rogovin's effort to document workers beginning in the 1960s nearly picks up where the SONJ photographs left off in the 1950s and reflects the cultural transitions in industry as they were happening. Through Rogovin's photographs we see disadvantaged minorities, including women, filling positions in heavy industry once commonly held by white men who left the mines, factories, and plants for white-collar careers in the rapidly expanding corporate worlds of finance and technology. Rogovin's revisiting of his Buffa-lo steel plant subjects years after he took the initial photographs reflects the deindustrialization happening in America as the plants shut down and the workers became unemployed.

The third Roy Stryker–related collection held at the Photographic Ar-chives is the Jones and Laughlin (J&L) Steel Company Photographic Project, and it, too, connects directly with Rogovin's work. J&L was Stryker's last documentary project and was similar in design to the SONJ project, though much smaller in scale; Stryker directed a number of photographers to docu-ment the operations of the J&L Steel Company for its public-relations depart-ment. In fact, it is one of the images created for this project that prompted Milton Rogovin to begin photographing workers at their homes. According to Rogovin's son, Mark, an image of a J&L steel worker and his child at home feeding geese made Rogovin realize he needed to photograph the workers outside of their trade to get a fuller sense of each person.

The Fine Print Collection in the Photographic Archives holds a few thousand photographs, including many by masters who influenced Rogovin's work, along with those by others who echo his themes. The prints in this col-lection are used for study and display and help tell the broad history of pho-tography. Included is Paul Strand's series *The Mexican Portfolio* (1932–1933). Strand was one of Rogovin's mentors, and his influence on Rogovin is seen in the humanistic portraits within this portfolio. Also held in this portion of the archives is *Northumbrian Coal Miner at His Evening Meal, 1937* by Bill Brandt. Brandt photographed coal miners in the north of England during the indus-trial depression of the 1930s. His photographs of miners in their homes are directly associated to Rogovin's work. Also in the Fine Print Collection are images of coal mining by Louisville photographer Bob Hower, who has been shooting mining operations for himself and commercial clients since 1976. His workplace portraits of miners recall Rogovin's straightforward shots of workers conveying pride and confidence amid gritty, industrial backdrops. The Photographic Archives also have a number of prints by native Kentuck-ian Shelby Lee Adams, who has been photographing families in the Appala-chian Mountains of eastern Kentucky consistently for more than thirty-five years. Adams returns to Appalachia to shoot the same families year after year in and around their homes, much as Rogovin returned to photograph there every summer from 1962 to 1971. Both photographers' work communicates the dignity and endurance of the Appalachian people.

Upon speaking with Rogovin's son, Mark, I was surprised to learn that the University of Louisville Photographic Archives had been his father's first choice of repository to hold the archive of his life's work, in part because of Rogovin's friendship with founder Robert Doherty but principally because the Roy Stryker Papers and Standard Oil documentary project are housed here. Unfortunately, at the time Rogovin approached the archives, the size of his collection was much more than the staff and facilities could manage (the bulk of the Rogovin archive eventually landed in the Library of Congress, with another significant group of prints going to the Center for Creative Photography at the University of Arizona). That a large portion of Rogovin's prints have come to reside in the archives among the work of many of the photographer's greatest influences is comforting to me. And now with the inclusion of Milton Rogovin's work, the path of social documentary photography from Hine to Stryker to Rogovin to photographers after him can be studied firsthand in the University of Louisville Photographic Archives.

Note

1. James Agee and Walker Evans, *Let Us Now Praise Famous Men* (Boston: Houghton Mifflin, 1941).

Photo Gallery

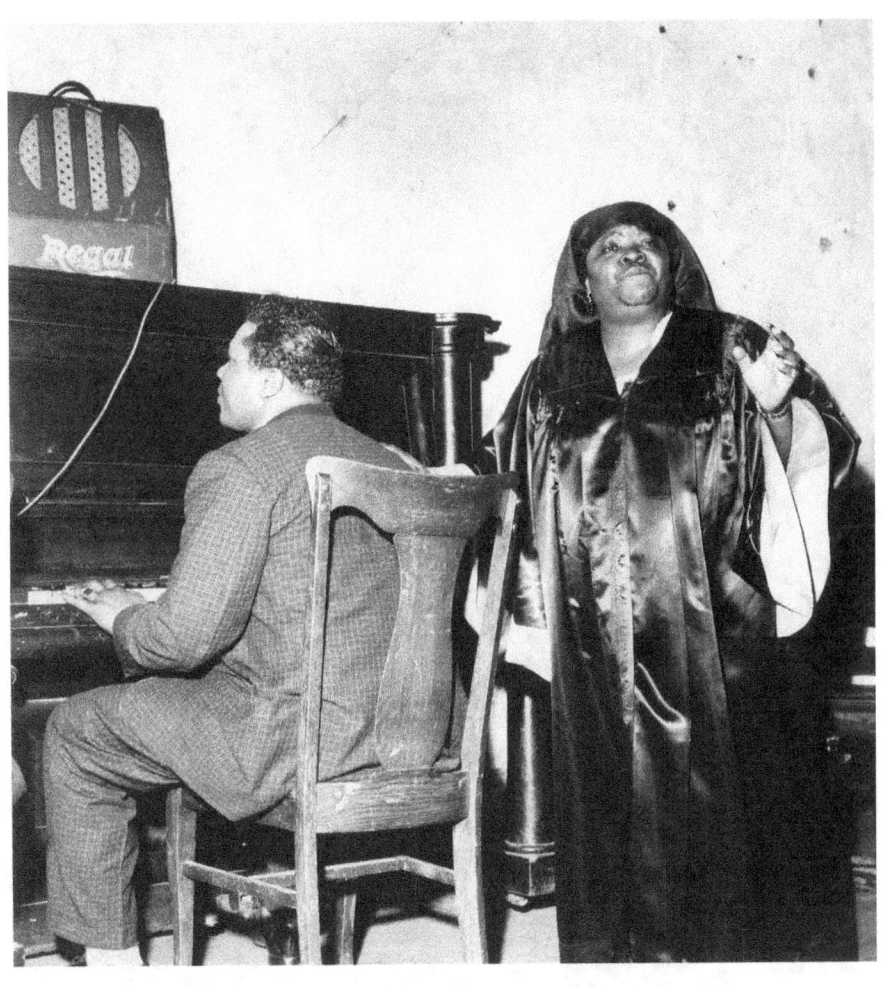

Untitled, *Storefront Churches,* 1958–1961. The Rogovin Collection, Chicago. Copyright © Milton Rogovin. Courtesy, Center for Creative Photography, University of Arizona Foundation.

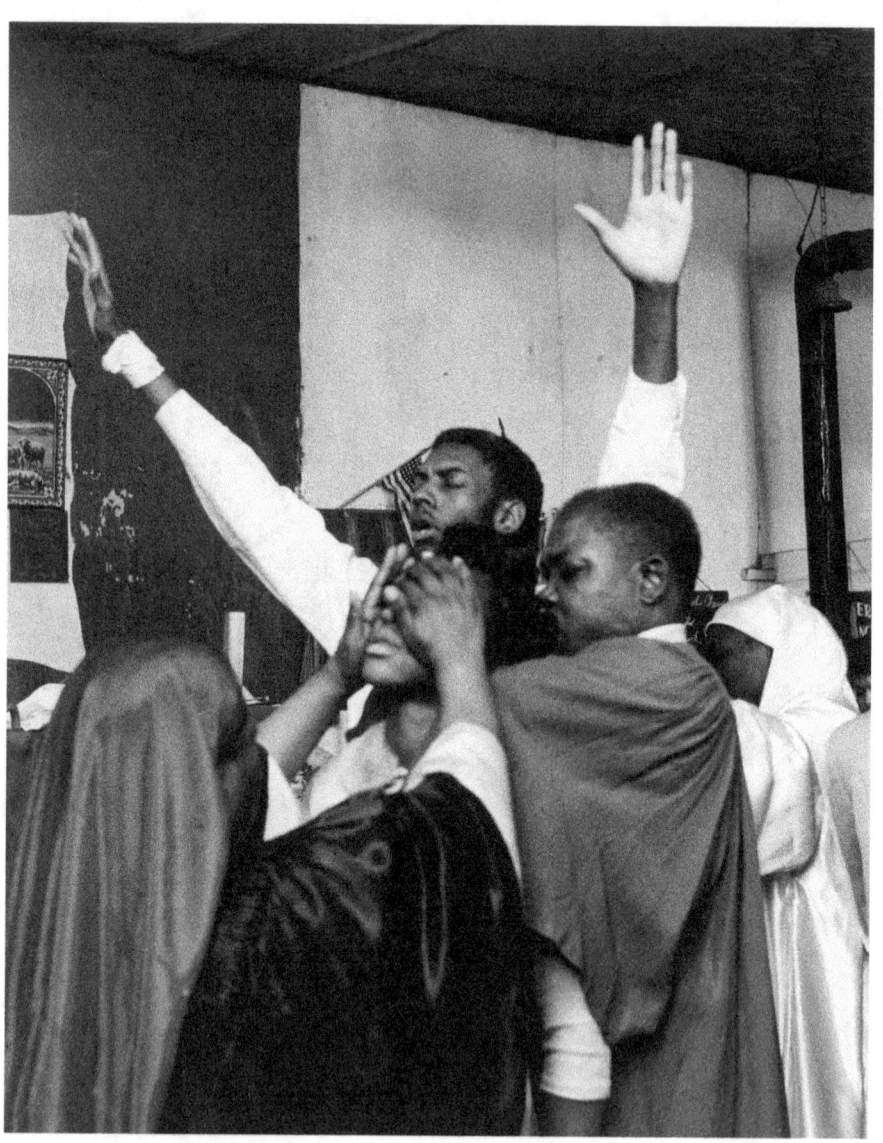

Untitled, *Storefront Churches,* 1958–1961. The Rogovin Collection, Chicago. Copyright © Milton Rogovin. Courtesy, Center for Creative Photography, University of Arizona Foundation.

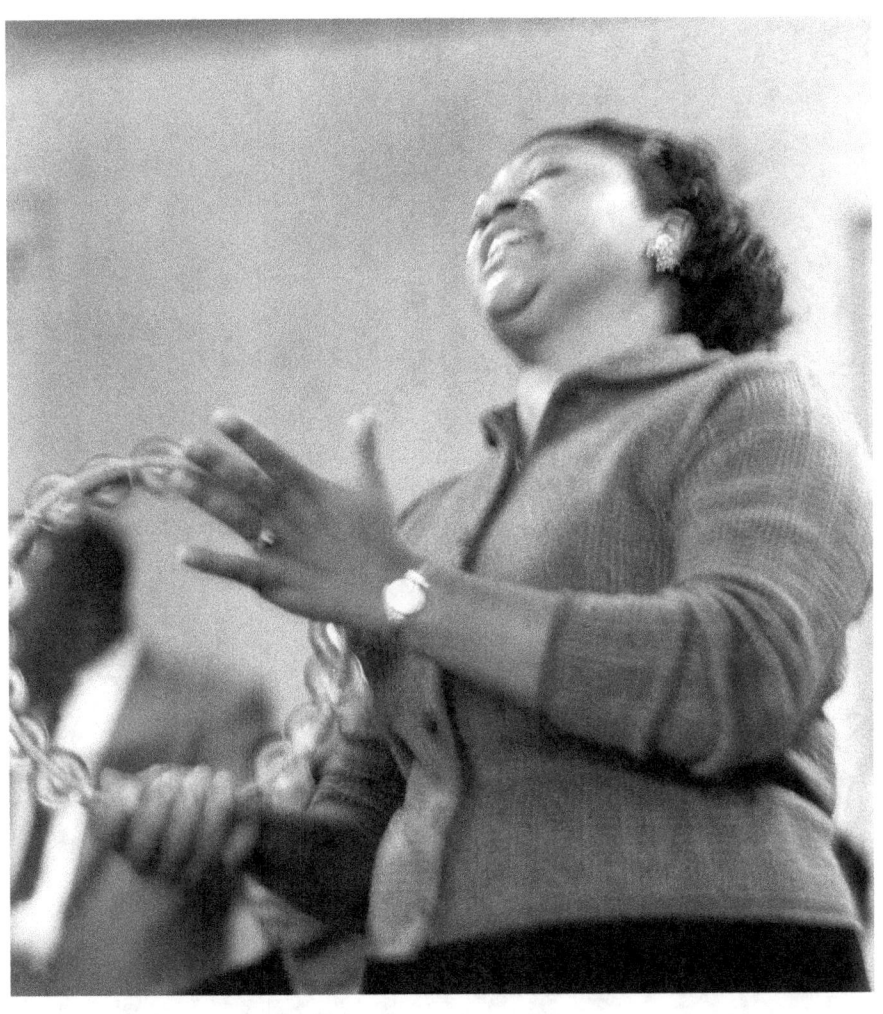

Untitled, *Storefront Churches*, 1958–1961. The Rogovin Collection, Chicago. Copyright © Milton Rogovin. Courtesy, Center for Creative Photography, University of Arizona Foundation.

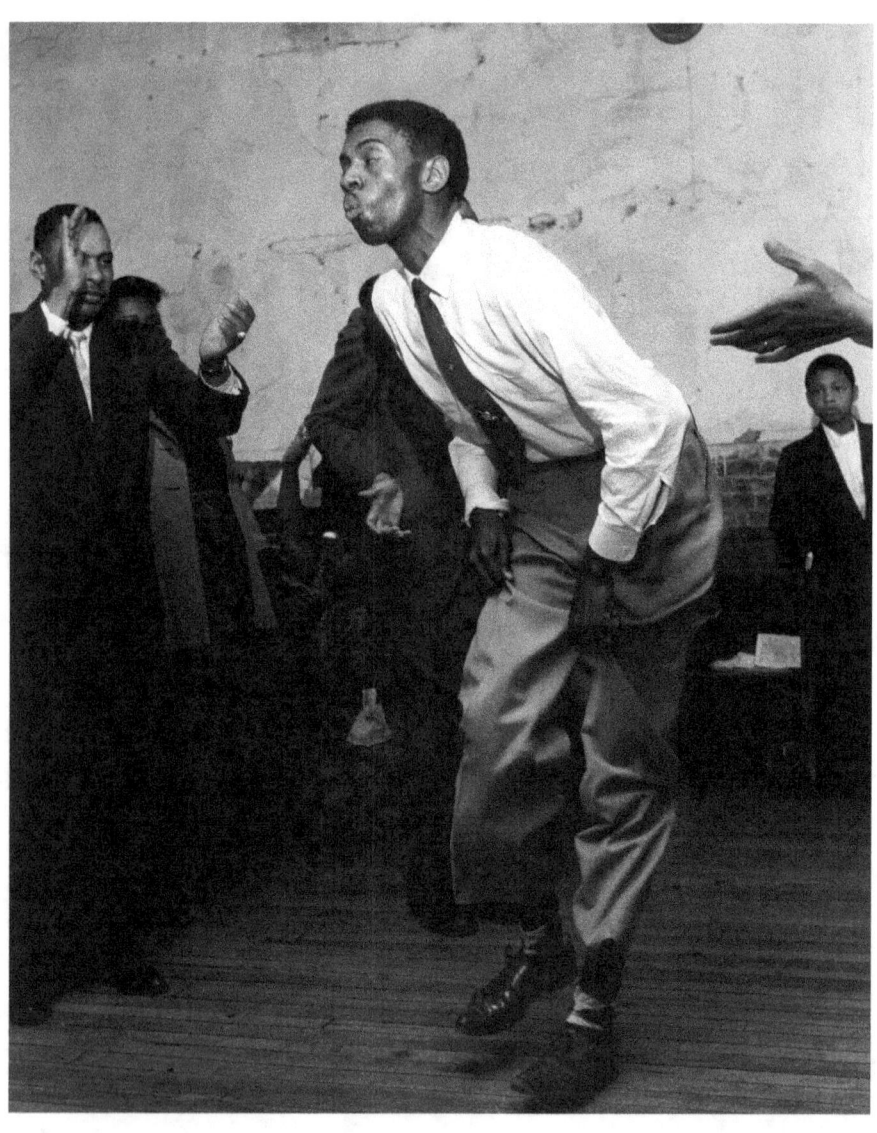

Untitled, *Storefront Churches,* 1958–61. The Rogovin Collection, Chicago. Copyright © Milton Rogovin. Courtesy, Center for Creative Photography, University of Arizona Foundation.

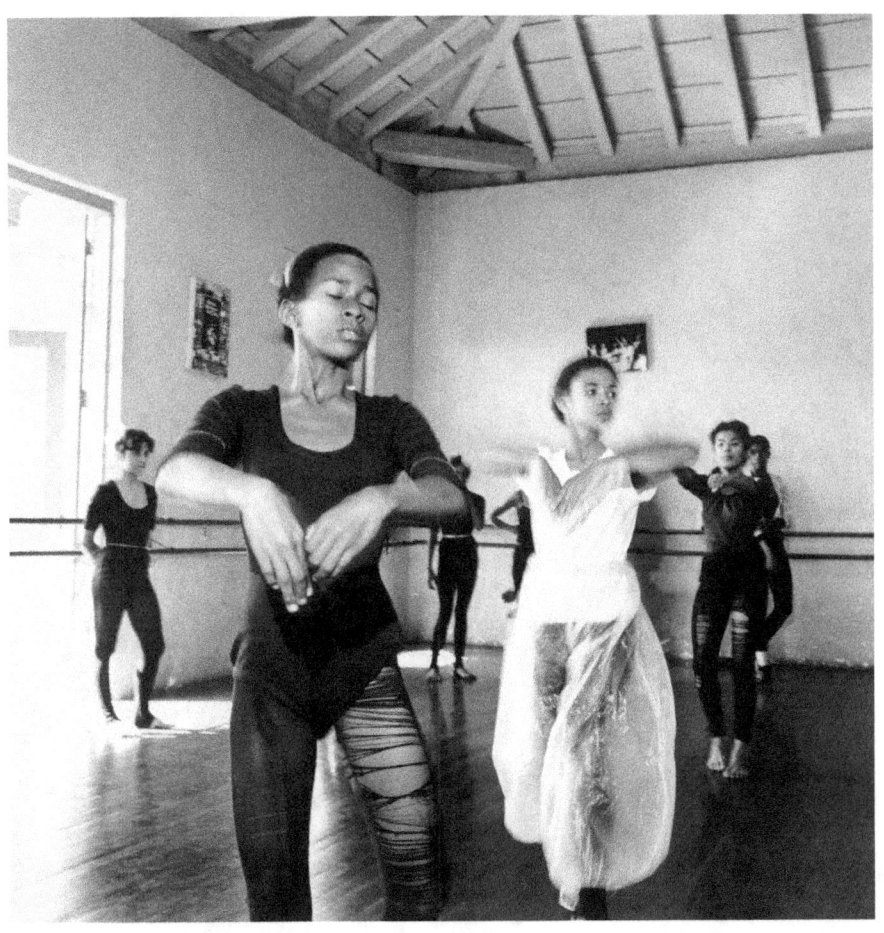

Untitled (Cuba), *Family of Miners*, 1984. Photographic Archives, University of Louisville. Copyright © Milton Rogovin. Courtesy, Center for Creative Photography, University of Arizona Foundation.

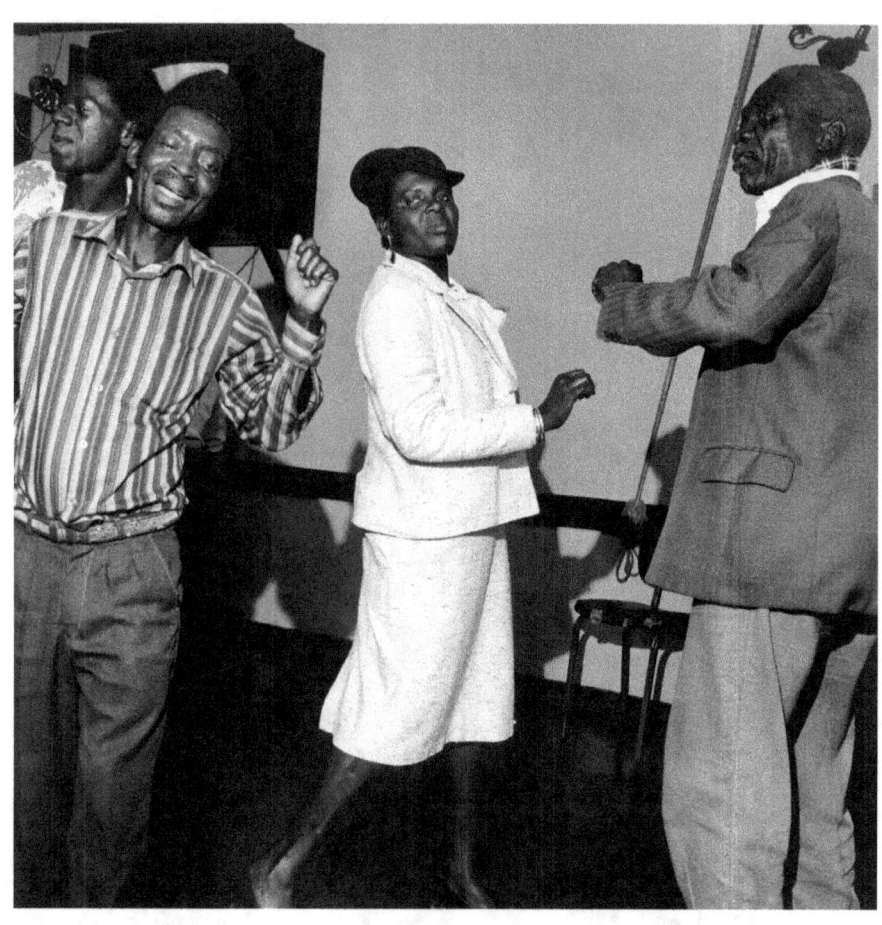

Untitled (Zimbabwe), *Family of Miners,* 1989. Photographic Archives, University of Louisville. Copyright © Milton Rogovin. Courtesy, Center for Creative Photography, University of Arizona Foundation.

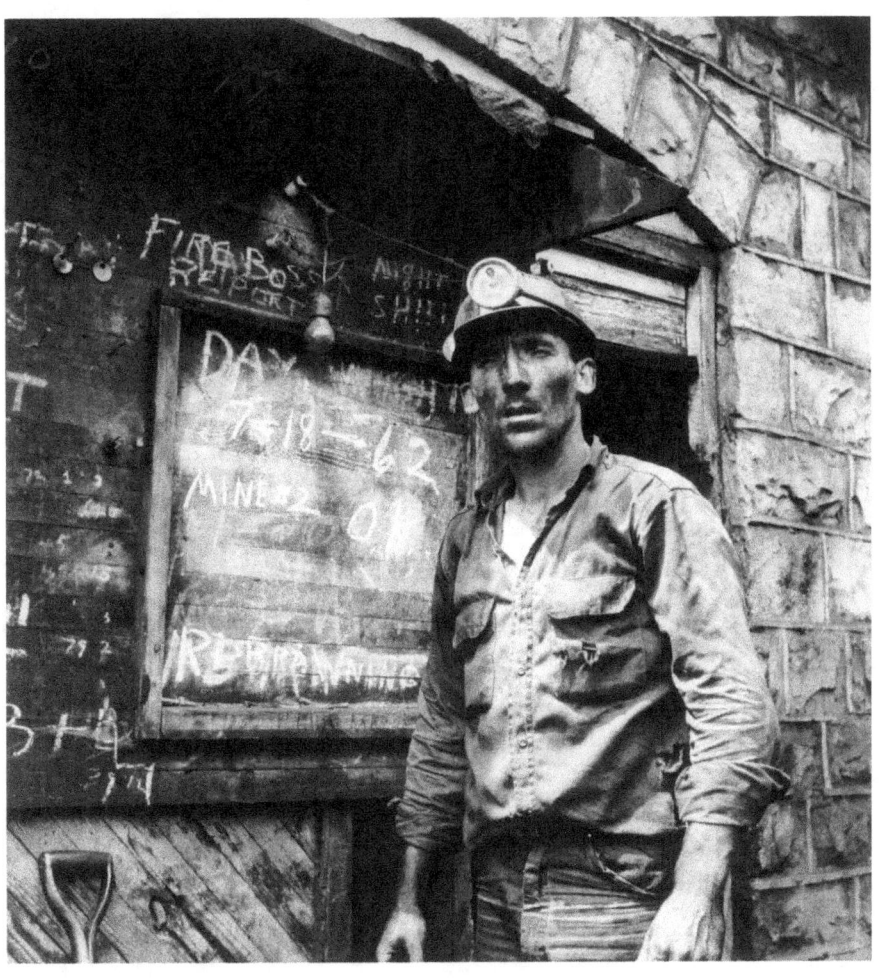

Untitled, *Appalachia,* 1962. Photographic Archives, University of Louisville. Copyright © Milton Rogovin. Courtesy, Center for Creative Photography, University of Arizona Foundation.

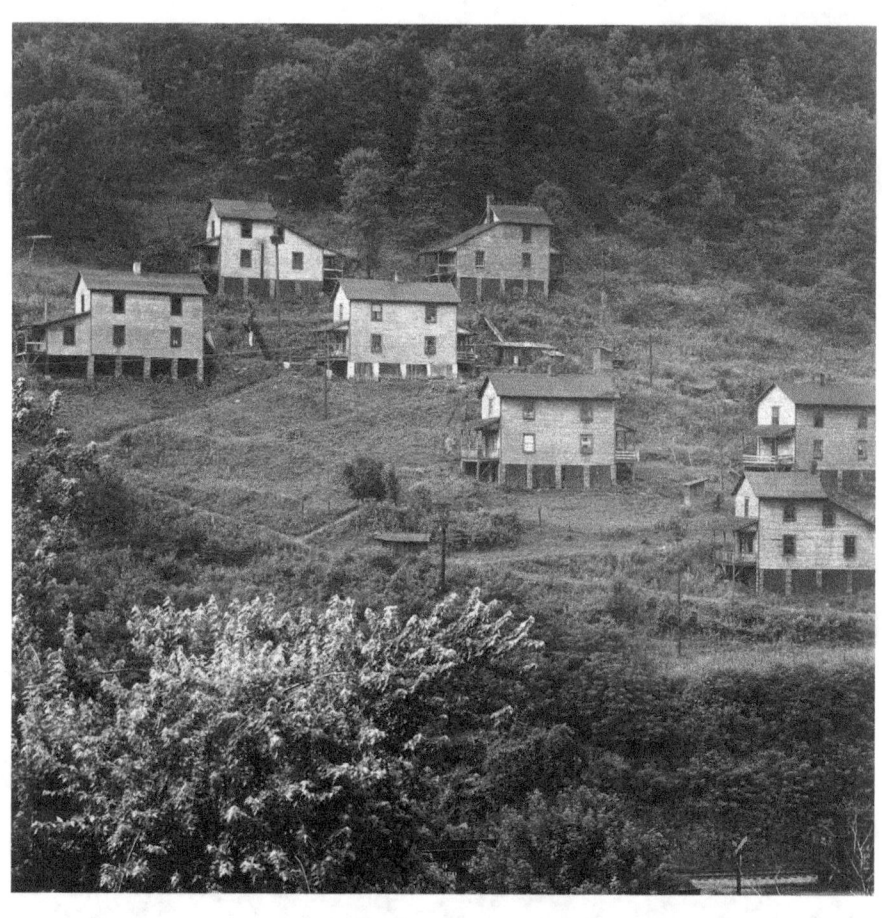

Untitled, *Appalachia,* 1962. The Rogovin Collection, Chicago. Copyright © Milton Rogovin.
Courtesy, Center for Creative Photography, University of Arizona Foundation.

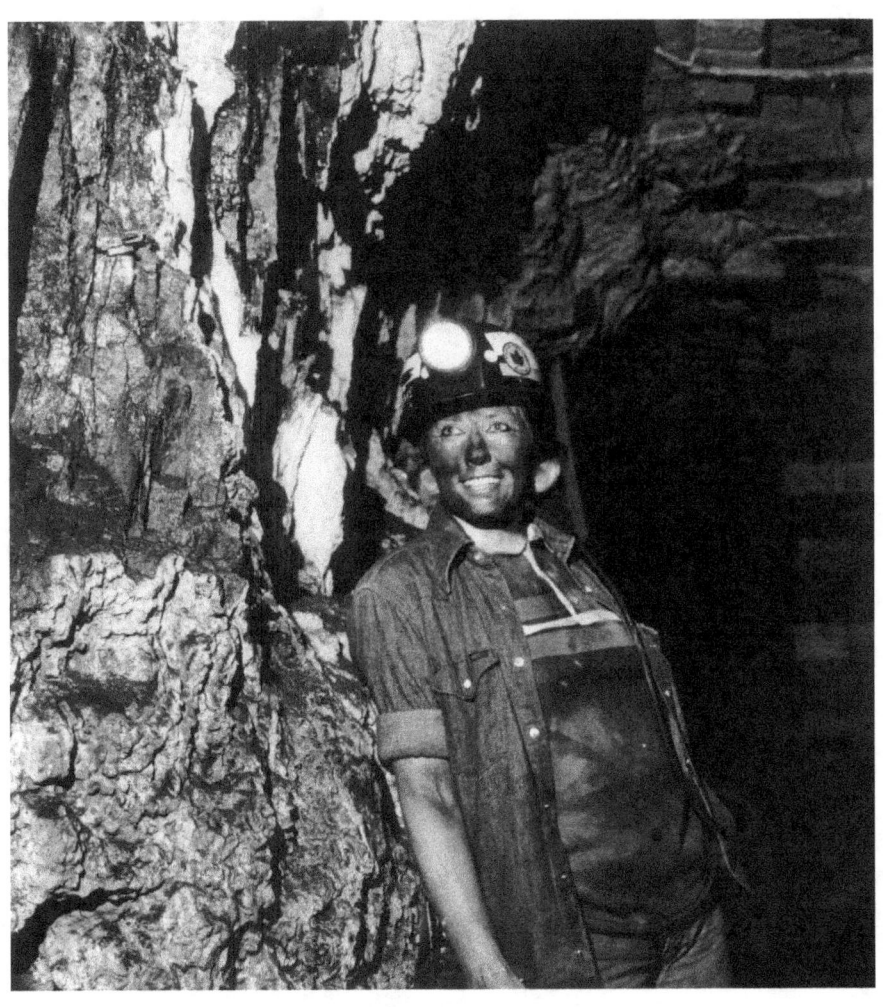

Untitled, *Appalachia*, 1981. Photographic Archives, University of Louisville. Copyright © Milton Rogovin. Courtesy, Center for Creative Photography, University of Arizona Foundation.

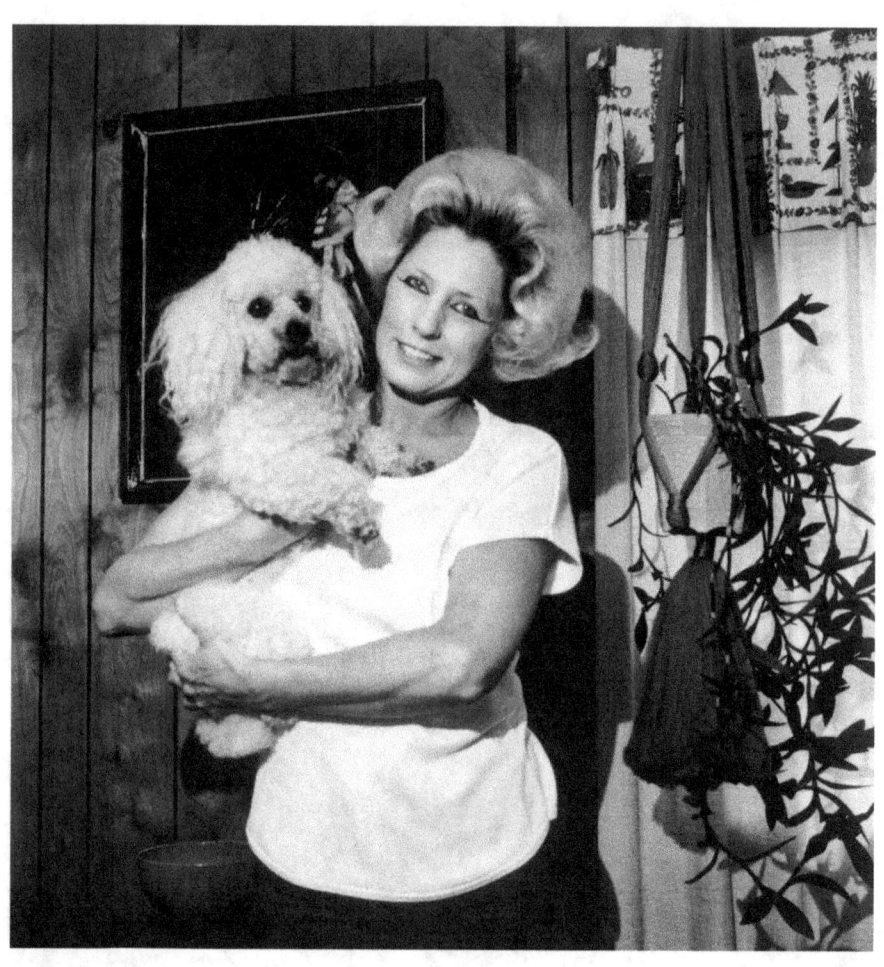

Untitled, *Appalachia*, 1981. Photographic Archives, University of Louisville. Copyright © Milton Rogovin. Courtesy, Center for Creative Photography, University of Arizona Foundation.

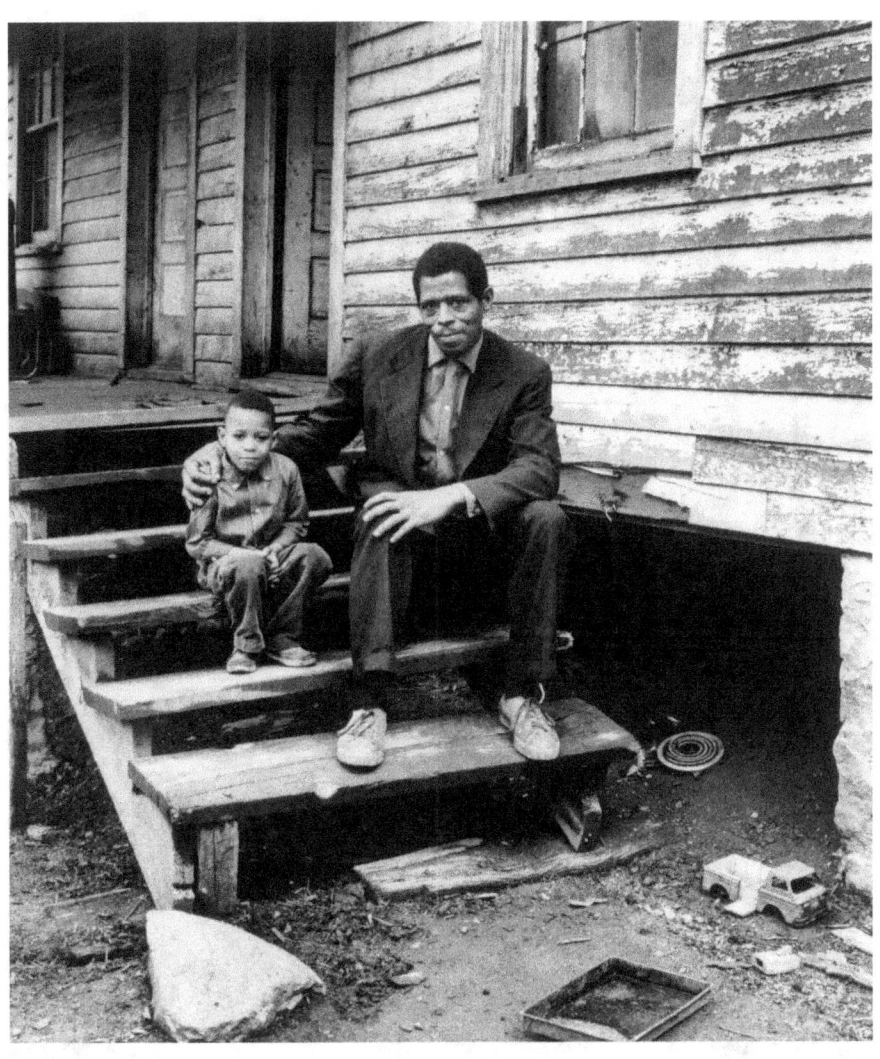

Untitled, *Appalachia*, 1965. Photographic Archives, University of Louisville. Copyright © Milton Rogovin. Courtesy, Center for Creative Photography, University of Arizona Foundation.

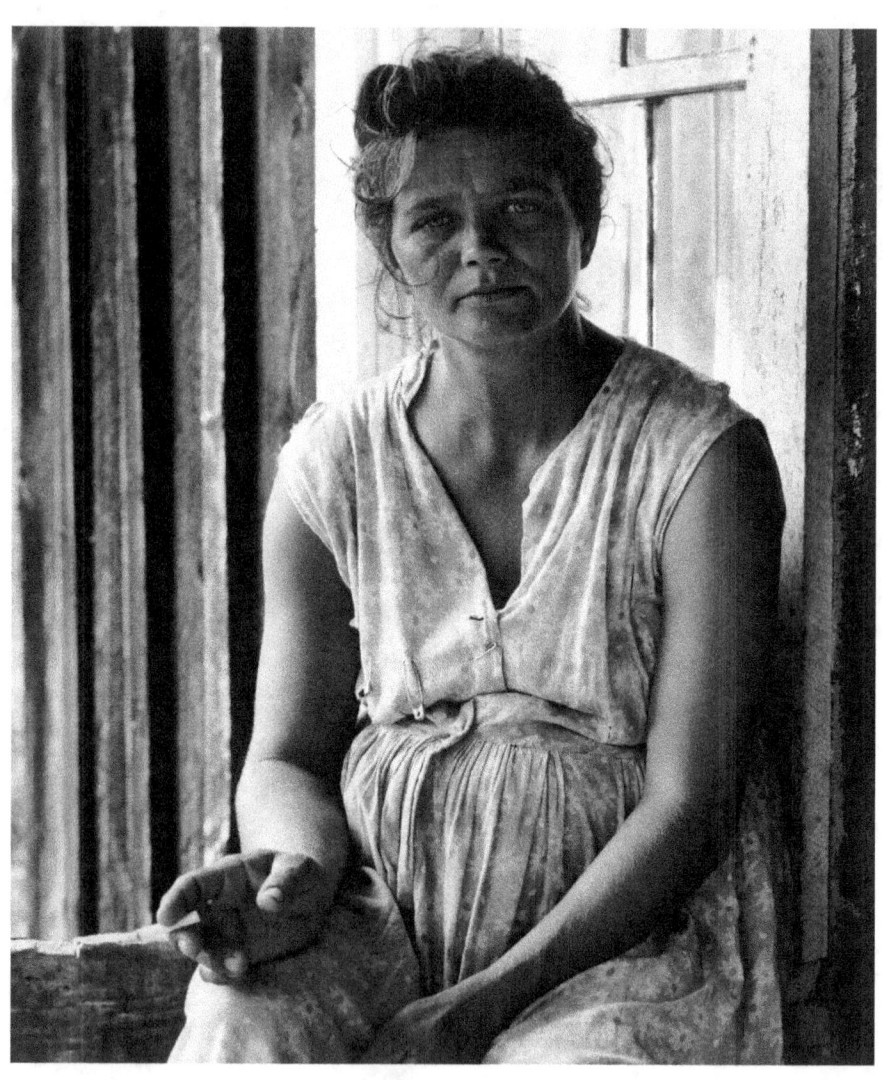

Untitled, *Appalachia*, 1964. Photographic Archives, University of Louisville. Copyright © Milton Rogovin. Courtesy, Center for Creative Photography, University of Arizona Foundation.

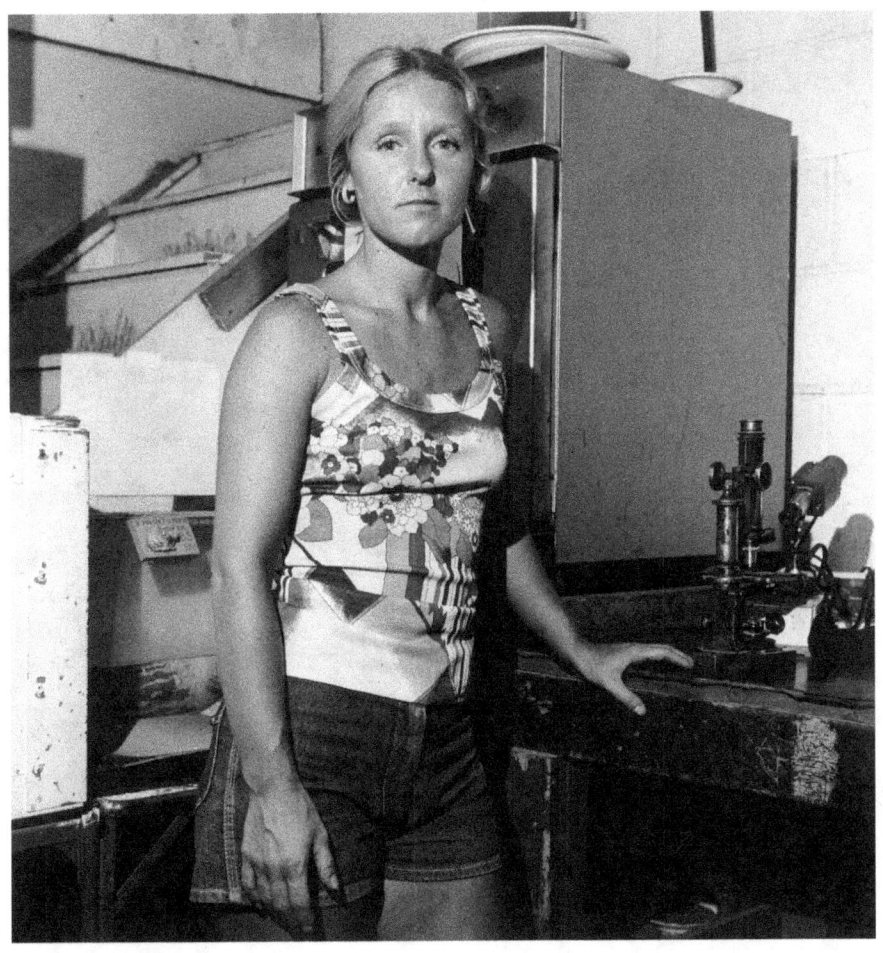

Untitled (Buffalo China), *Working People,* 1978. Photographic Archives, University of Louisville. Copyright © Milton Rogovin. Courtesy, Center for Creative Photography, University of Arizona Foundation.

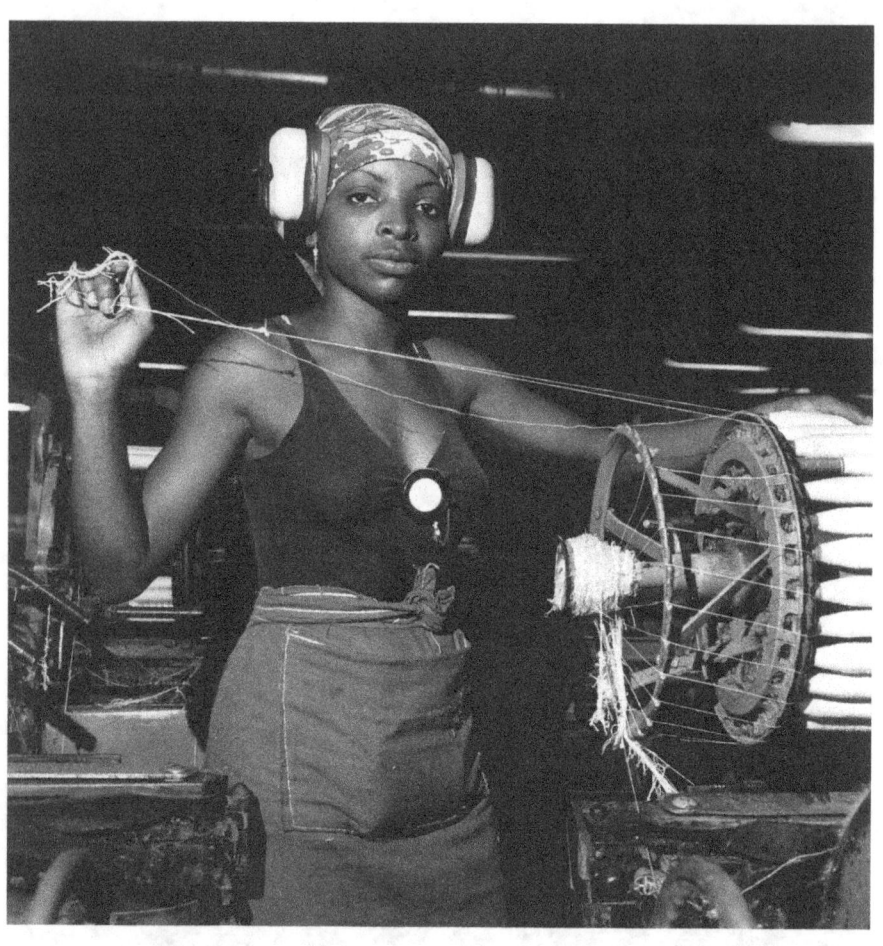

Untitled (Cuba), *Family of Miners,* 1984. The Rogovin Collection, Chicago. Copyright © Milton Rogovin. Courtesy, Center for Creative Photography, University of Arizona Foundation.

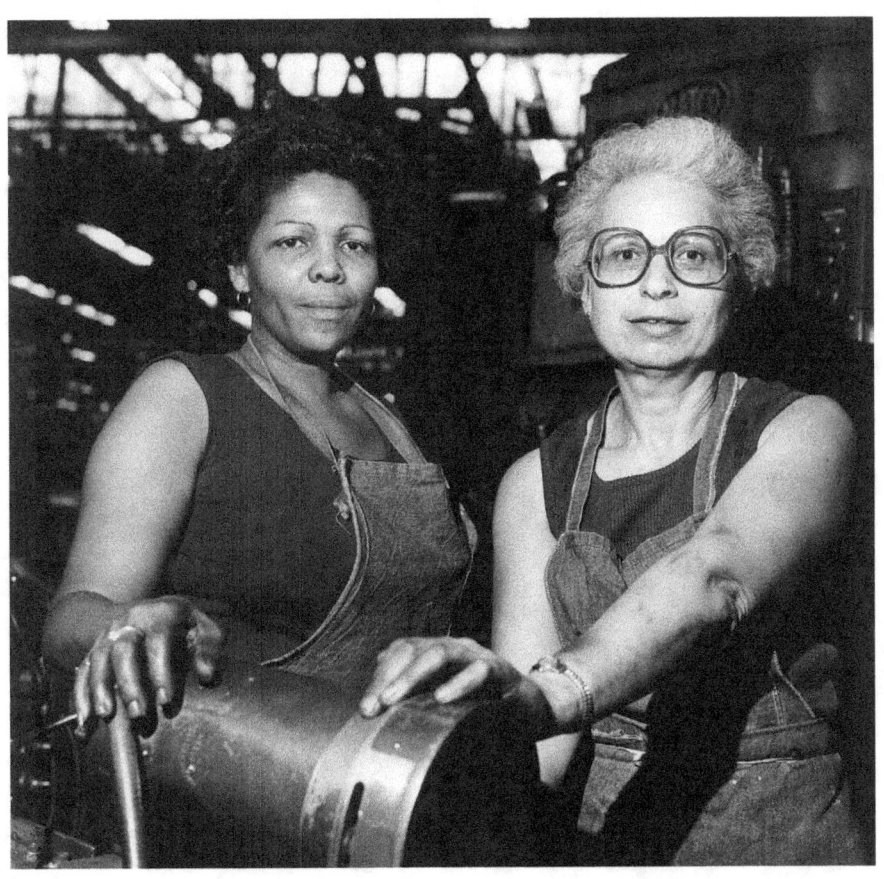

Untitled (Westinghouse Electric Company, Motor and Industrial Control Division), *Working People,* 1978. The Rogovin Collection, Chicago. Copyright © Milton Rogovin. Courtesy, Center for Creative Photography, University of Arizona Foundation.

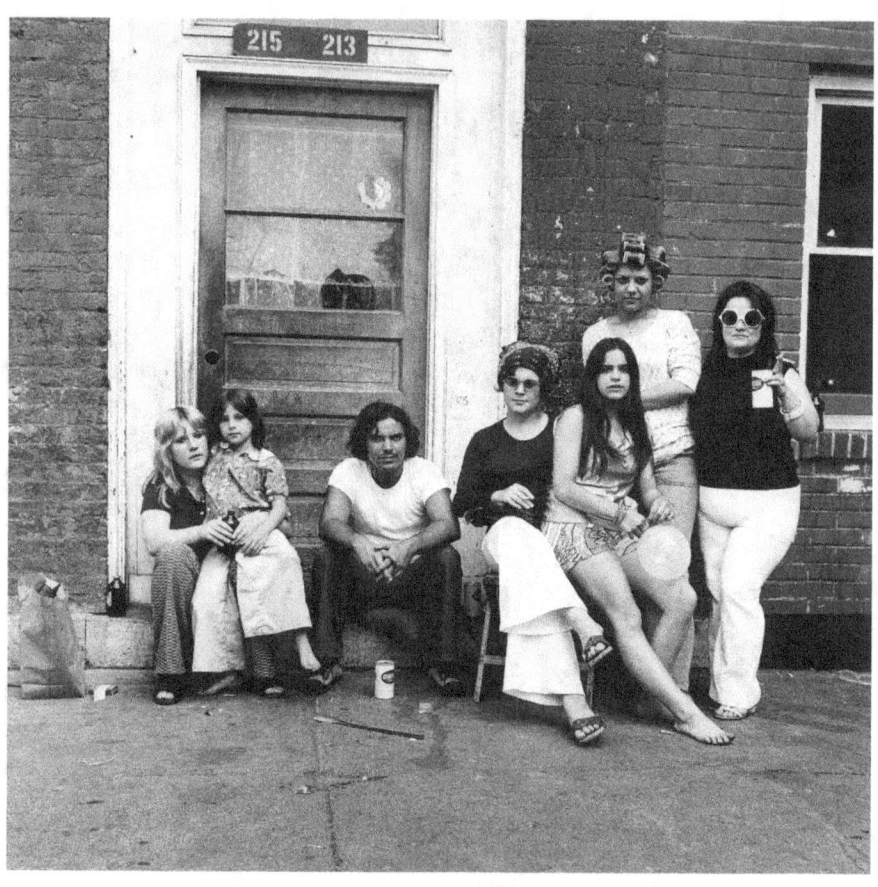

Untitled, *Lower West Side—Revisited,* 1983–1985. The Rogovin Collection. Copyright © Milton Rogovin. Courtesy, Center for Creative Photography, University of Arizona Foundation.

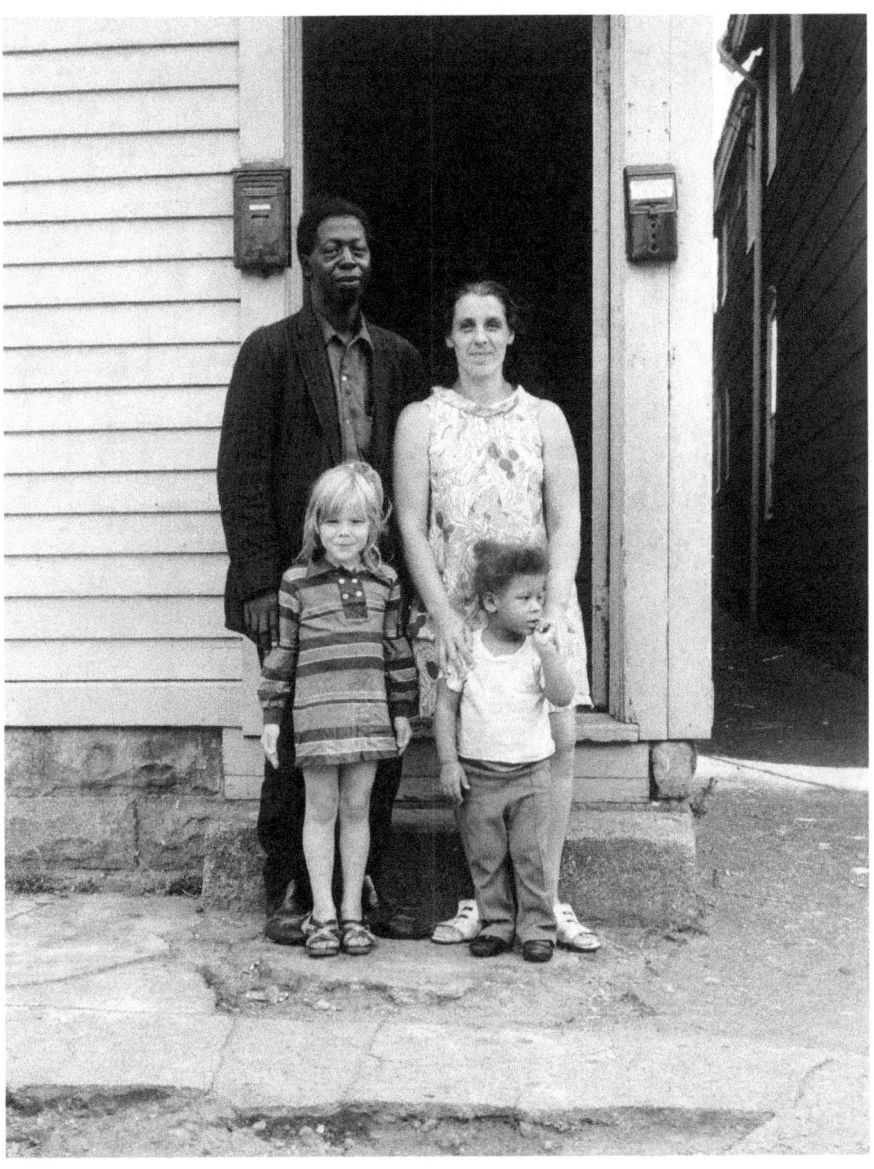

Untitled, *Lower West Side,* 1972. Photographic Archives, University of Louisville. Copyright © Milton Rogovin. Courtesy, Center for Creative Photography, University of Arizona Foundation.

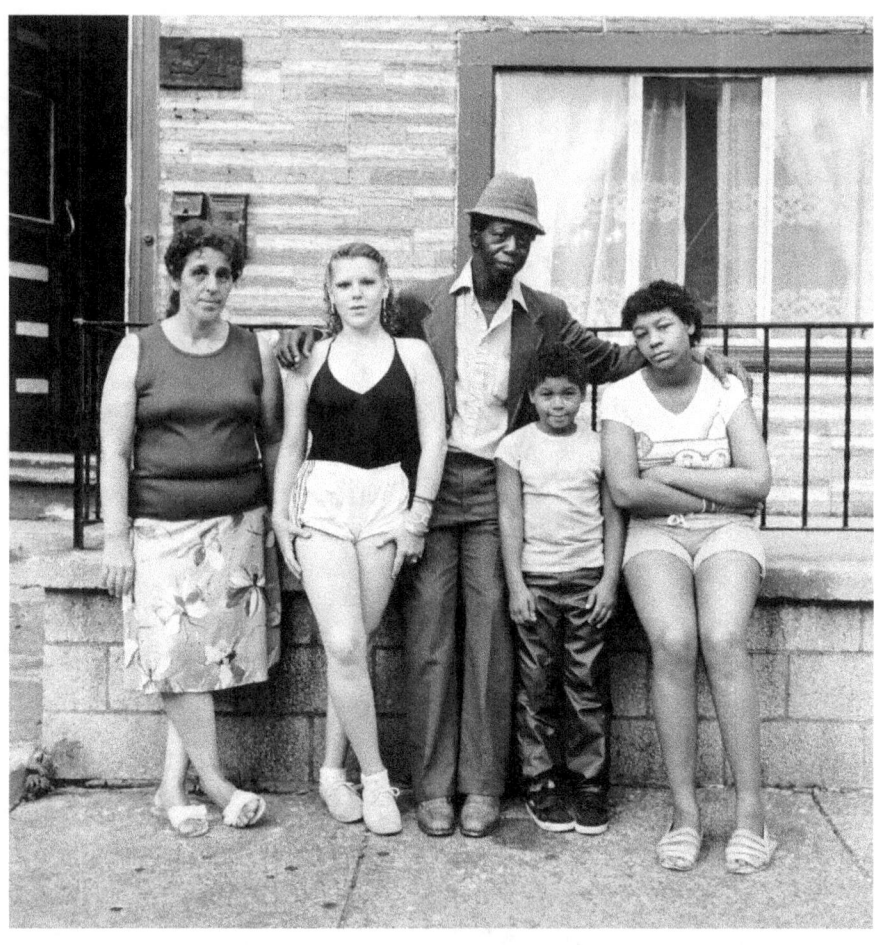

Untitled, *Lower West Side—Revisited,* 1985. Photographic Archives, University of Louisville. Copyright © Milton Rogovin. Courtesy, Center for Creative Photography, University of Arizona Foundation.

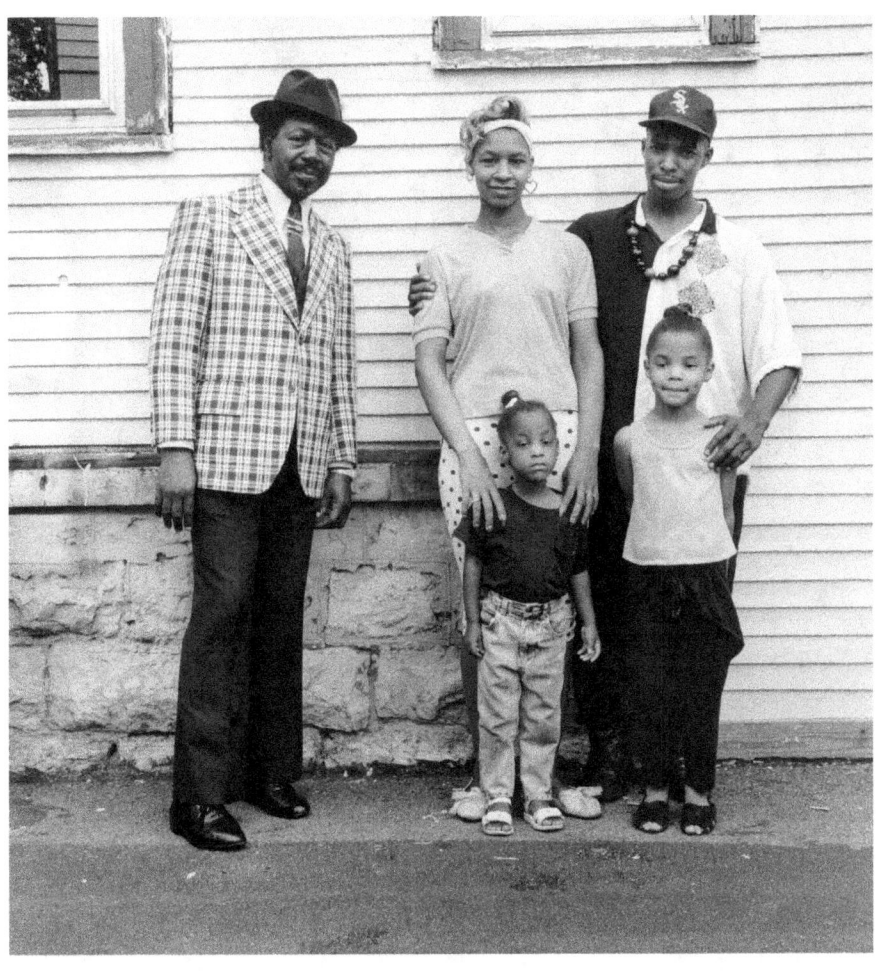

Untitled, *Lower West Side—Triptychs,* 1992. Photographic Archives, University of Louisville. Copyright © Milton Rogovin. Courtesy, Center for Creative Photography, University of Arizona Foundation.

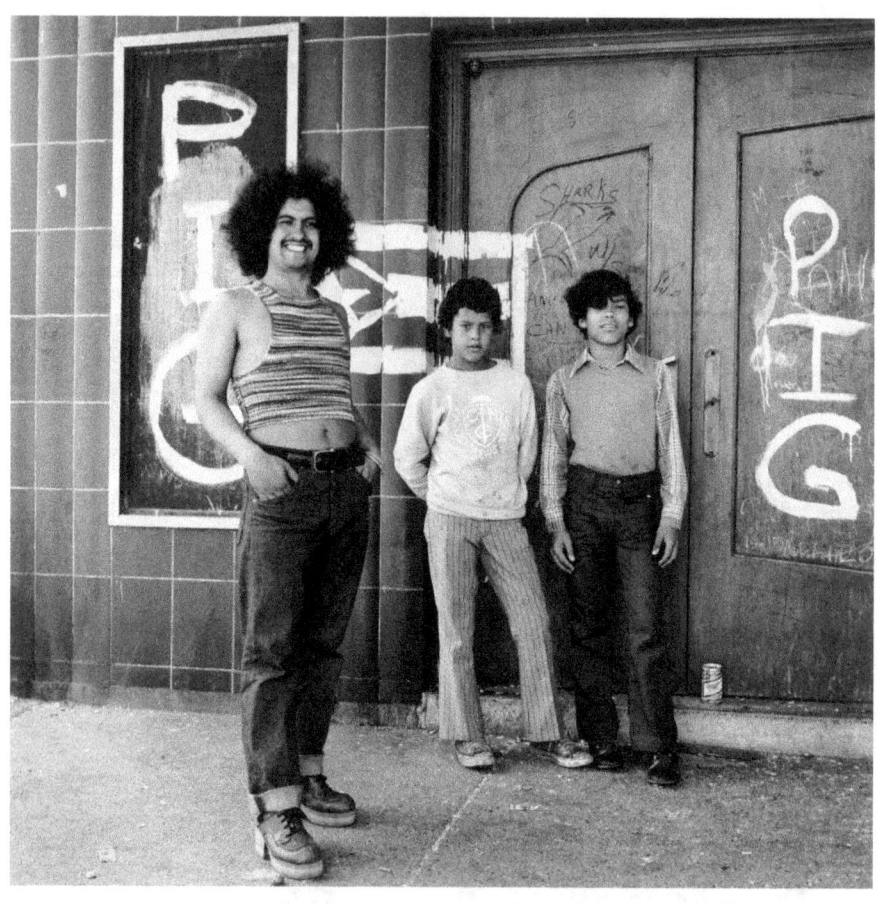

Untitled, *Lower West Side—Revisited,* c. 1983–1985. Photographic Archives, University of Louisville. Copyright © Milton Rogovin. Courtesy, Center for Creative Photography, University of Arizona Foundation.

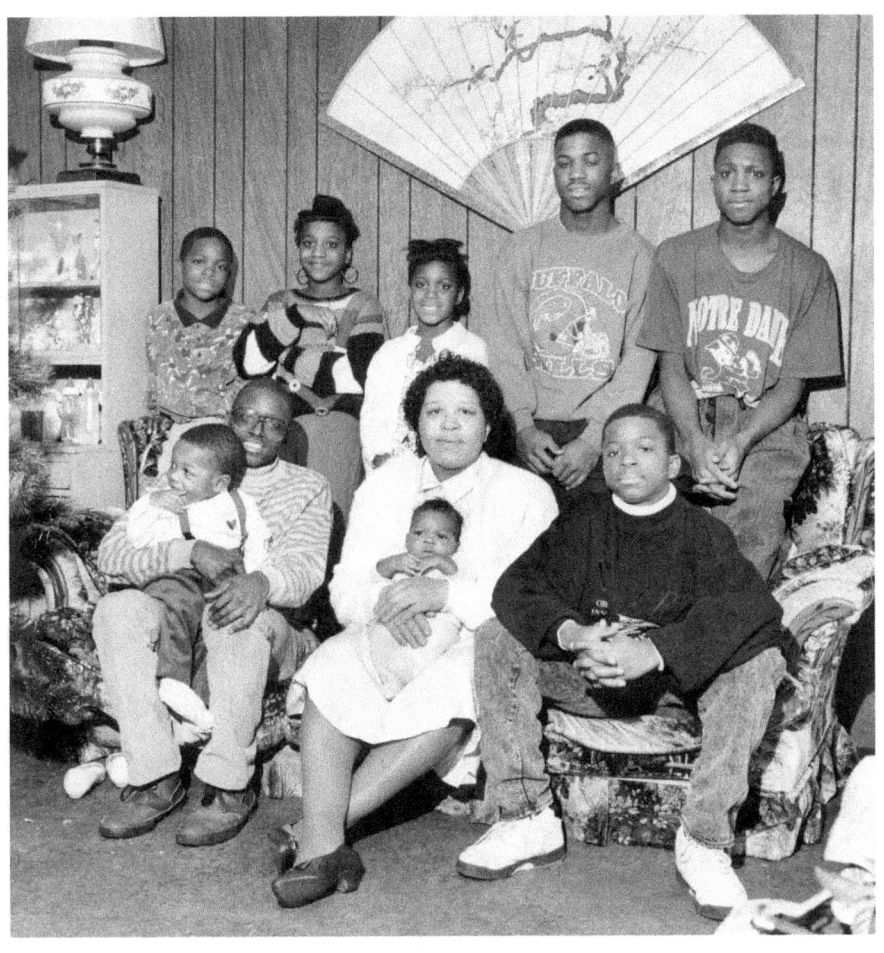

Untitled, *Lower West Side—Triptychs,* 1992. Photographic Archives, University of Louisville. Copyright © Milton Rogovin. Courtesy, Center for Creative Photography, University of Arizona Foundation.

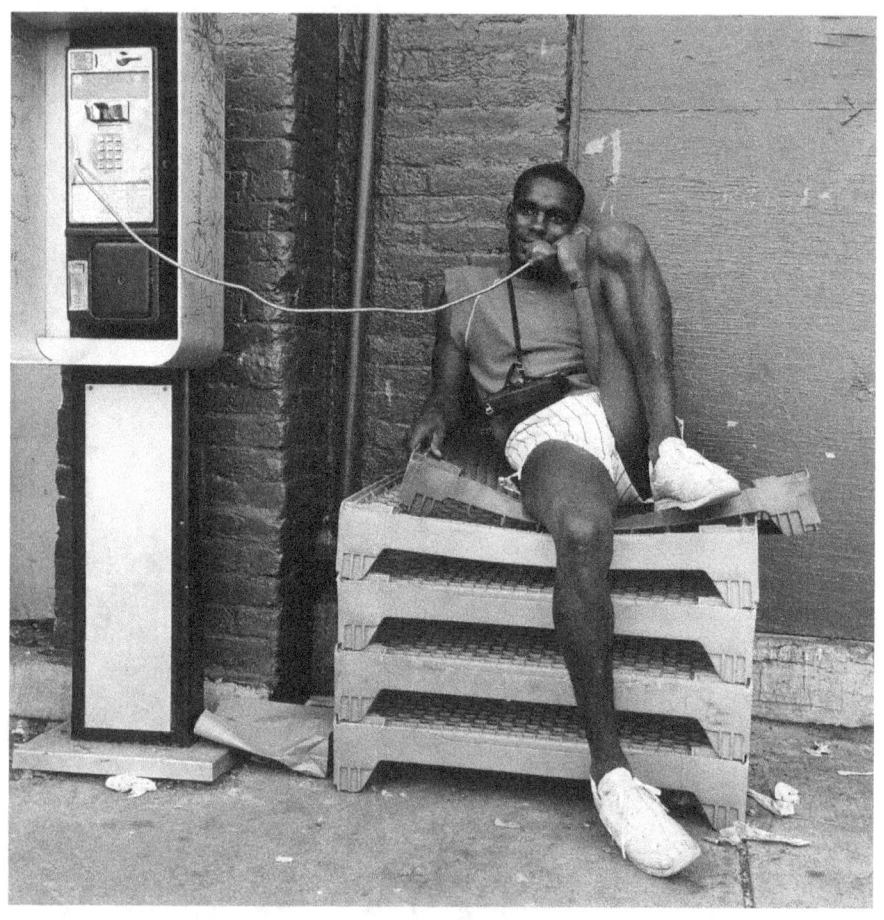

Untitled, *Lower West Side—Revisited*, 1985. The Rogovin Collection, Chicago. Copyright © Milton Rogovin. Courtesy, Center for Creative Photography, University of Arizona Foundation.

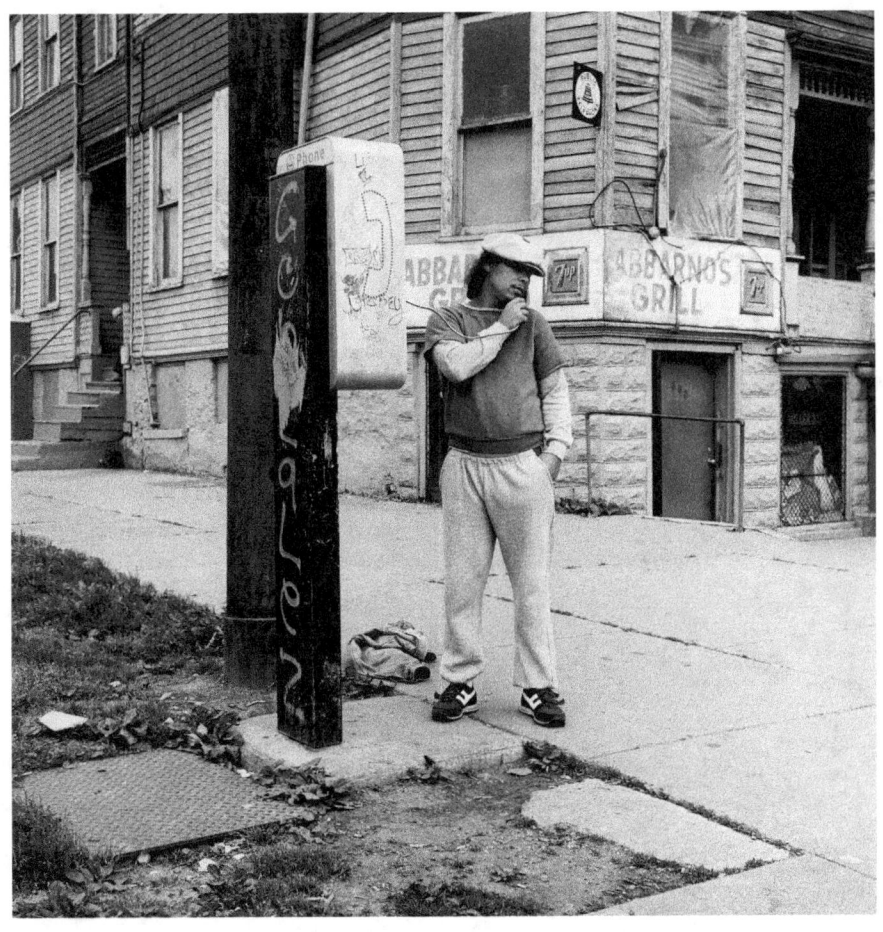

Untitled, *Lower West Side—Revisited,* 1985. The Rogovin Collection, Chicago. Copyright © Milton Rogovin. Courtesy, Center for Creative Photography, University of Arizona Foundation.

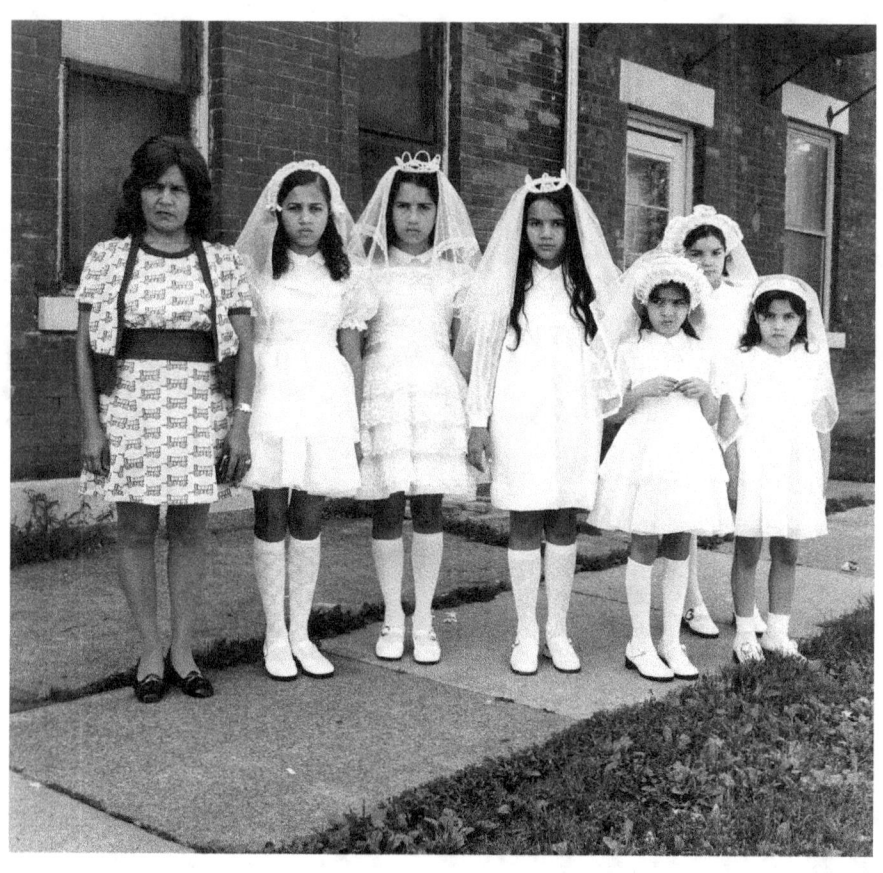

Untitled, *Lower West Side,* 1973. The Rogovin Collection, Chicago. Copyright © Milton Rogovin. Courtesy, Center for Creative Photography, University of Arizona Foundation.

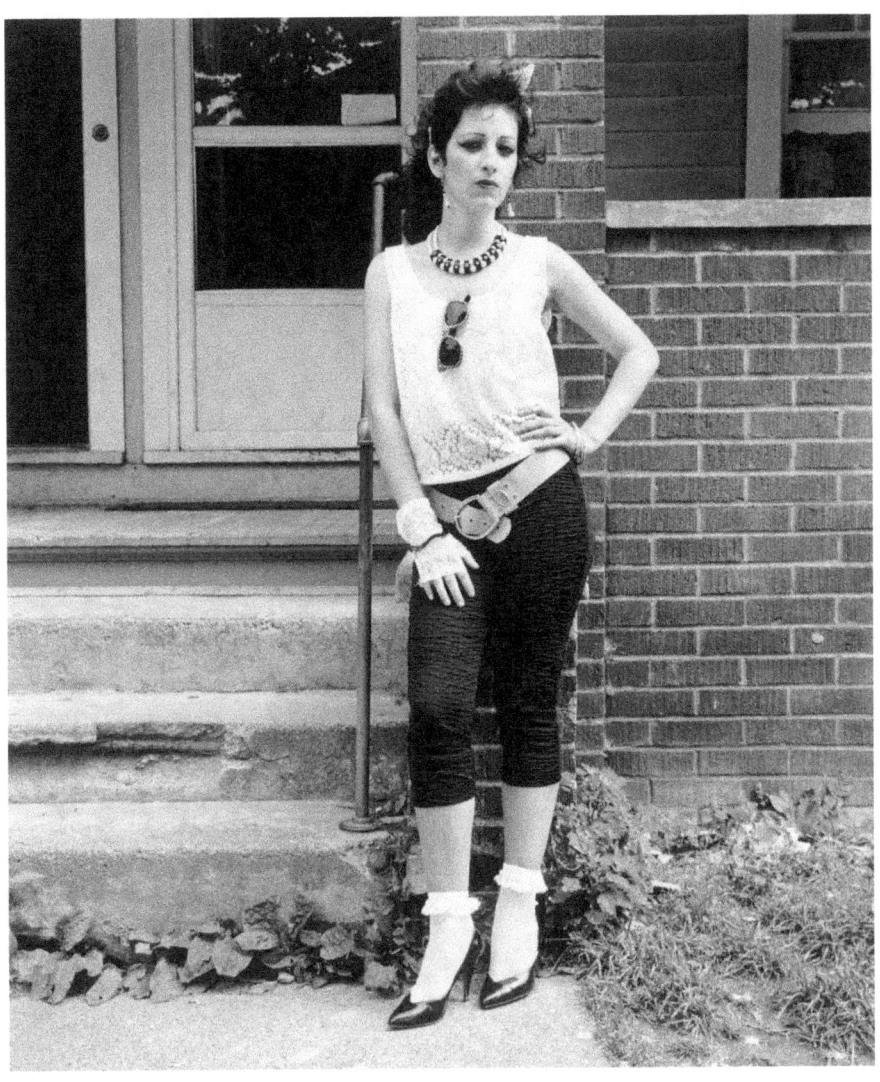

Untitled, *Lower West Side—Revisited,* 1984. Photographic Archives, University of Louisville. Copyright © Milton Rogovin. Courtesy, Center for Creative Photography, University of Arizona Foundation.

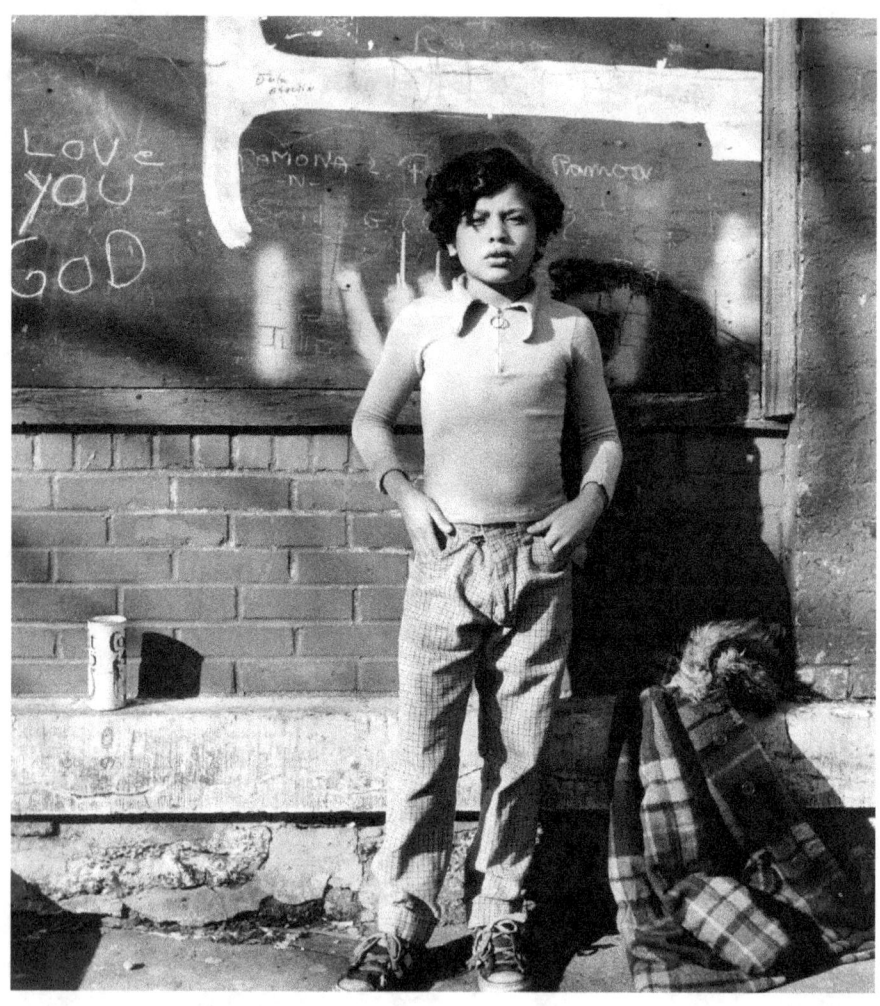

Untitled, *Lower West Side,* 1972–1975. The Rogovin Collection, Chicago. Copyright © Milton Rogovin. Courtesy, Center for Creative Photography, University of Arizona Foundation.

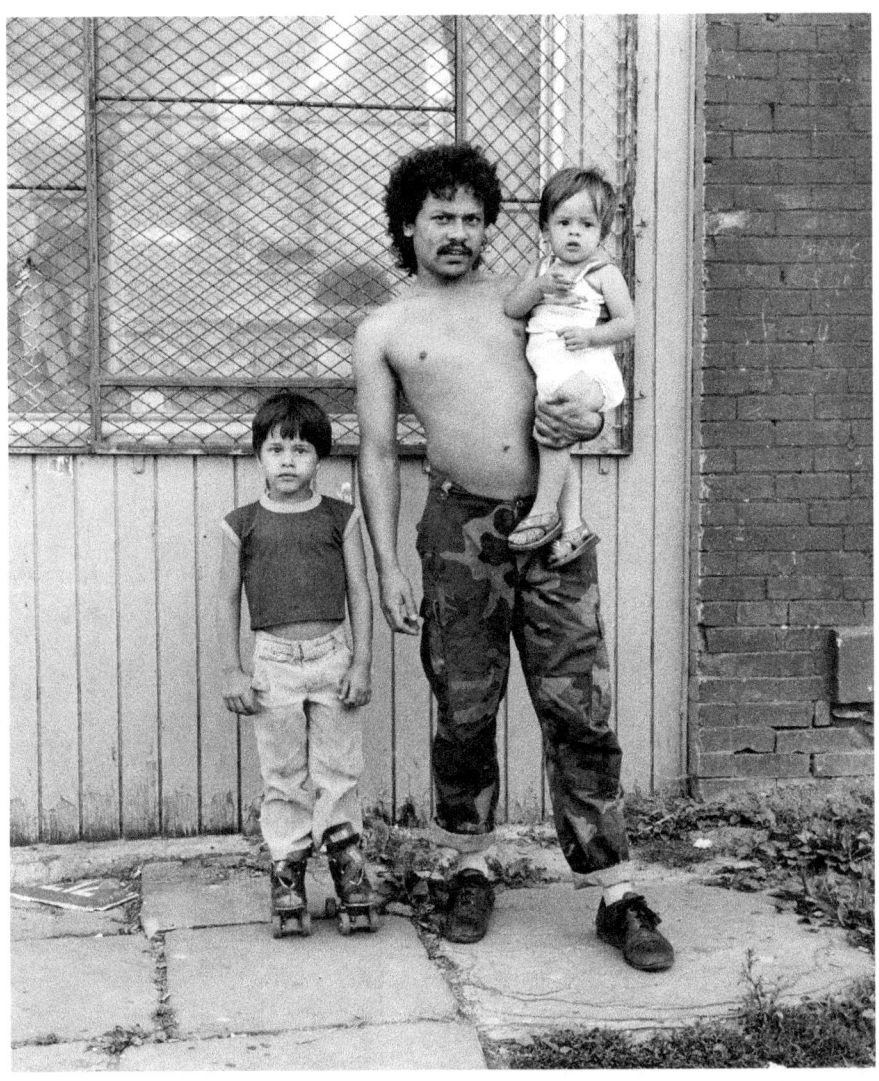

Untitled, *Lower West Side—Revisited*, 1983–1985. The Rogovin Collection, Chicago. Copyright © Milton Rogovin. Courtesy, Center for Creative Photography, University of Arizona Foundation.

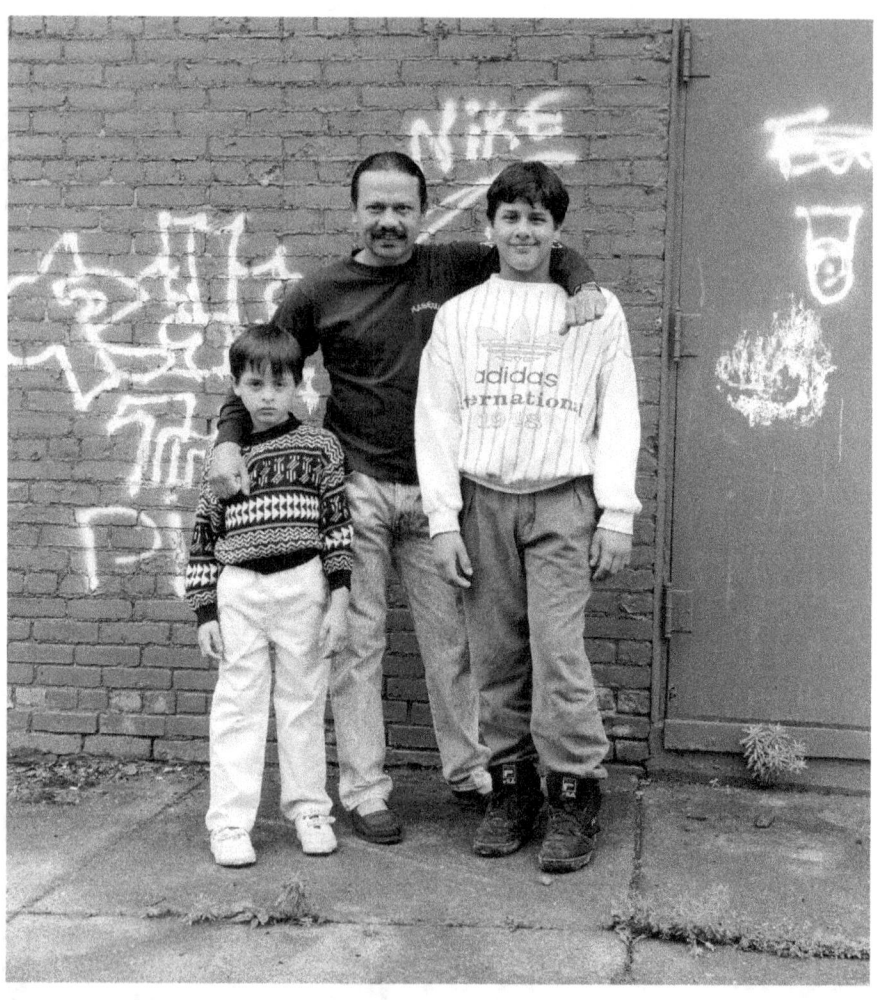

Untitled, *Lower West Side—Triptychs,* 1992. The Rogovin Collection, Chicago. Copyright © Milton Rogovin. Courtesy, Center for Creative Photography, University of Arizona Foundation.

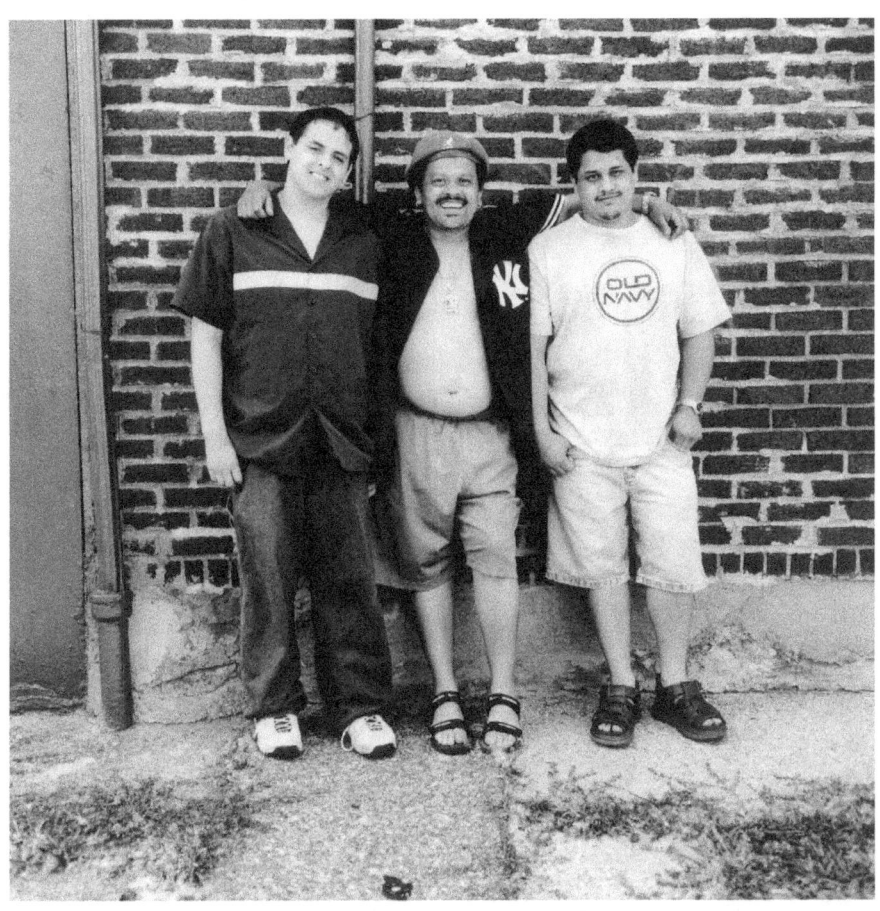

Untitled, *Lower West Side—Quartets,* 2000–2002. The Rogovin Collection, Chicago. Copyright © Milton Rogovin. Courtesy, Center for Creative Photography, University of Arizona Foundation.

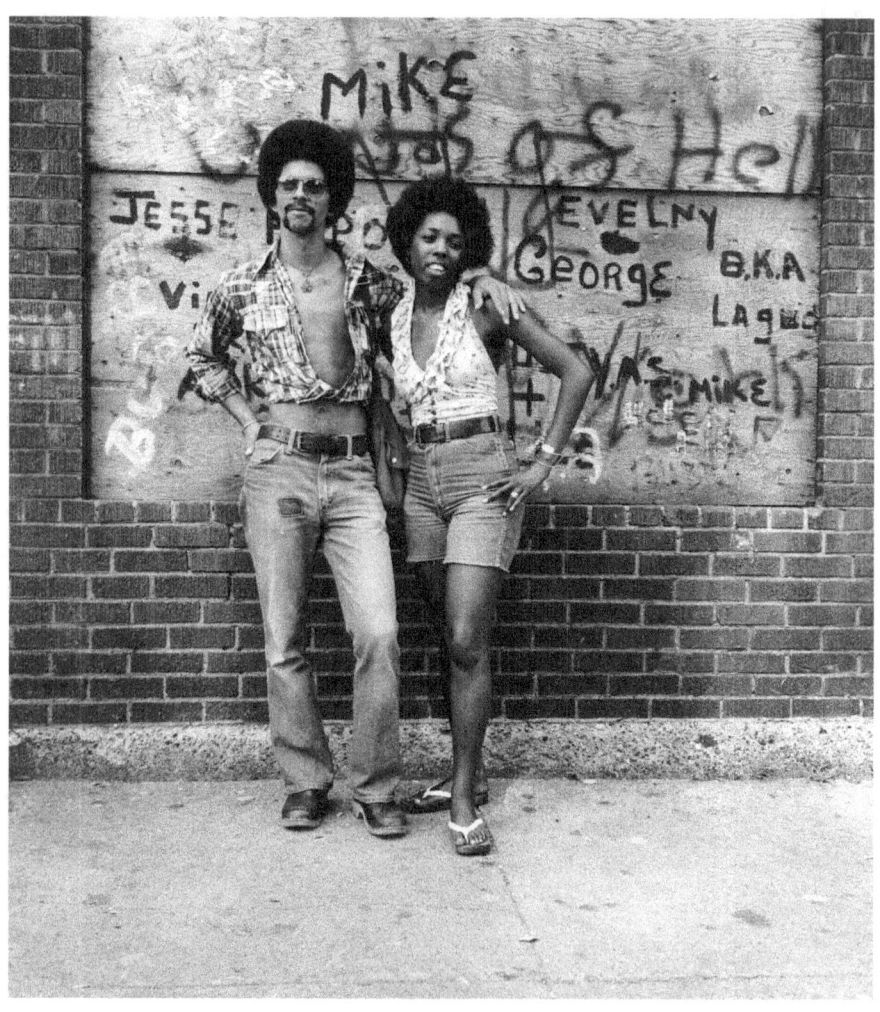

Untitled, *Lower West Side,* 1972–1975. The Rogovin Collection, Chicago. Copyright © Milton Rogovin. Courtesy, Center for Creative Photography, University of Arizona Foundation.

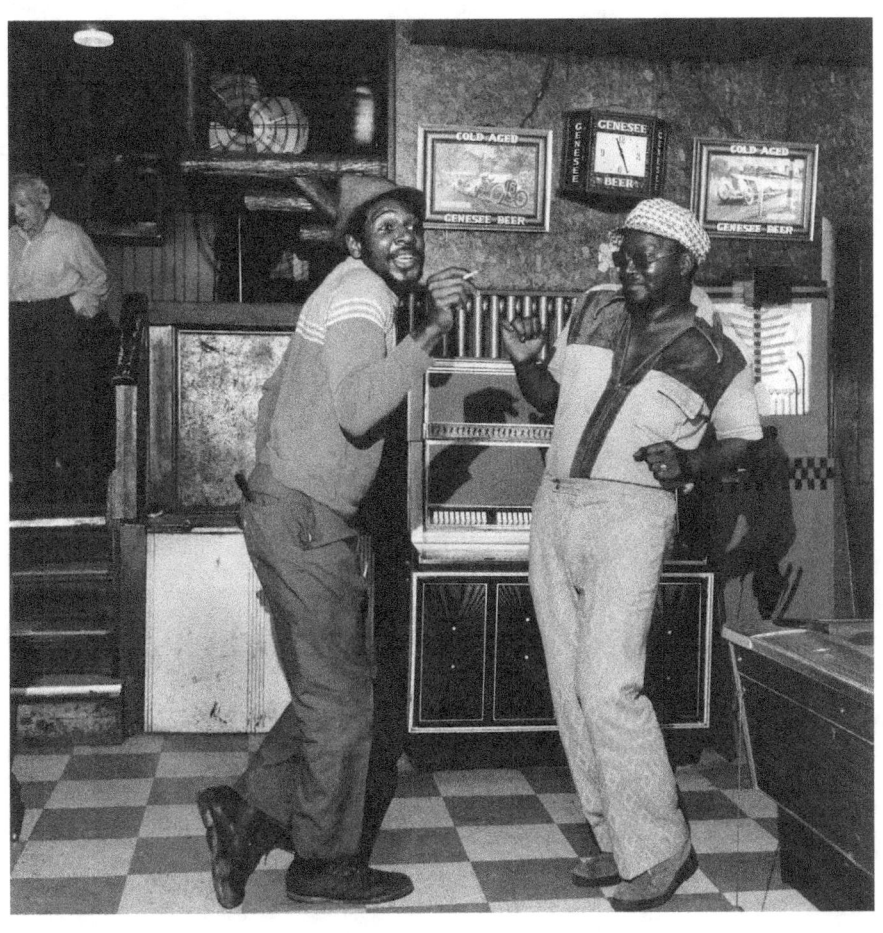

Untitled, *Lower West Side*, 1972–1975. The Rogovin Collection, Chicago. Copyright © Milton Rogovin. Courtesy, Center for Creative Photography, University of Arizona Foundation.

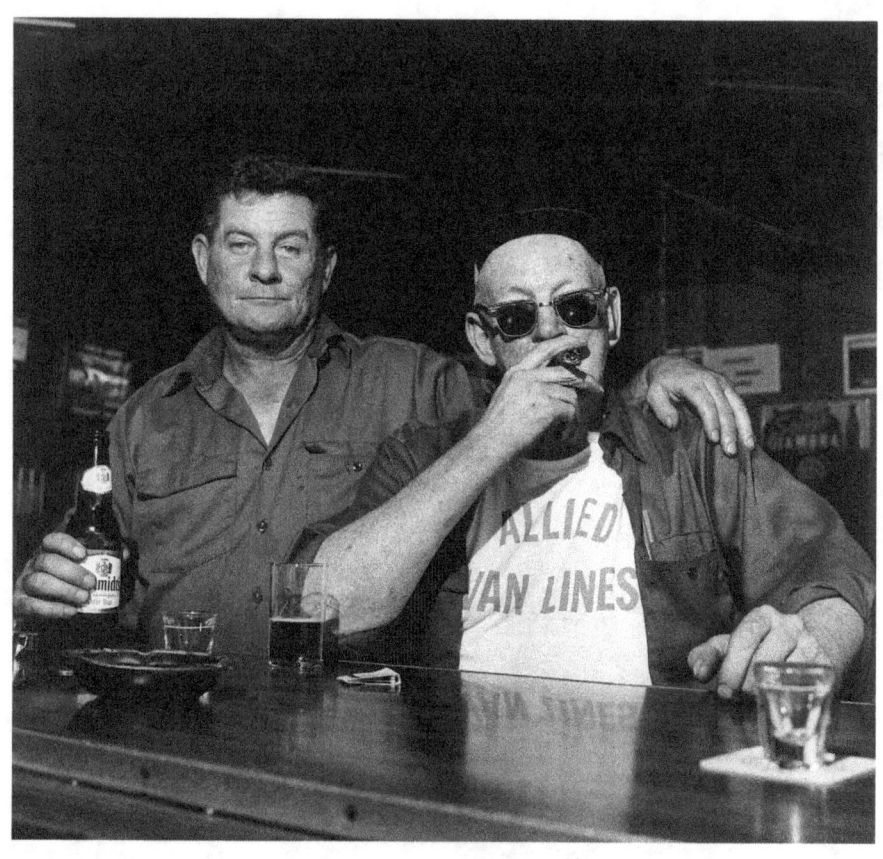

Untitled, *Lower West Side—Revisited,* 1983–1985. The Rogovin Collection, Chicago. Copyright © Milton Rogovin. Courtesy, Center for Creative Photography, University of Arizona Foundation.

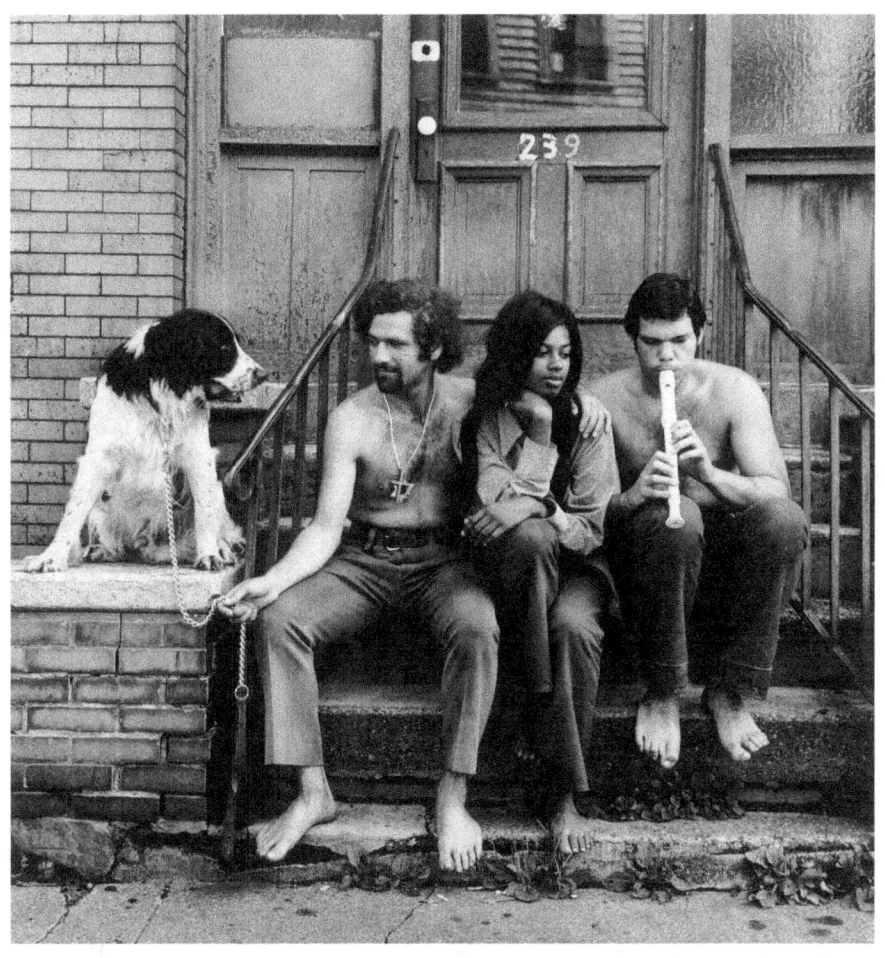

Untitled, *Lower West Side,* 1972–1975. Photographic Archives, University of Louisville. Copyright © Milton Rogovin. Courtesy, Center for Creative Photography, University of Arizona Foundation.

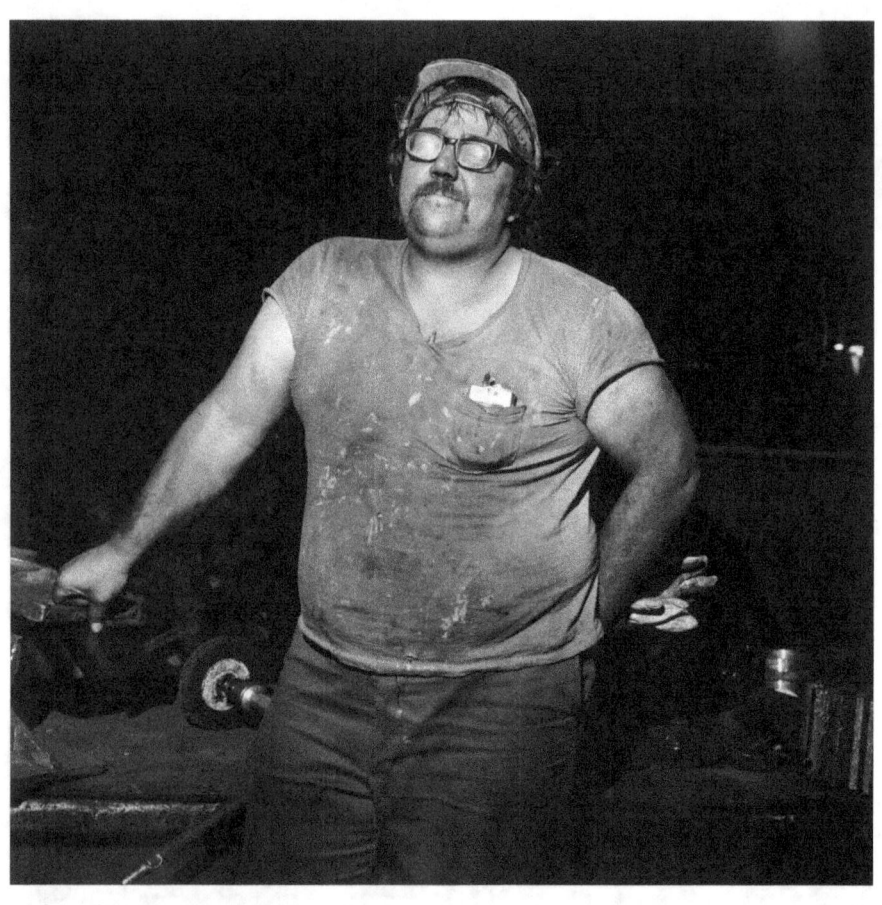

Untitled (Atlas Steel Casting Company), *Working People,* 1976. Photographic Archives, University of Louisville. Copyright © Milton Rogovin. Courtesy, Center for Creative Photography, University of Arizona Foundation.

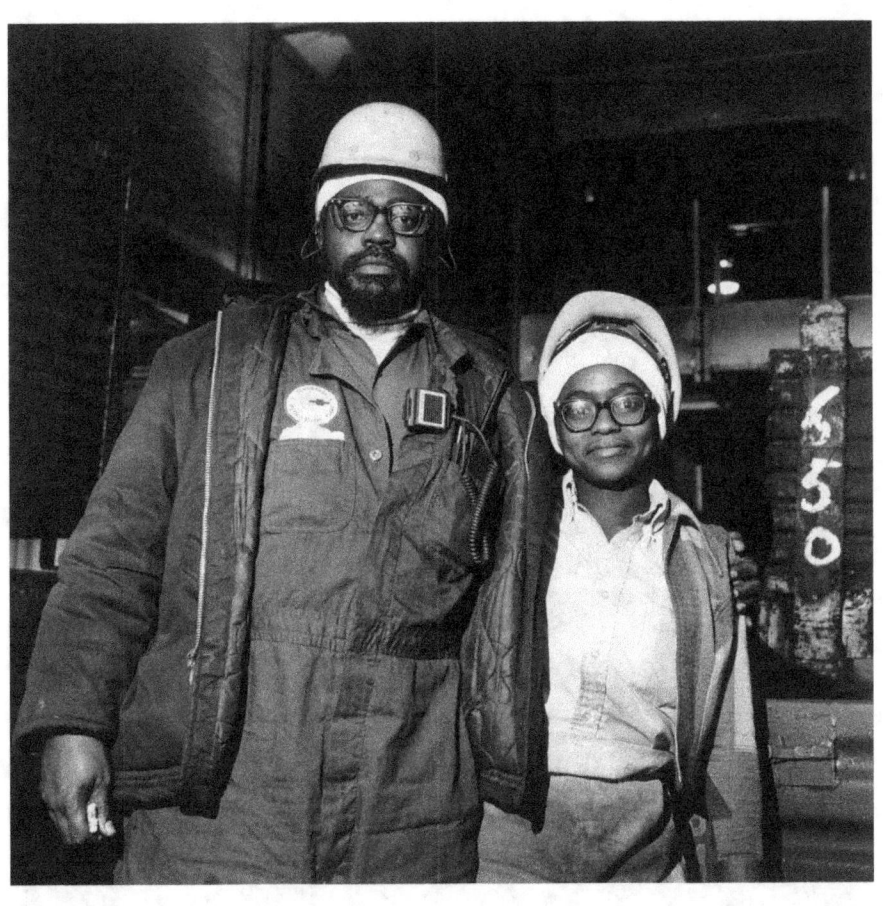

Untitled (Chevrolet Metal Casting Plant), *Working People,* 1977–1978. Photographic Archives, University of Louisville. Copyright © Milton Rogovin. Courtesy, Center for Creative Photography, University of Arizona Foundation.

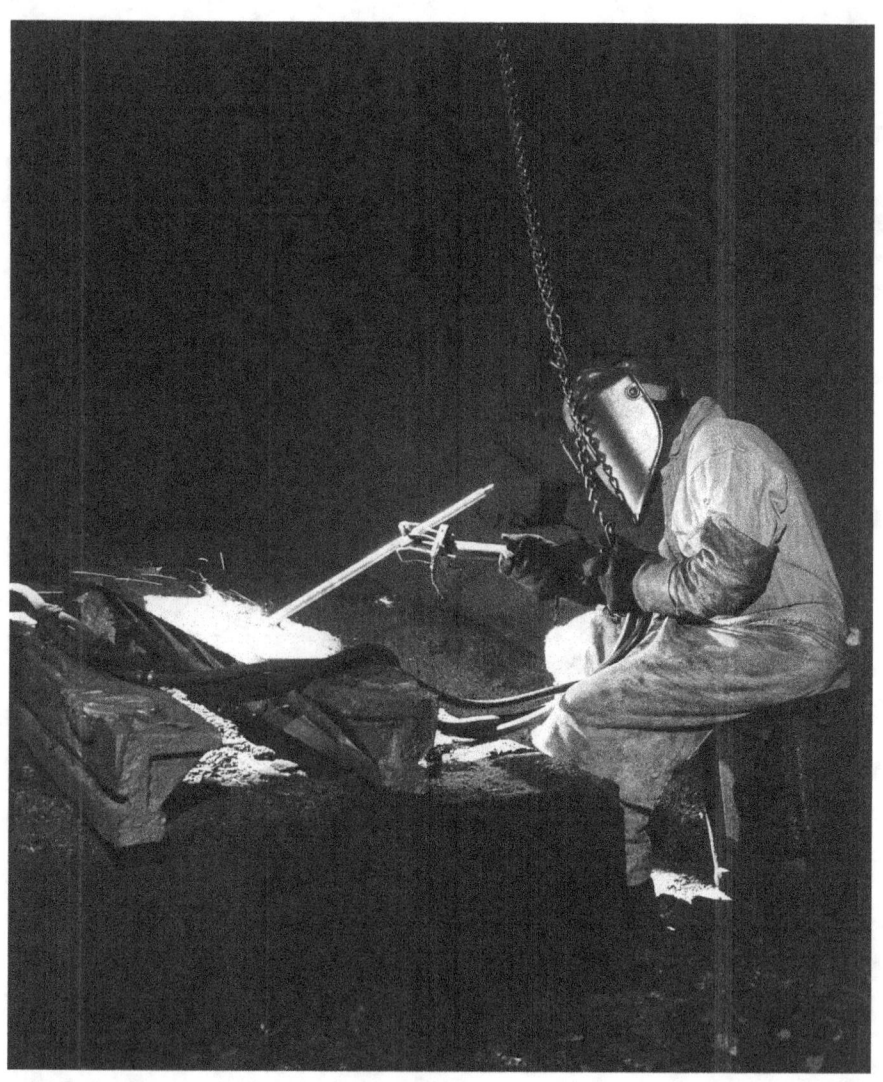

Untitled (Atlas Steel Casting Company), *Working People*, 1978–1979. The Rogovin Collection, Chicago. Copyright © Milton Rogovin. Courtesy, Center for Creative Photography, University of Arizona Foundation.

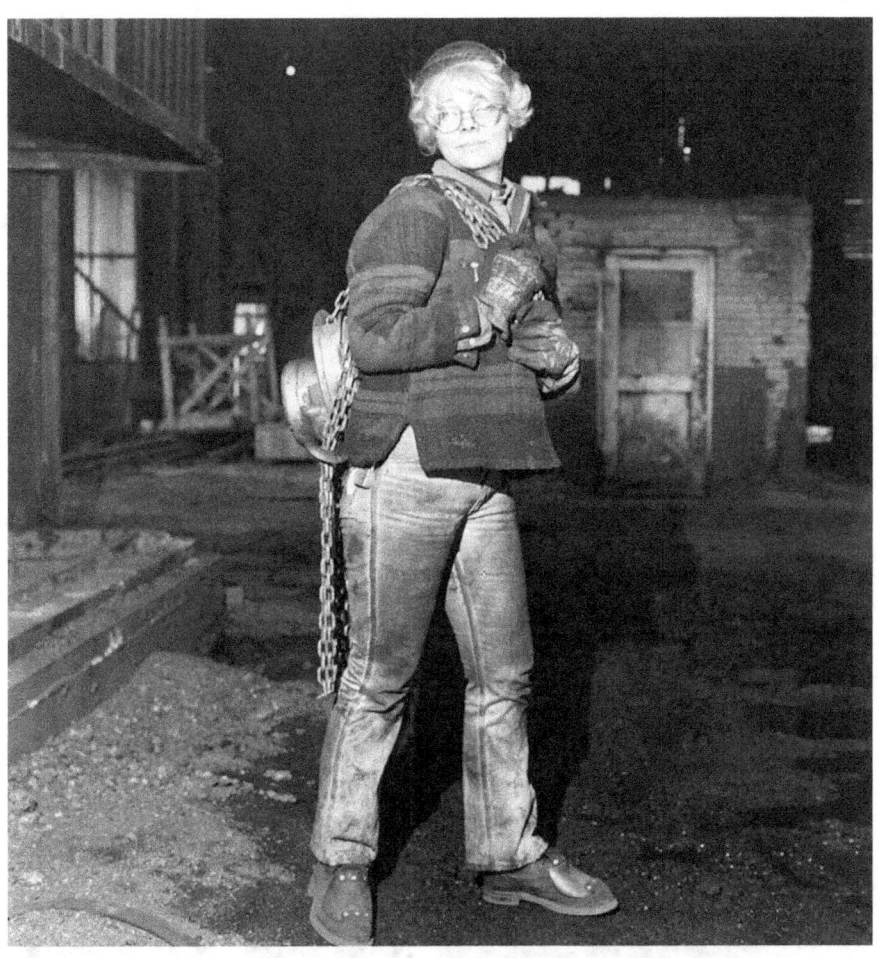

Untitled (Republic Steel), *Working People,* 1978. The Rogovin Collection, Chicago. Copyright © Milton Rogovin. Courtesy, Center for Creative Photography, University of Arizona Foundation.

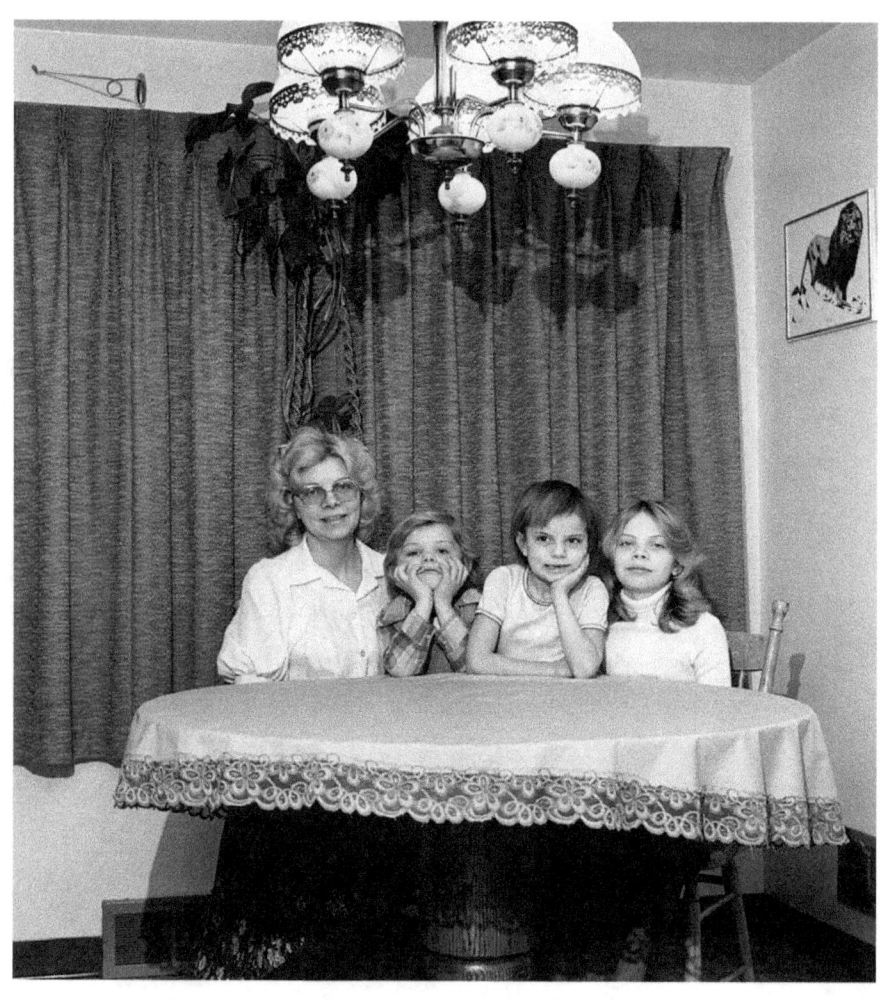

Untitled (Republic Steel), *Working People*, 1979. The Rogovin Collection, Chicago. Copyright © Milton Rogovin. Courtesy, Center for Creative Photography, University of Arizona Foundation.

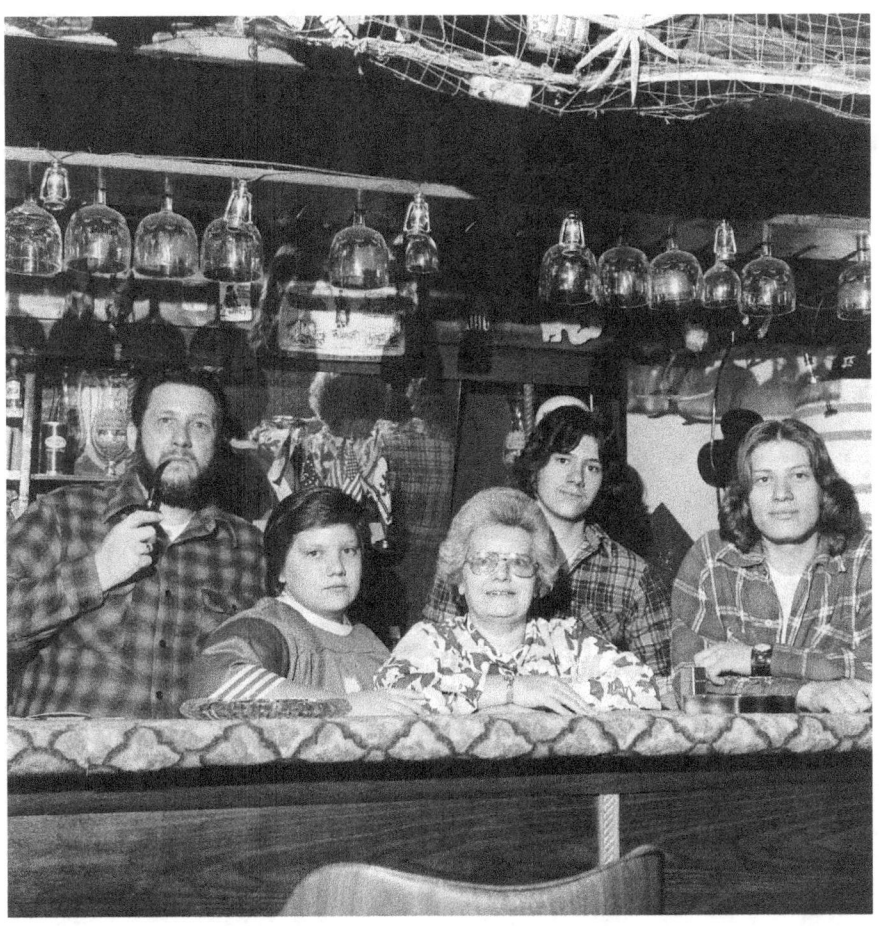

Untitled (Shenango, Inc., Steel Ingot Molds Division), *Working People*, 1978–1981. The Rogovin Collection, Chicago. Copyright © Milton Rogovin. Courtesy, Center for Creative Photography, University of Arizona Foundation.

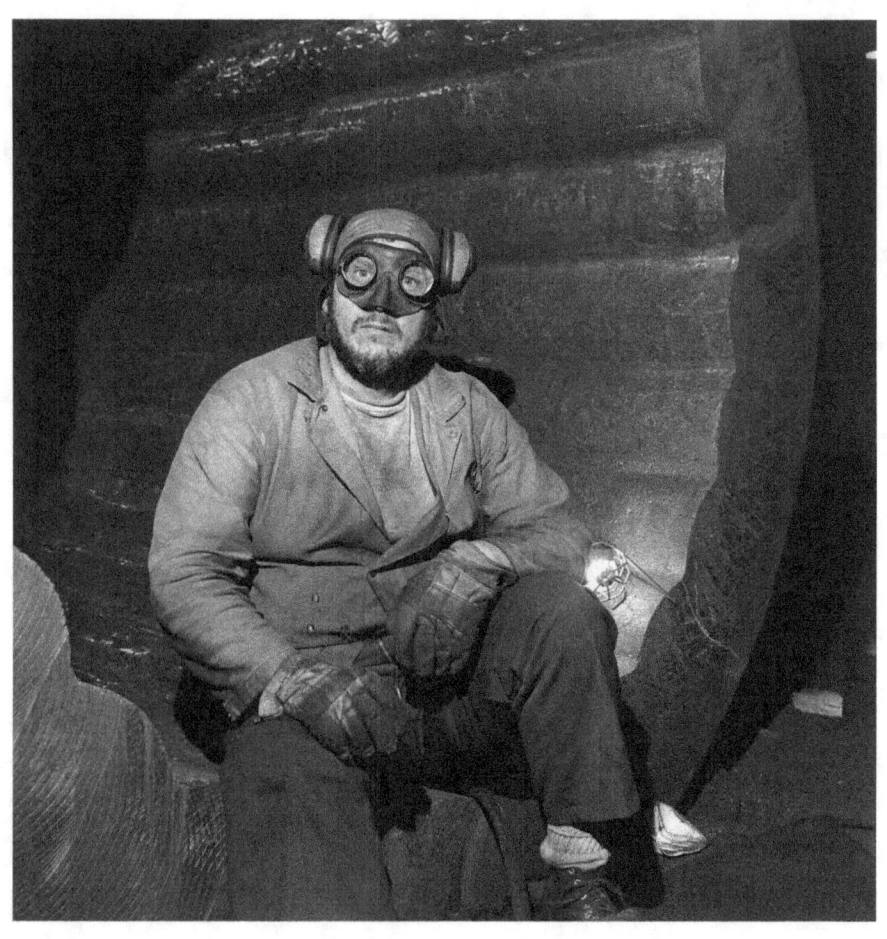

Untitled (Shenango, Inc., Steel Ingot Molds Division), *Working People,* 1978–1981. The Rogovin Collection, Chicago. Copyright © Milton Rogovin. Courtesy, Center for Creative Photography, University of Arizona Foundation.

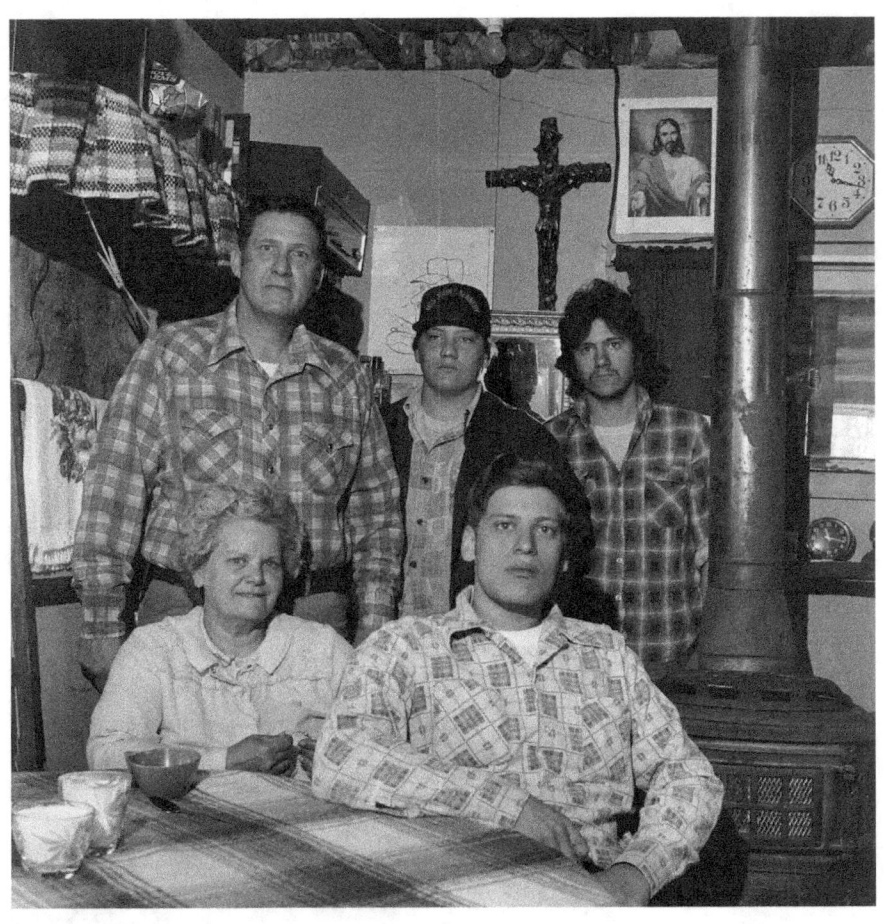

Untitled (Shenango, Inc., Steel Ingot Molds Division), *Working People*, 1983. The Rogovin Collection, Chicago. Copyright © Milton Rogovin. Courtesy, Center for Creative Photography, University of Arizona Foundation.

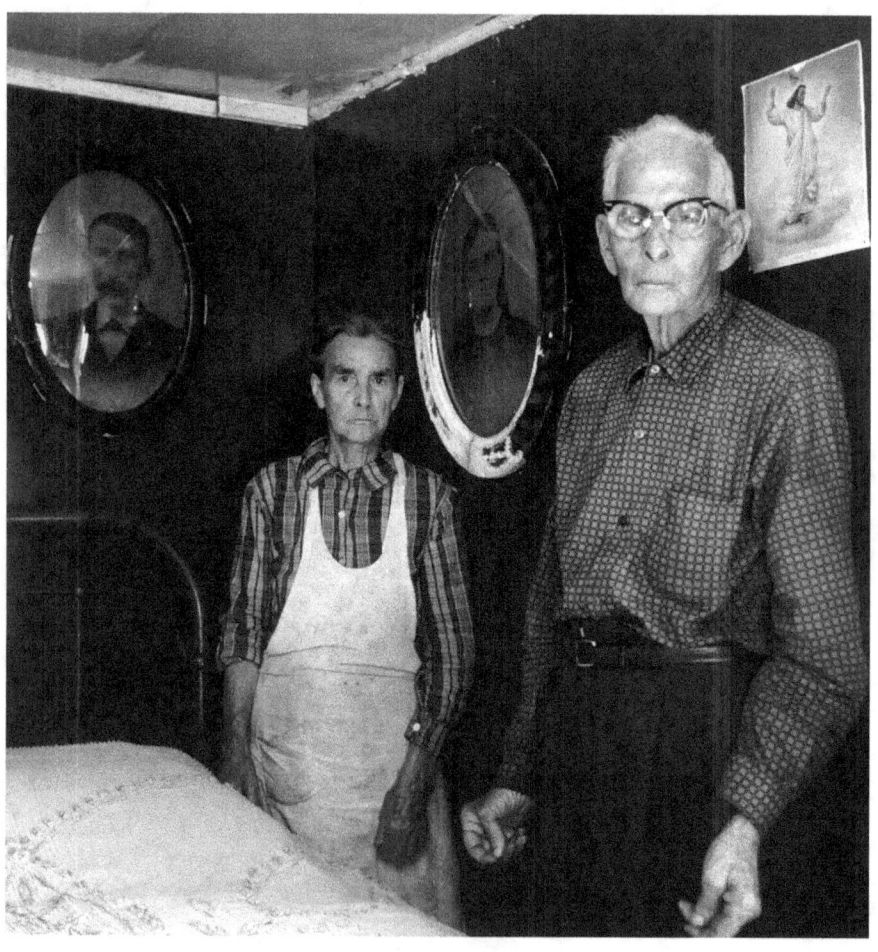

Untitled, *Appalachia,* 1964. Photographic Archives, University of Louisville. Copyright © Milton Rogovin. Courtesy, Center for Creative Photography, University of Arizona Foundation.

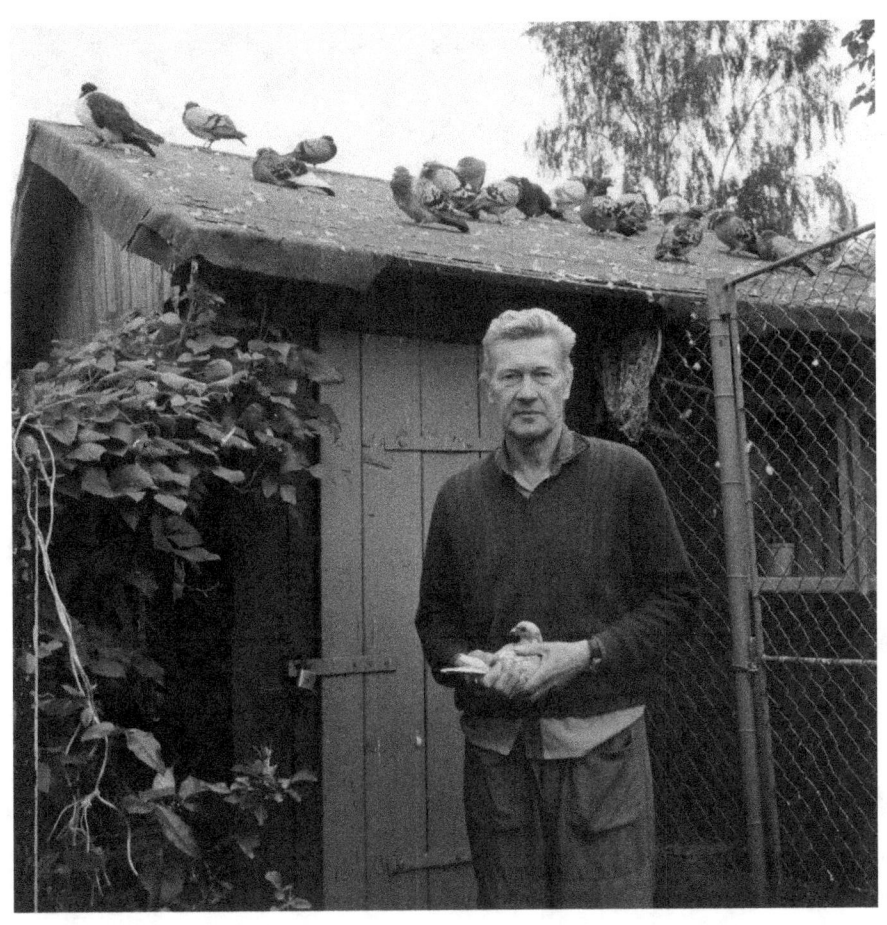

Untitled (West Germany), *Family of Miners,* 1984. Photographic Archives, University of Louisville. Copyright © Milton Rogovin. Courtesy, Center for Creative Photography, University of Arizona Foundation.

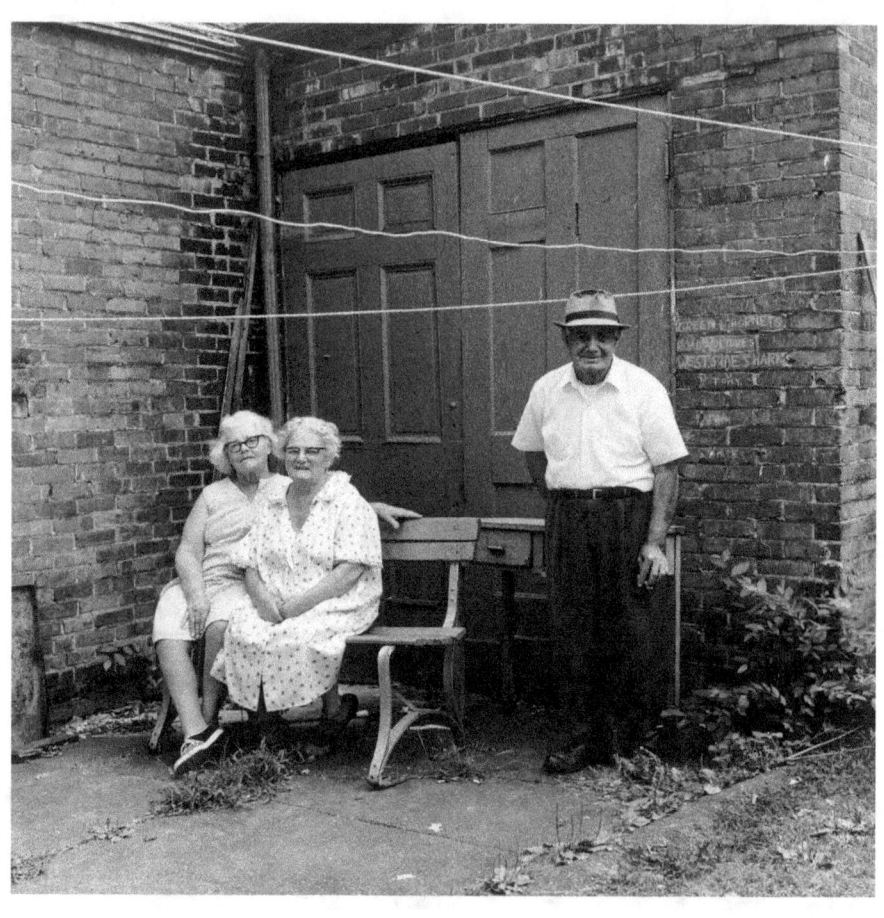

Untitled, *Lower West Side,* 1972–1975. Photographic Archives, University of Louisville. Copyright © Milton Rogovin. Courtesy, Center for Creative Photography, University of Arizona Foundation.

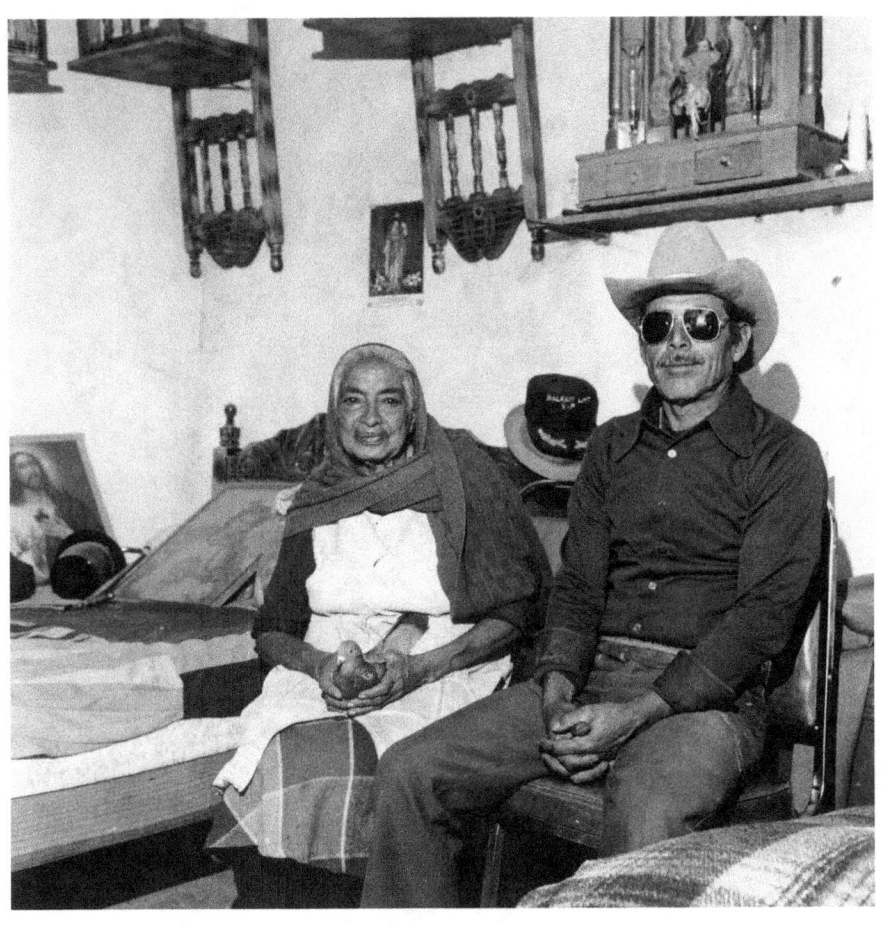

Untitled (Mexico), *Family of Miners,* 1988. Photographic Archives, University of Louisville. Copyright © Milton Rogovin. Courtesy, Center for Creative Photography, University of Arizona Foundation.

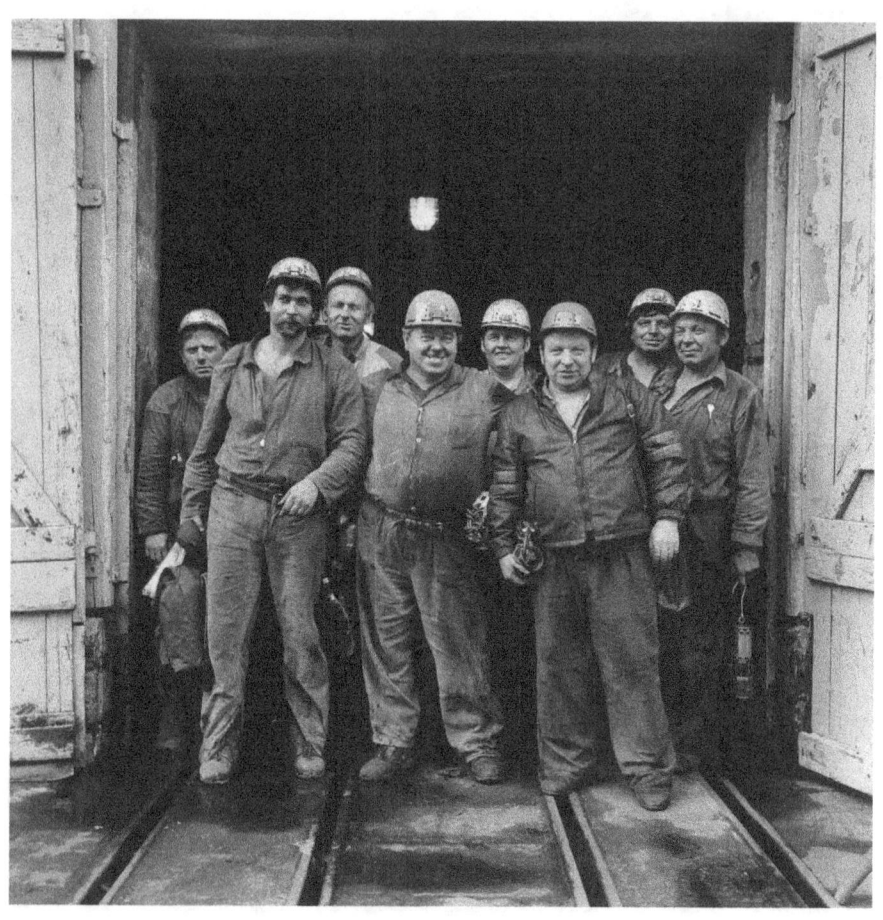

Untitled (Czechia), *Family of Miners,* 1990. The Rogovin Collection, Chicago. Copyright © Milton Rogovin. Courtesy, Center for Creative Photography, University of Arizona Foundation.

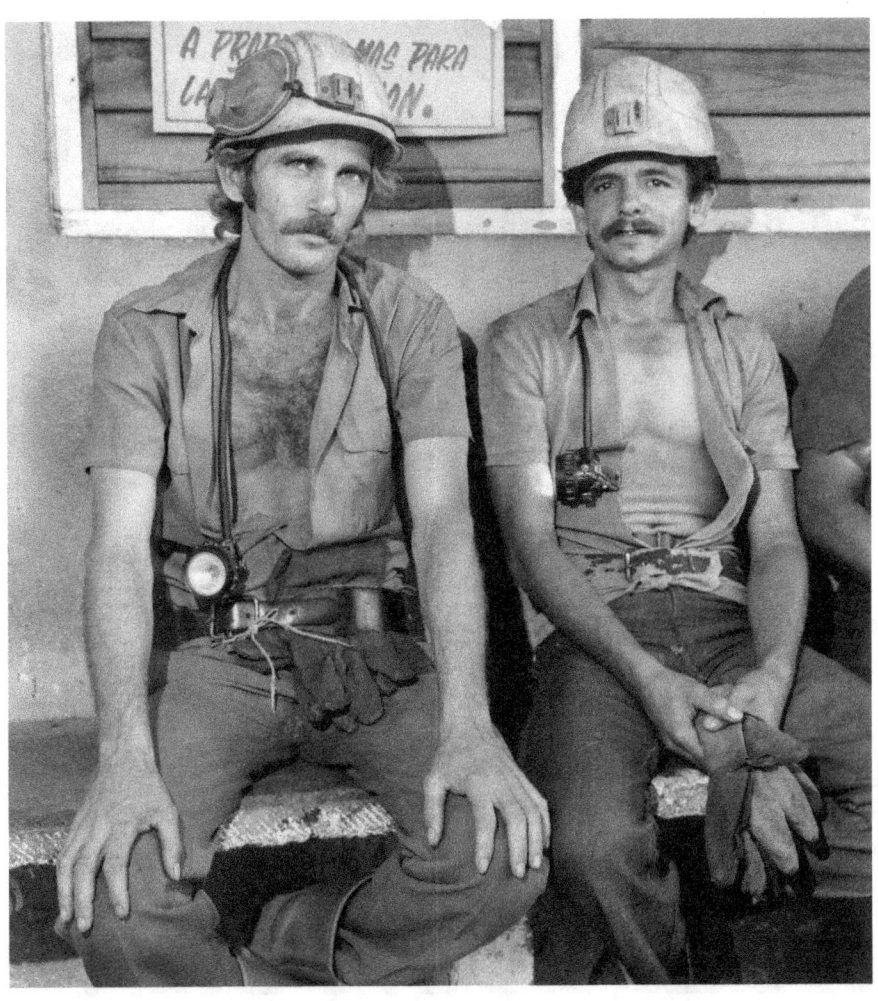

Untitled (Cuba), *Family of Miners*, 1989. Photographic Archives, University of Louisville. Copyright © Milton Rogovin. Courtesy, Center for Creative Photography, University of Arizona Foundation.

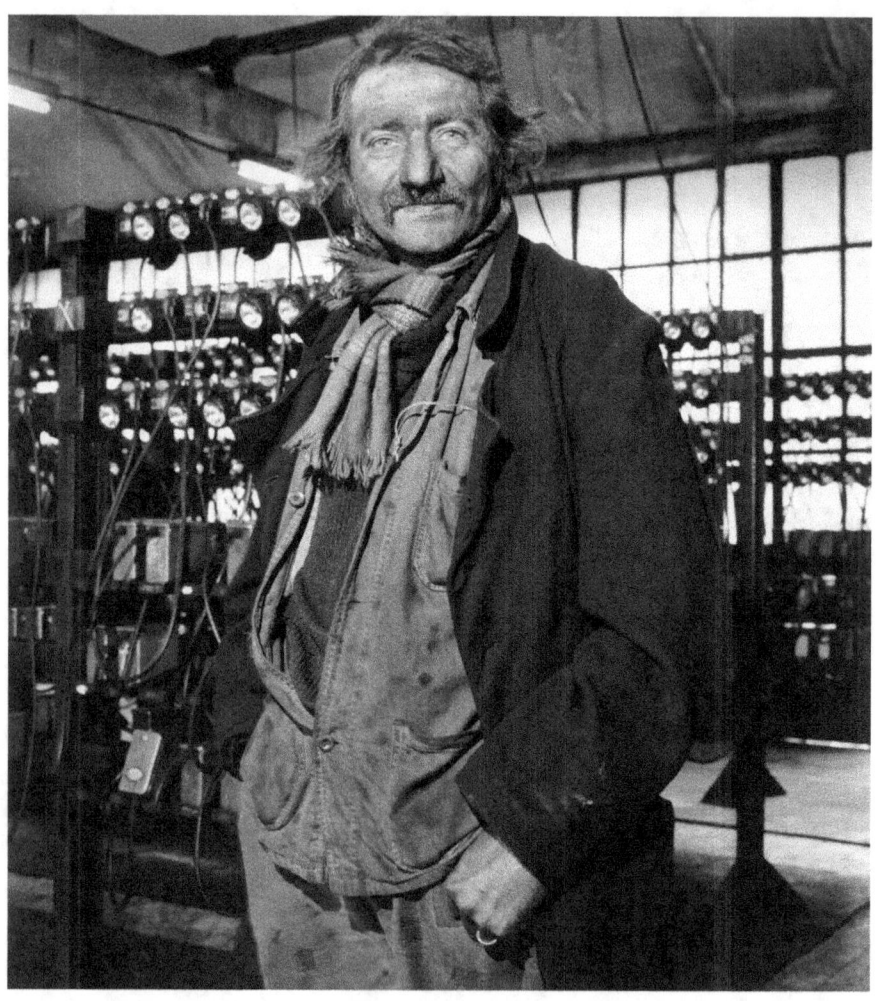

Untitled (France), *Family of Miners,* 1981. Photographic Archives, University of Louisville. Copyright © Milton Rogovin. Courtesy, Center for Creative Photography, University of Arizona Foundation.

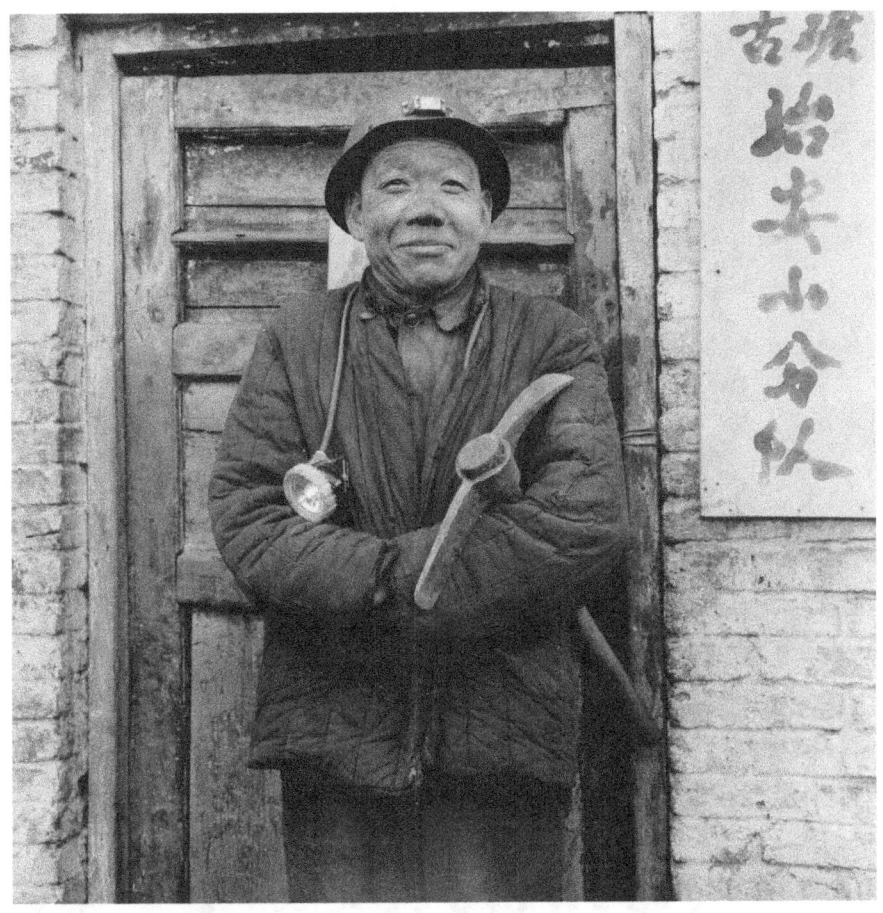

Untitled (China), *Family of Miners,* 1986. The Rogovin Collection, Chicago. Copyright © Milton Rogovin. Courtesy, Center for Creative Photography, University of Arizona Foundation.

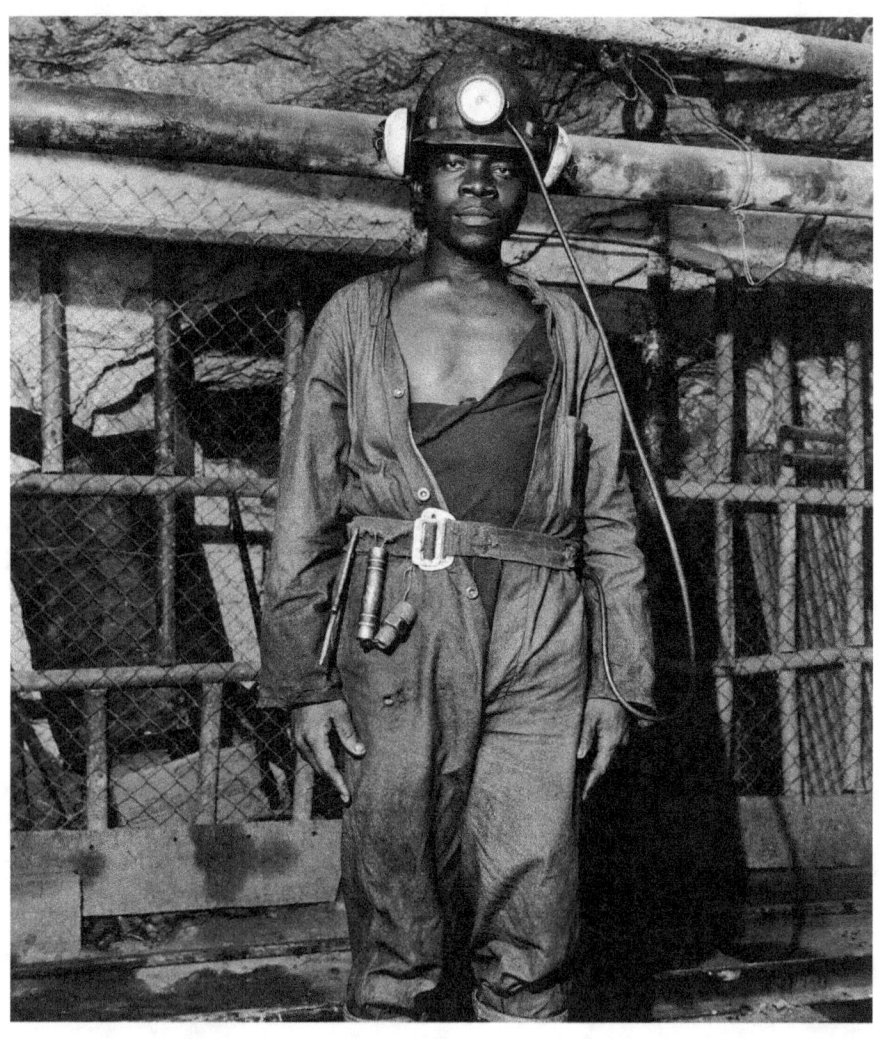

Untitled (Zimbabwe), *Family of Miners*, 1989. The Rogovin Collection, Chicago. Copyright © Milton Rogovin. Courtesy, Center for Creative Photography, University of Arizona Foundation.

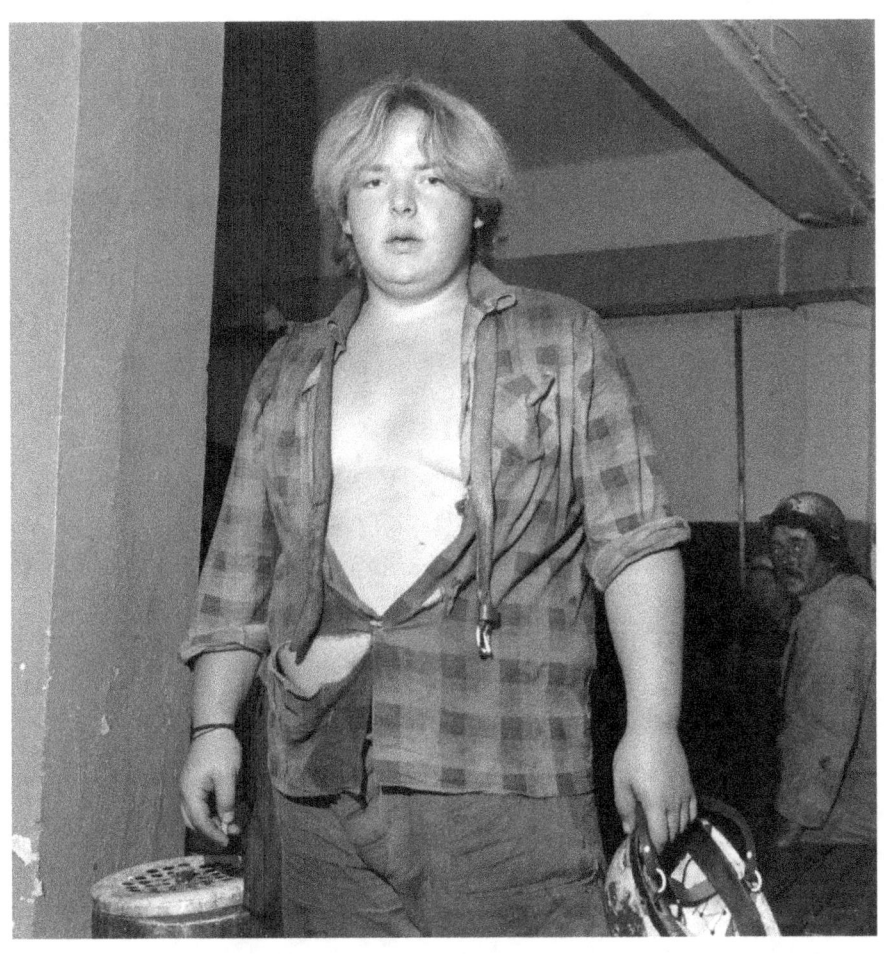

Untitled (Czechia), *Family of Miners,* 1990. Photographic Archives, University of Louisville. Copyright © Milton Rogovin. Courtesy, Center for Creative Photography, University of Arizona Foundation.

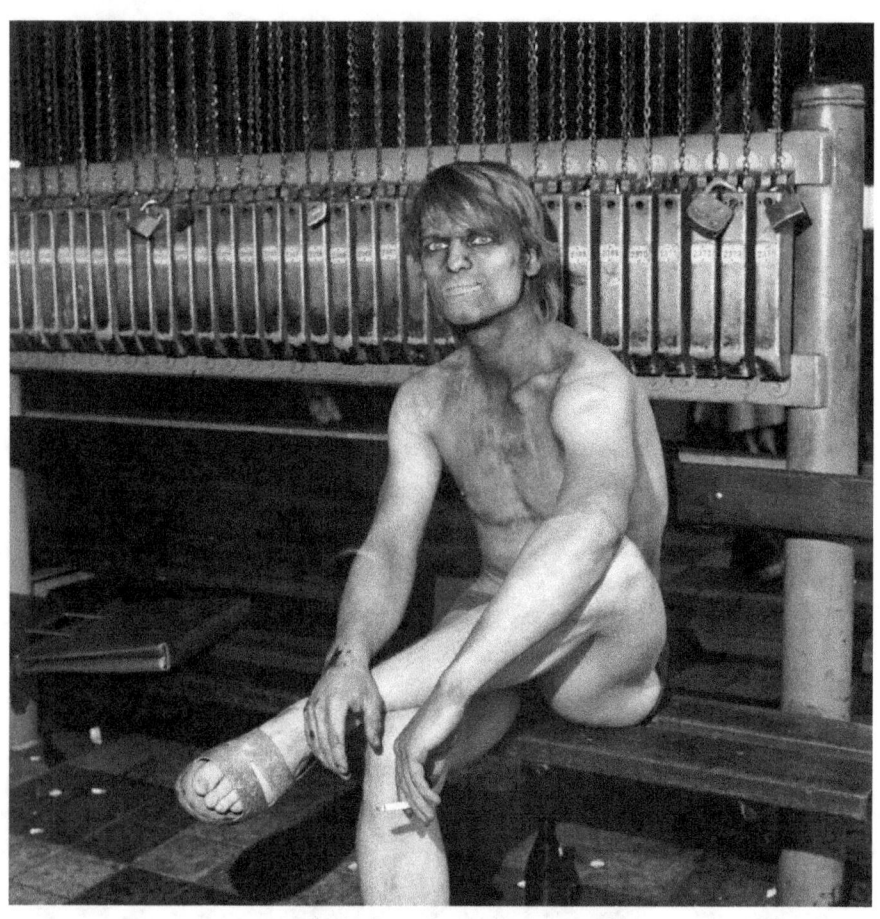

Untitled (West Germany), *Family of Miners*, 1984. Photographic Archives, University of Louisville. Copyright © Milton Rogovin. Courtesy, Center for Creative Photography, University of Arizona Foundation.

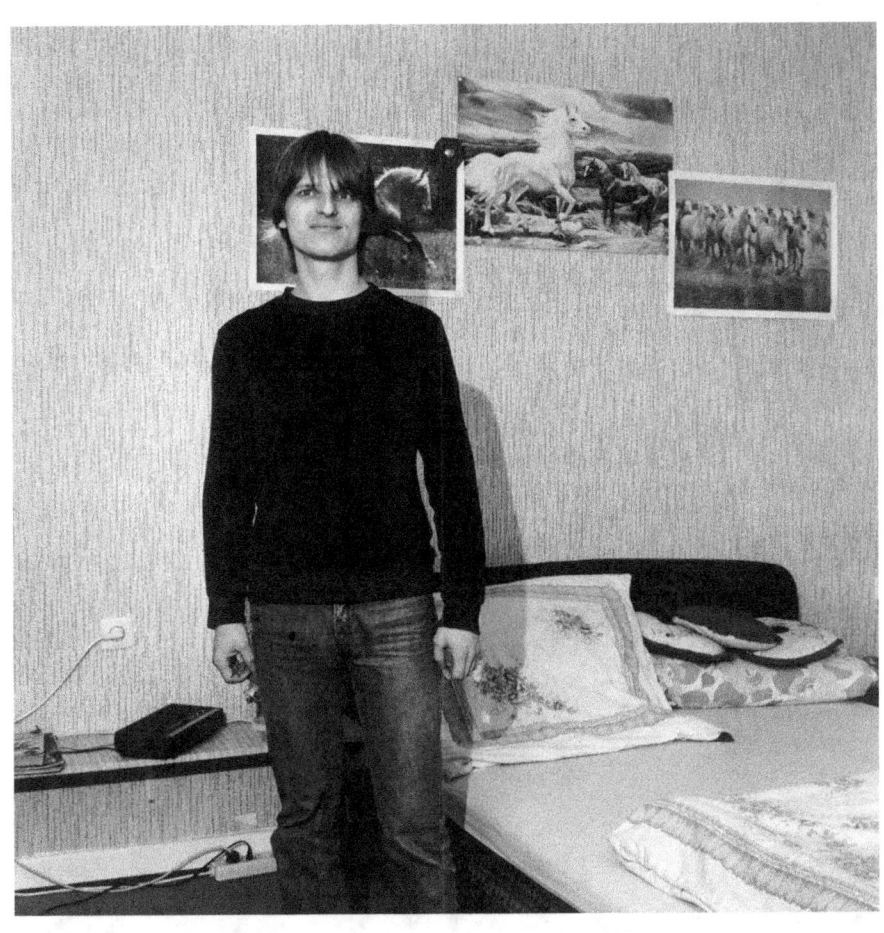

Untitled (West Germany), *Family of Miners,* 1984. Photographic Archives, University of Louisville. Copyright © Milton Rogovin. Courtesy, Center for Creative Photography, University of Arizona Foundation.

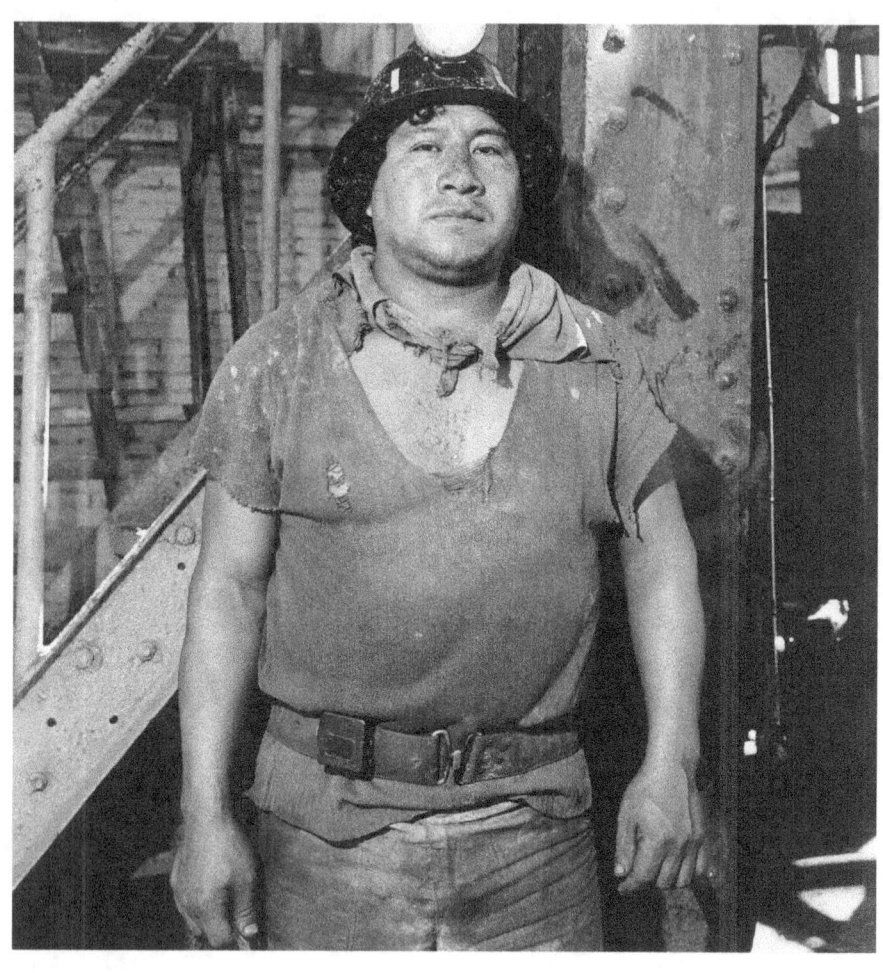

Untitled (Mexico), *Family of Miners,* 1988. The Rogovin Collection, Chicago. Copyright © Milton Rogovin. Courtesy, Center for Creative Photography, University of Arizona Foundation.

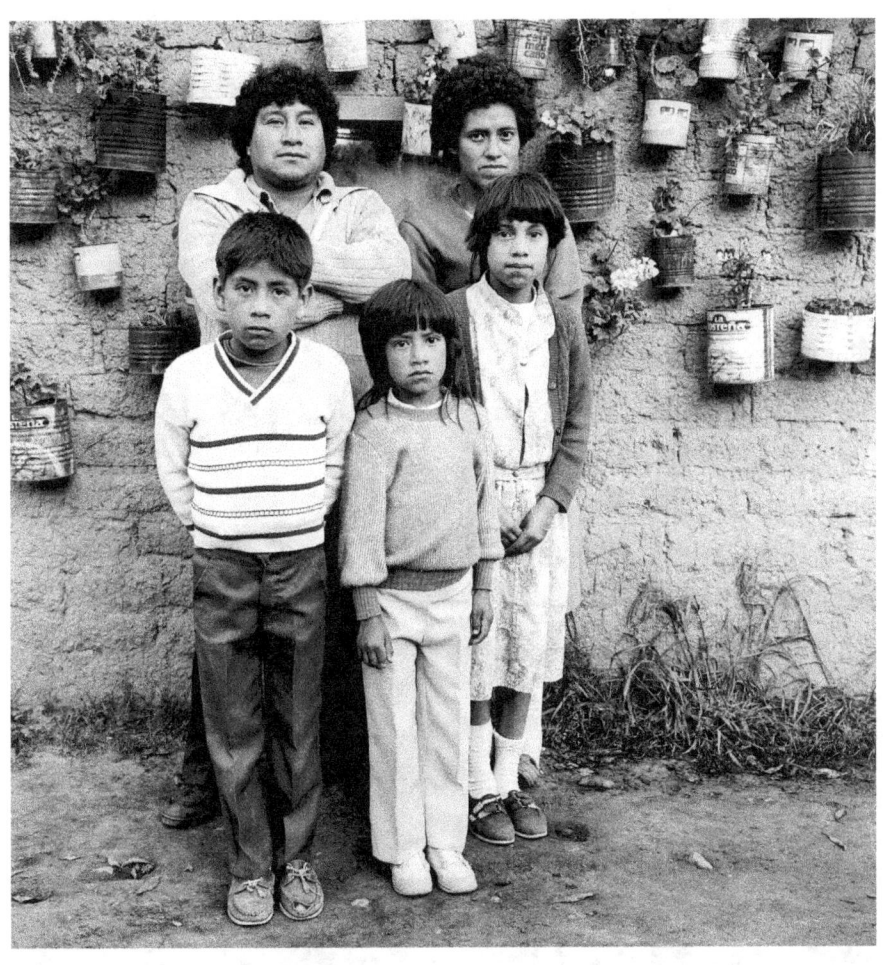

Untitled (Mexico), *Family of Miners,* 1988. The Rogovin Collection, Chicago. Copyright © Milton Rogovin. Courtesy, Center for Creative Photography, University of Arizona Foundation.

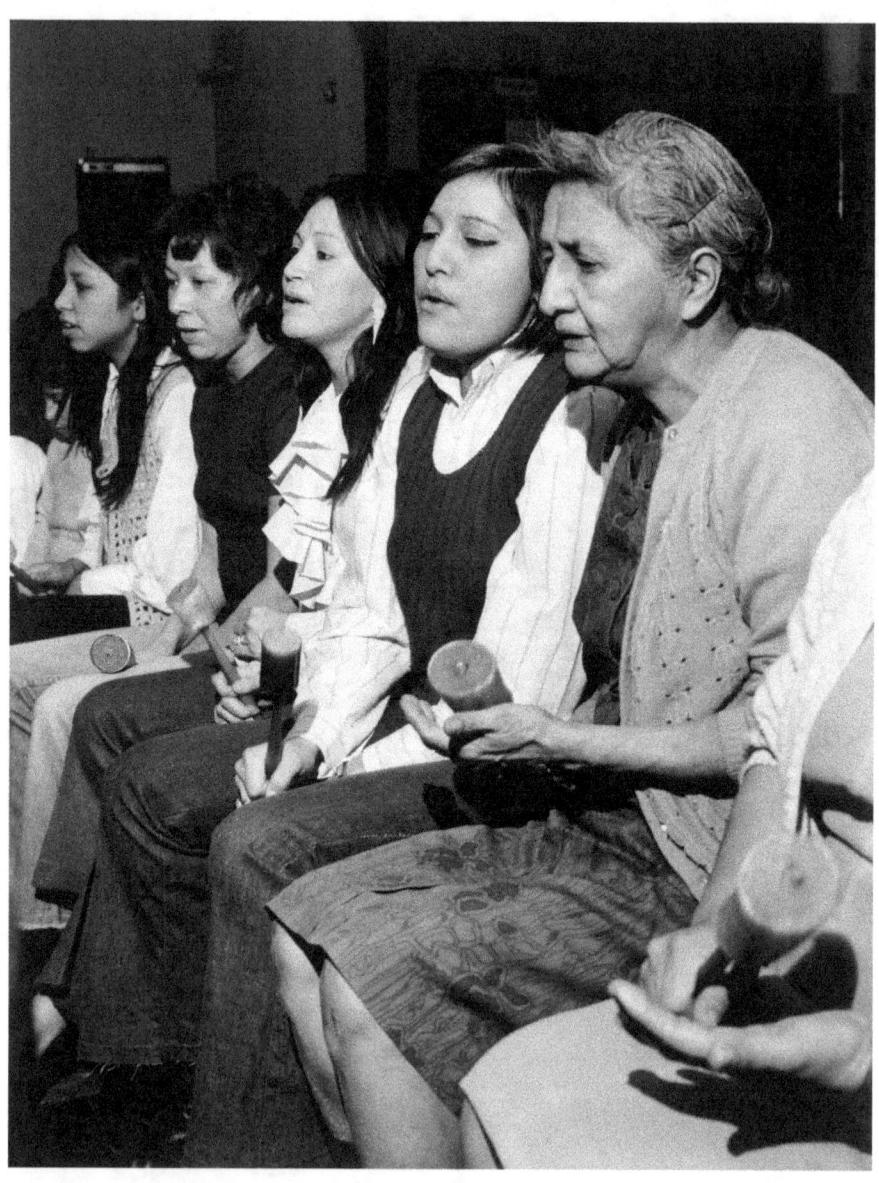

Untitled, *Native Americans,* undated. Photographic Archives, University of Louisville. Copyright © Milton Rogovin. Courtesy, Center for Creative Photography, University of Arizona Foundation.

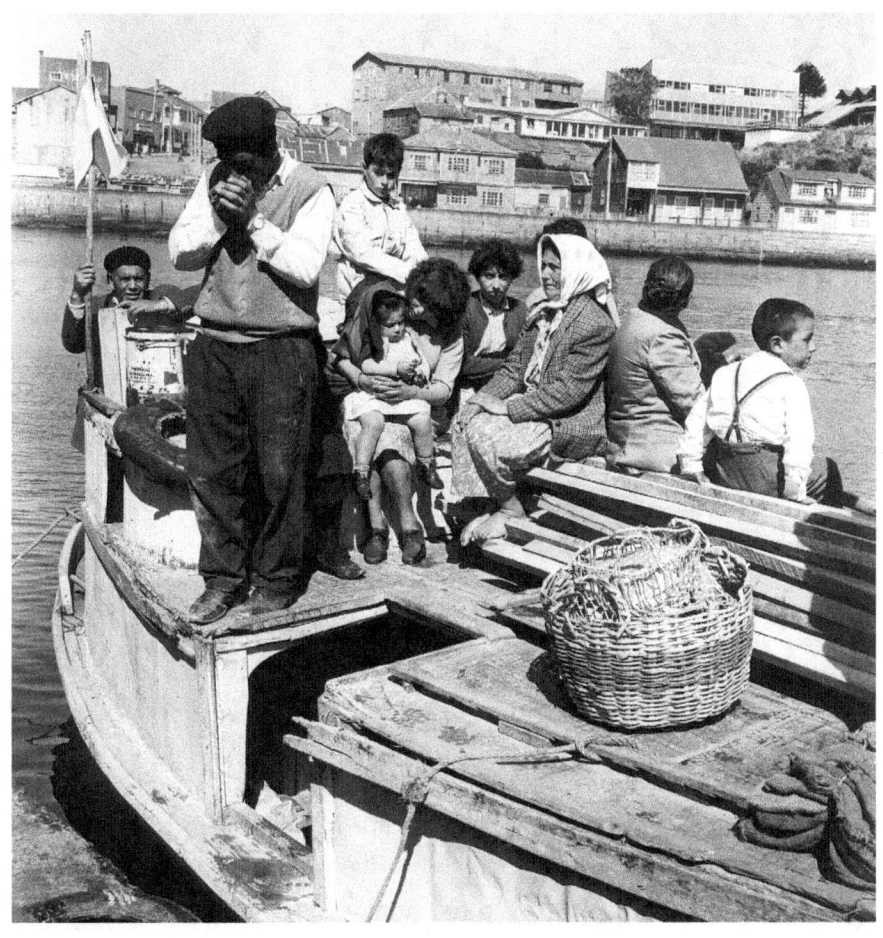

Untitled, *Chile,* 1967. The Rogovin Collection, Chicago. Copyright © Milton Rogovin. Courtesy, Center for Creative Photography, University of Arizona Foundation.

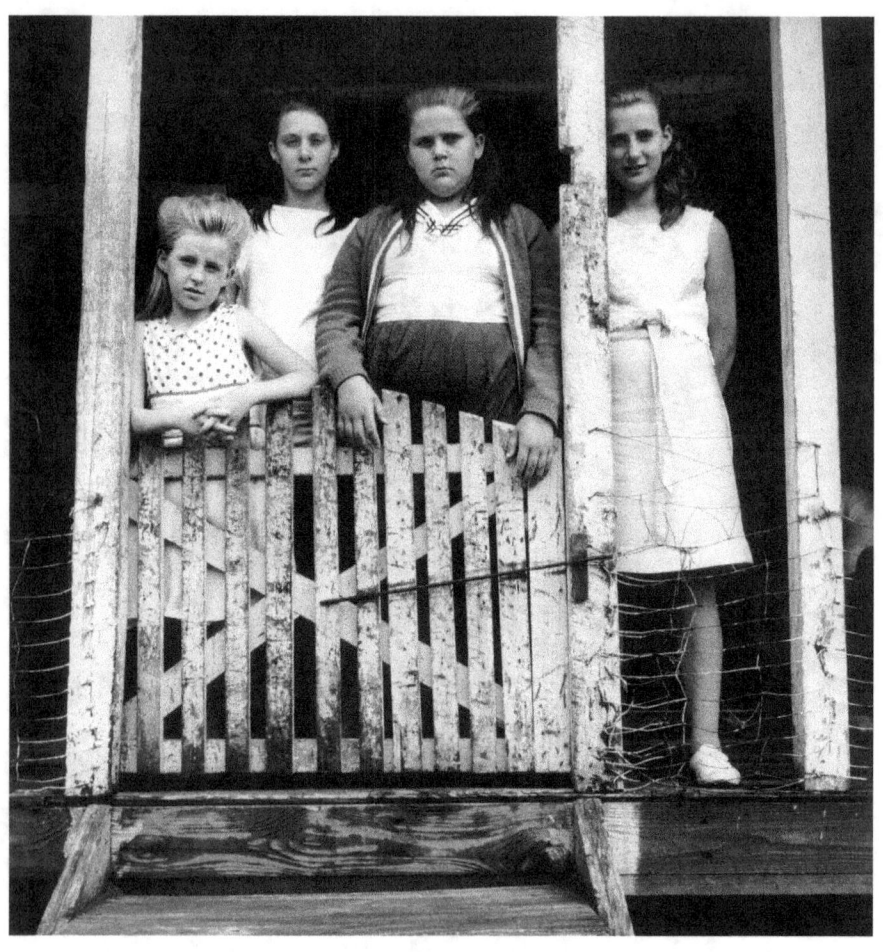

Untitled, *Appalachia*, 1964. Photographic Archives, University of Louisville. Copyright © Milton Rogovin. Courtesy, Center for Creative Photography, University of Arizona Foundation.

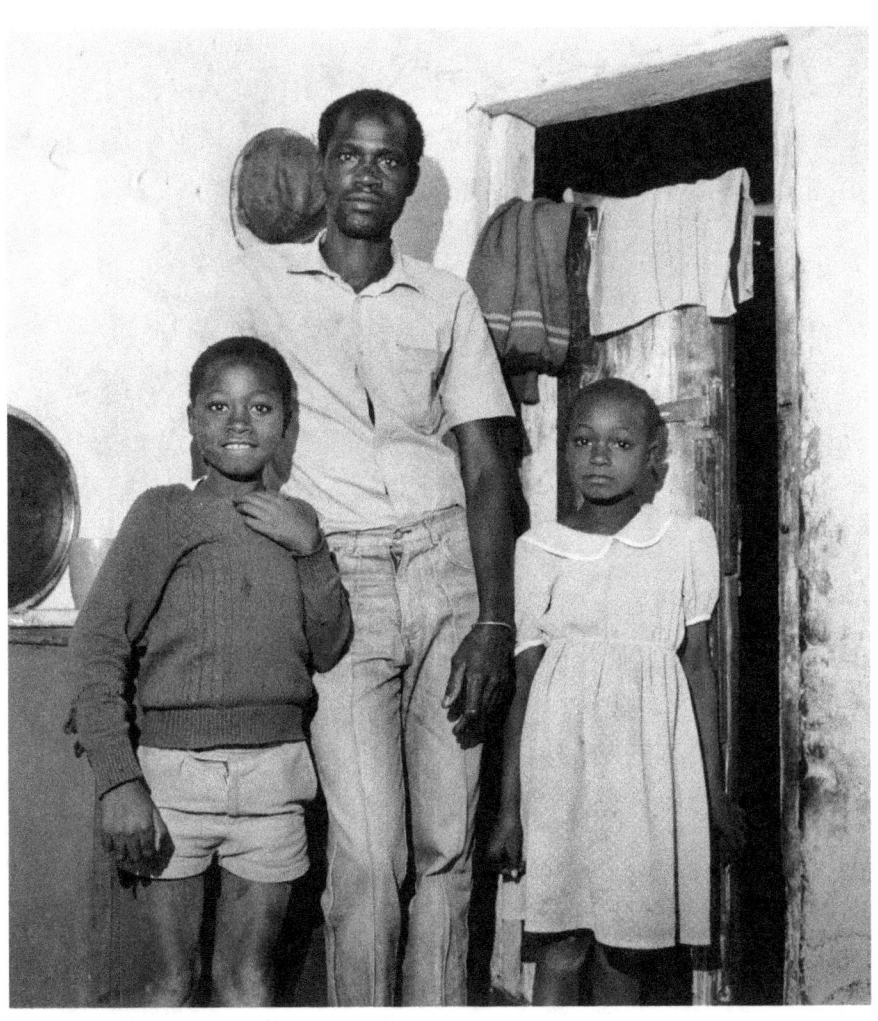

Untitled (Zimbabwe), *Family of Miners,* 1989. Photographic Archives, University of Louisville. Copyright © Milton Rogovin. Courtesy, Center for Creative Photography, University of Arizona Foundation.

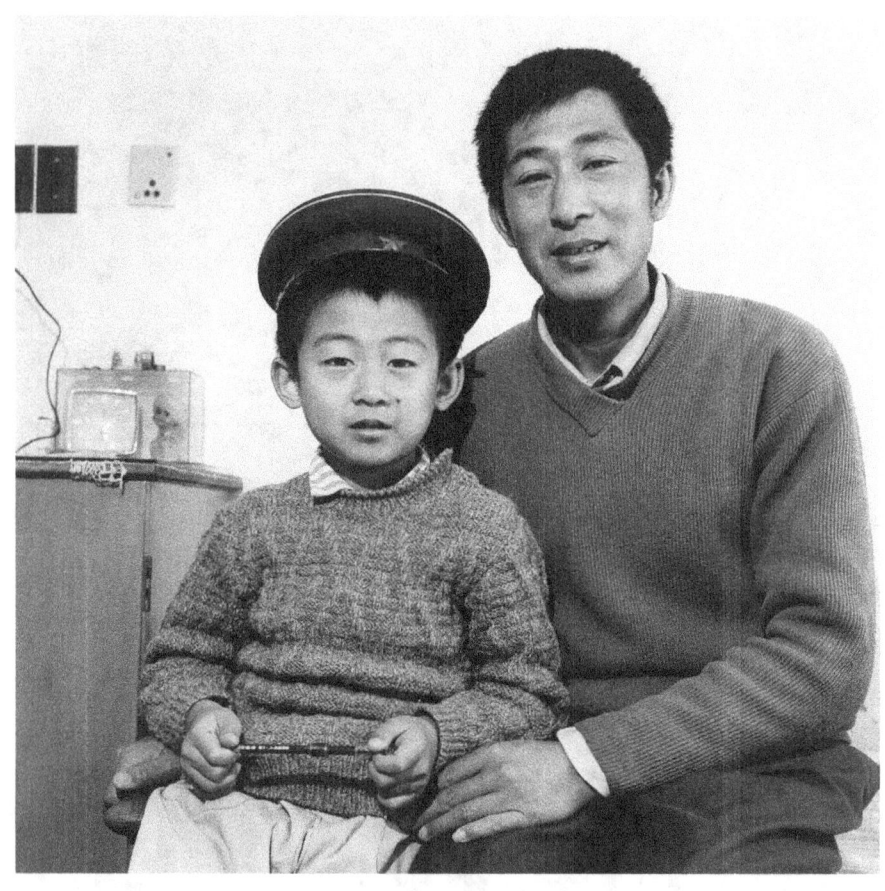

Untitled (China), *Family of Miners*, 1986. The Rogovin Collection, Chicago. Copyright © Milton Rogovin. Courtesy, Center for Creative Photography, University of Arizona Foundation.

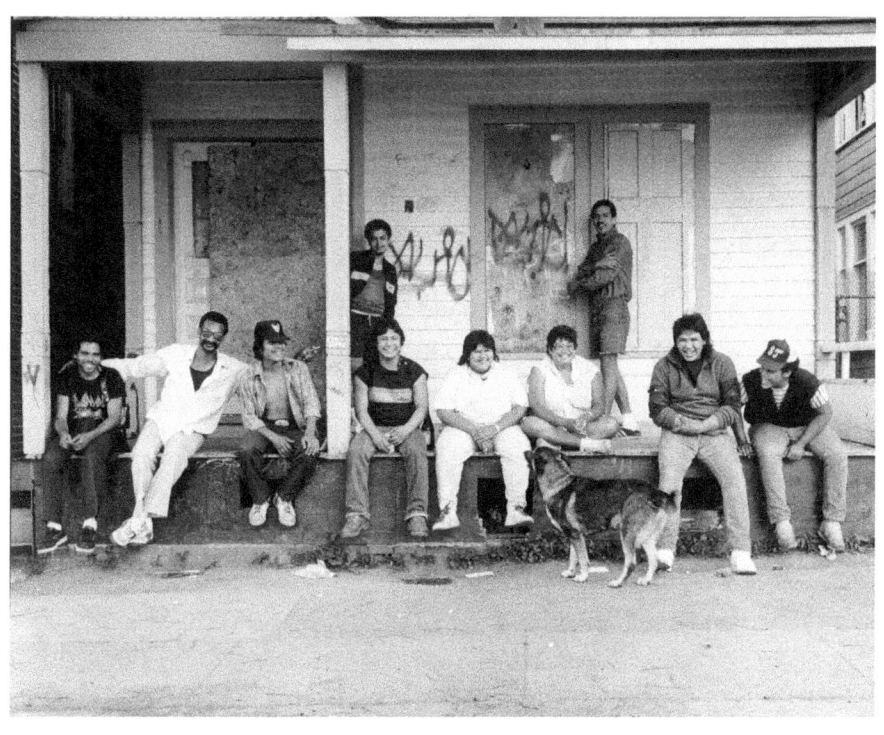

Untitled, *Lower West Side*, 1972–1975. Photographic Archives, University of Louisville. Copyright © Milton Rogovin. Courtesy, Center for Creative Photography, University of Arizona Foundation.

Humanism, Radicalism, and the Angel of History

Milton Rogovin's *Family of Miners*

Thomas B. Byers

AS THE ROGOVIN COLLECTION in the University of Louisville Photographic Archives illustrates, Milton Rogovin conceptualized most of his work in terms of long-term projects, some of which went on for decades. One of the most famous of these projects, featured prominently in the volume *The Forgotten Ones,* is the *Lower West Side—Quartets* series. It portrays the same individuals in photos taken during Rogovin's visits to their Buffalo, New York, neighborhood in four different time periods between 1972 and 2002. Like a project from a very different social stratum, Nicholas Nixon's *Brown Sisters* (1975–present), the *Lower West Side—Quartets* series has as a primary theme the effects of time on particular individuals.

A quite different project is at the heart of *Family of Miners,* another of Rogovin's most celebrated series and the primary focus of this essay. Though he took these photographs between 1962 and 1989, a time period almost as long as that for the *Lower West Side—Quartets* series, the *Miners* photos downplay temporal differences and instead address spatial ones. Rather than returning to the same sites to photograph the same individuals, Rogovin traveled around the world to photograph different individuals who made their living at the same activity. The series began in Appalachia but eventually, thanks to funding provided by the International Center of Photography's W. Eugene Smith Memorial Fund Award for Documentary Photography in 1983, Rogovin was able to widen the project to include photos of miners in China, Cuba, Czechoslovakia (today's Czechia and Slovakia), France, Germany, Mexico, Scotland, Spain, and Zimbabwe.

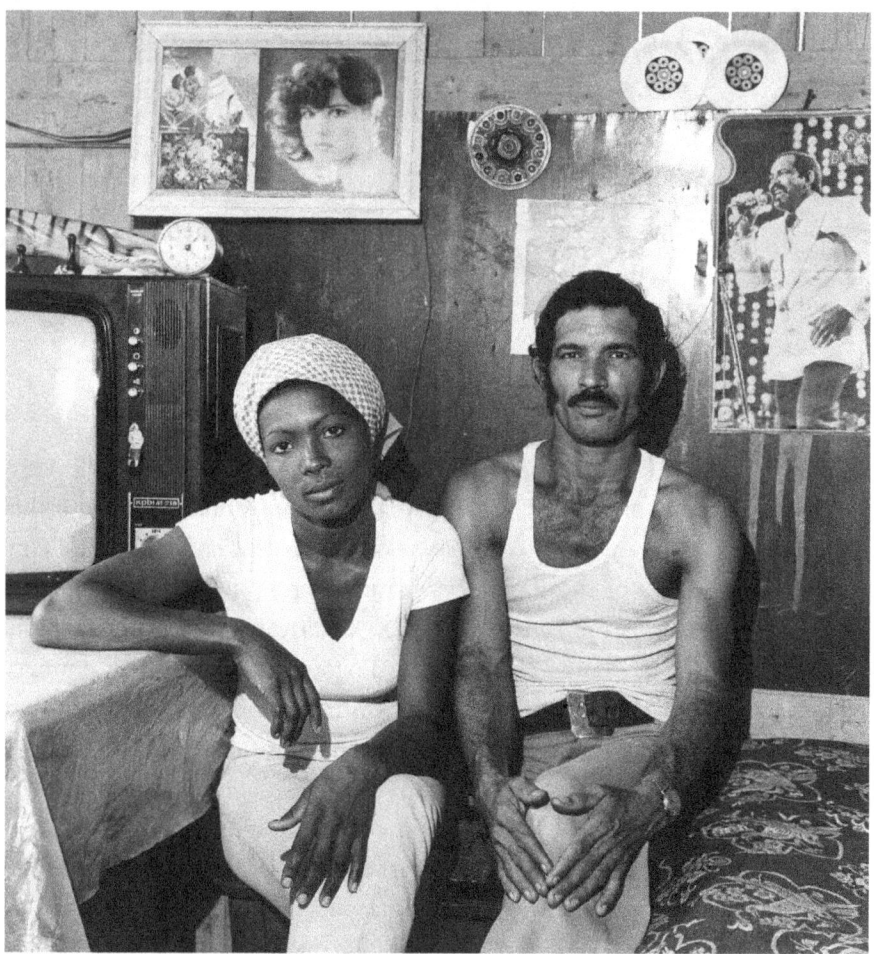

Untitled (Cuba), *Family of Miners*, 1984. The Rogovin Collection, Chicago. Copyright © Milton Rogovin. Courtesy, Center for Creative Photography, University of Arizona Foundation.

Rogovin, as we know, was a social documentarian; indeed, the official website constructed by his children to keep his memory alive is named Milton Rogovin: Social Documentary Photographer. For him, as for most such photographers, the documentary impulse is tightly intertwined with the social one; the pictures are not neutral documents but rhetorical ones, designed to make points, to plead cases, to persuade audiences. In this essay, I try to identify the particular cases being made in *Family of Miners*, to pinpoint a more radical agenda than most commentators discuss, and, finally, to suggest certain ways in which the photographs' subjects may complicate or even impede the images' rhetorical effect. But to do all this requires, first of all, some context from Rogovin's own biography, from the history of photography, and from the most famous document of Marxist rhetoric.

Rogovin's background was what Karl Marx might have identified as petit bourgeois: his Russian Empire Jewish immigrant parents (his mother was born in Lithuania, his father in Belarus) were small-business owners, operating a dry-goods business in New York City. During the early years of the Great Depression, they lost the rental properties they had acquired, and then the store went bankrupt, "which," Rogovin said, "had a devastating effect on my father. In 1931, four months before I was to graduate from Columbia [with a degree in optometry], my father died of a heart attack."[1] By the photographer's own testimony, he "was a product of the Great Depression, and what I saw and experienced myself [including his father's death] made me politically active."[2] And not only active, but radical: having served as education director of the Communist Party USA in Buffalo, New York, Rogovin was called in 1957 to testify before the House Un-American Activities Committee (HUAC) and invoked his rights under the First and Fifth Amendments in refusing to answer questions the committee put to him. The headline in his local paper, the *Buffalo Evening News*, proclaimed the next day, October 4, "Rogovin, Named as Top Red in Buffalo, Balks at Nearly All Queries." As a result, his optometry practice collapsed, and his family was ostracized. Though his FBI file reveals that he chose not to re-enroll in the party in 1958, he remained a lifelong political leftist and advocate for the working class and the poor.[3]

Perhaps because of the real, material damage done to him and his family during the persecution of him for his political beliefs, most of the commentary on Rogovin tends to downplay the radical aspect of those beliefs in favor of portraying him as a socially conscious humanist.[4] At times—even, as we shall see, at times when he speaks about *Family of Miners*—his own utterances feed this tendency; certainly, his family's portrayal of his work on the official website does so. The website declares that "Rogovin's sole purpose, as timeless as it is universal, is to help the viewer see the people in his photographs in a new light, as people of dignity and strength."[5] The humanist language of timelessness and universality here stands in implicit opposition to the historicizing and particularizing discourse of class struggle in the work of Karl Marx and Friedrich Engels. I want to suggest, however, that the more radical strain persists in Rogovin's work, sometimes in unresolved tension with the universalizing humanism. Ultimately, the suppression of the more radical strain uncannily repeats the McCarthyite silencing of Rogovin's voice in the 1950s. Moreover, to accept this suppression is to see him as a less complex figure than he actually was.

In general, commentators follow the lead of Rogovin himself in placing his work in the tradition of social documentary, and it certainly belongs there. His line of descent is traced from Jacob Riis through Lewis Hine (and sometimes August Sander) to Walker Evans, Dorothea Lange, and the other photographers of the Farm Security Administration project and to such independent photographers as Margaret Bourke-White and Paul Strand, the latter of whom identified this lineage in his appreciation of Rogovin's *Lower West Side* series.[6] Although the commentary in general does consistently recognize Rogovin's social activism, it tends to lump together all of these photographers, failing to distinguish the range of positions they took, from the politically conservative Riis and the relatively apolitical Evans through the liberal social reformer Hine to the more left-leaning Bourke-White and Strand. When critical discourse fails to make such distinctions, it keeps us from accurate specific knowledge of important aspects of photographers and their work and prevents us from placing the work accurately. It also often has the effect of "domesticating" more radical work to keep from discomfiting the viewer by implying any serious threat of social change.

I think the same kind of domestication is at work, perhaps unconsciously, in Rogovin's own statement of goals for the *Family of Miners* series: "I'm hoping that when people see these photographs, they will realize that wherever these people are from, they're just like we are. They're people with the same desires. They love their children just as much or as little as we do, they want to live in peace . . . no matter whether it's socialist or whatever. . . . I'm trying to show that underneath it all we're all brothers and sisters."[7]

On one hand, all of this is no doubt so, and it may be because of such quotations that Judith Keller speculates in her contribution to *Milton Rogovin: The Mining Photographs* that Rogovin chose the title *Family of Miners* "perhaps in honor of Edward Steichen's exhibition of 1955, *The Family of Man*."[8] It is possible that Keller's supposition is correct. On the other hand, it is equally plausible to read Rogovin's title as a kind of corrective response to Steichen's.

Steichen's exhibit—perhaps still the single most famous photo exhibit ever mounted in the United States—opened at the Museum of Modern Art in 1955, two years before Rogovin's HUAC testimony and while he was still a member of the Communist Party.[9] Although the exhibit was widely celebrated, there were dissenters, perhaps the best known of whom is the French critic and theorist Roland Barthes. Barthes reviewed the show under its Paris title, which translates as *The Great Family of Man*, and his review is collected in his book *Mythologies*, which first appeared in French in 1957 and in an English translation in 1972. Barthes criticizes the exhibition as basically an example of what the volume's now classic theoretical essay, "Myth Today," defines as "myth." In Barthes's analysis, myth "has the task of giving an historical intention a natural justification, and making contingency appear eternal." In it, "a conjuring trick has taken place; it has turned reality inside out, it has emptied it of history and filled it with nature."[10]

Writing specifically on *The Great Family of Man*, Barthes says:

> This myth functions in two stages: first the difference be-
> tween human morphologies is asserted, exoticism is insistently
> stressed, the infinite variations of the species, the diversity in
> skins, skulls and customs are made manifest, the image of Babel
> is complacently projected over that of the world. Then, from this
> pluralism, a type of unity is magically produced: man is born,
> works, laughs and dies everywhere in the same way; and if there
> still remains in these actions some ethnic peculiarity, at least
> one hints that there is underlying each one an identical "nature,"
> that their diversity is only formal and does not belie the exis-
> tence of a common mould.[11]

All in all, then, the effect of the myth and of what John O'Brian calls "[t]he overriding proposition of the exhibition . . . was that people are the same the world over, regardless of differences in geography and culture. At its crudest, the exhibition proposed that indigenous peoples living in Hokkaido are no different than Upper East Side millionaires living in New York."[12]

It seems unlikely that the humanist Rogovin would deny "the existence of a common mould." But it seems equally unlikely, given his Marxist background, that he would agree that the "diversity" of the poor and the rich "is only formal." For a Marxist, that diversity is crucially *historical*—and historically crucial. As *The Communist Manifesto* famously announces, "The history of all hitherto existing society is the history of class struggles."[13] From that perspective, universalizing notions such as "the family of man" only cover over the pressing, brutal realities of historical difference and class oppression. In that light, "the Family of Miners" can be seen as a much more particularizing designation than "the Family of Man"—the miners are a family based not on a universal human essence but on the historical specificity of their occupation, which defines a specific relation to industrial production. Like the subjects of Rogovin's series *Working People* (1976–1987), focused largely on steel workers such as those found in his book *Portraits in Steel*,[14] the miners are members of the proletariat, the class that Marx and Engels saw as destined to overthrow the bourgeoisie and institute communism and the class to whom they addressed *The Communist Manifesto*.

The *Manifesto* ends with the famous rallying cry, "Working Men of All Countries, Unite!" It implies that classes transcend national boundaries. Hence, the great anthem of the Communist and socialist Left is "The Internationale," whose very title places it in opposition to all national anthems. The *Family of Miners* series, with its emphasis both on commonalities of subject across national lines and on stylistic unity in the portrayal of social diversity, asserts the unity of the working people and implicitly invites them to recognize it. The subdued style, eschewing dramatic effects of lighting and variety in framing, generally captures the subjects head-on, with the camera—Rogovin's trusted Rolleiflex—positioned a little below their faces. The shots of them at work are generally framed in what film criticism calls *plan américain* (roughly from the knees up); the companion shots in their homes tend to be from a little farther back, so as to show something of their domestic milieu (and often other family members) and also, perhaps, not to be too invasive of their space. The photographs neither look down on the miners, inviting liberal pity, nor sentimentally glorify them in the tradition of Stalinist socialist realism. Rather, they portray them, at a respectful distance, in the dignity of their common humanity and their common lot. If the series' address to a bourgeois audience invites us to see that, as Rogovin said, the miners are "just like we are" because of such ubiquitous human emotions as love for children or desire for peace, the series' address to the miners themselves says, first and foremost, that they are like each other on the basis of their work and their class position—and that their differences not only of nationality but also of race and ethnicity are trivial in comparison to this work and class identity.

While Rogovin may have emphasized a humanist theme for the *Miners* series in an interview with his local paper,[15] we should recognize that this is the same paper that thirty-three years earlier had damaged him and his family by branding him "Buffalo's Top Red." He would have had ample reason to be careful about how he glossed the series for the *Buffalo Evening News*. But the series' title and visual rhetoric perfectly fit the basic Marxist principles and slogans with which *The Communist Manifesto* begins and ends, and in that light it seems anything but far-fetched to suggest that the title might be read not (or not only) as a tribute to *The Family of Man* but rather (or also) as a historically specific, class-focused corrective to it. Whether we interpret this more radical possibility as an element of Rogovin's post–Communist Party political unconscious or as a matter of a deliberately partially concealed conscious intention or simply as a symptom of the ways in which traditional humanist and more radical leftist discourses often at once overlap and conflict, it seems difficult to argue that the series does not invite or will not sustain such a reading.

If we push farther in this direction, we notice that the series suggests the unity of miners regardless not only of national boundaries but also of differences in race, ethnicity, and gender. (Indeed, for the traditional orthodox Marxist, the oppressions based on these latter differences are secondary to class oppression and will be remedied by the triumph of the unified proletariat.) Rhetorical readings of the *Family of Miners* series from both humanist and Marxist perspectives tend to see it as proposing the basic unity of the series' subjects, regardless of all these divisions. Its message is, in a double sense, utopian. On the one hand, it proposes the dream of a better world where that unity triumphs over differences. On the other hand, in a certain way it also serves as a reminder that a utopia is literally, etymologically, a place that is "no place." If we read the miners photographs with historical specificity, they may point toward a Marxist ideal of a world in which the workers are united, but they also are marked with reminders that such a world does not exist.

The *Miners* series depicts white European and European American miners, black African and African American miners, miners from Cuba and Mexico, and miners from China. These images of embodied racial and ethnic difference carry reminders of historical oppression that cannot be erased simply by the desire for workers' unity. For instance, images of miners from Zimbabwe cannot help but carry the historical traces of colonialism. Similarly, the history of African American, Latino, and Chinese miners in the United States includes enslavement and discriminatory indenture; lynchings such as those of scores of Latino miners in Sonora, California; massacres such as the murder of twenty-eight Chinese miners in Rock Springs, Wyoming; and other horrors. That such horrors are too often left out of the history textbooks does not mean that they did not exist or that they have disappeared without traces. The history also includes the mine owners' repeated pitting of one ethnic group against another, as in the use of minority miners as strikebreakers. In fairness, there are also many instances of miners' solidarity across racial and ethnic lines, particularly in labor actions. But the history of non-white "others" in the mines is all too often just another subset of the nation's long history of racial and ethnic oppression and conflict.

This history may be of profound importance for "the history of class struggles" in the United States. Starting with Marx and Engels, many commentators on US economic history have posed, as Seymour Martin Lipset and Gary Marks put it, "a specific question: Why did the United States, alone among industrial societies, lack a significant socialist movement or labor party?" According to Lipset and Marks, "Marx and Engels pointed to," among other factors, "the role of ethnic diversity in undermining class consciousness by giving native-born white workers a privileged position, thus enabling the bourgeoisie to play workers of different racial and ethnic

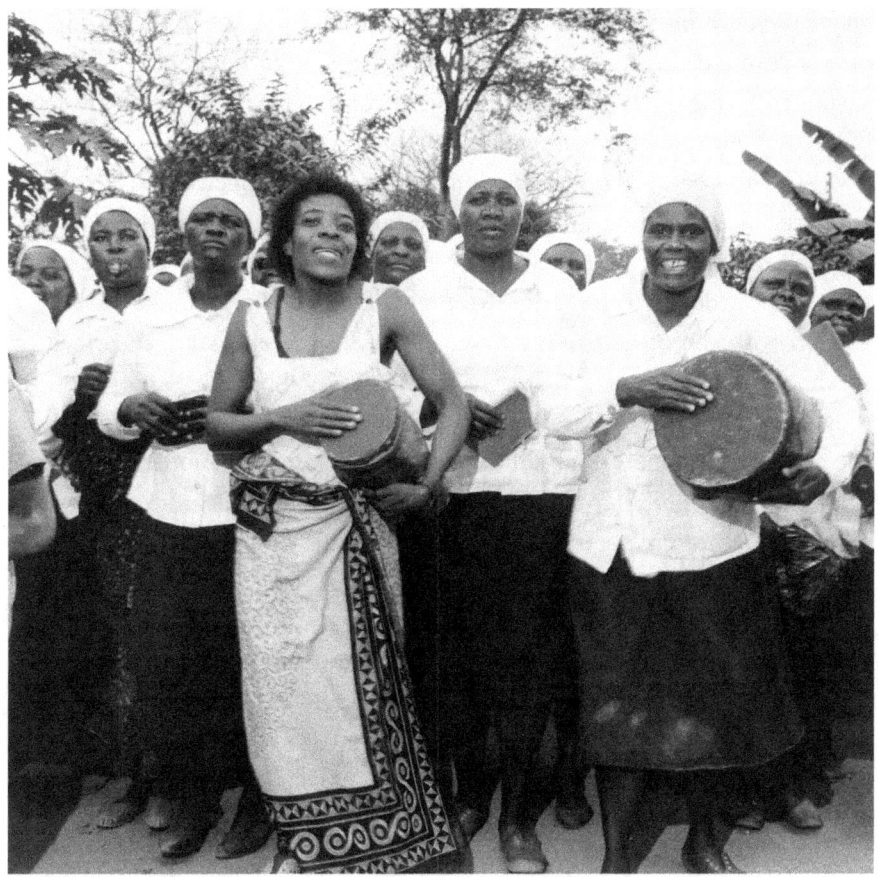

Untitled (Zimbabwe), *Family of Miners,* 1989. Photographic Archives, University of Louisville. Copyright © Milton Rogovin. Courtesy, Center for Creative Photography, University of Arizona Foundation.

backgrounds against one another. In a letter written in 1870 to two friends in New York, Marx noted that in America the 'working class is *split* into two *hostile* camps,' native and foreign-born. He recommended to his correspondents that they should press for a 'coalition among workers of different ethnic backgrounds.'"[16]

Although racial and ethnic divisions are only one of many explanations proposed by Marx and Engels, other commentators see these divisions as central; for instance, Michael Goldfield's book *The Color of Politics: Race and the Mainsprings of American Politics* is dedicated to the thesis, as one reviewer summarized it, that "the failure of the US working class to develop sustained forms of class organization and consciousness is the result of the failure to confront white supremacy."[17]

The photographs of the *Family of Miners* series implicitly call us to overcome racial and ethnic differences to establish unity. The impulse behind this call may be the humanist desire to celebrate the family of man or the more radical desire to unite the working class—or it may be both, each in tension with the other. In any case, the very differences are inscribed on the bodies of the miners themselves, and the photographs—will they, nil they—offer visual evidence of these divisions. Though race and ethnicity are social constructs, their signs continue to be legible, and their effects continue to be very materially real. Rogovin's photographs may mean to orient us to a future we must create, in which the family heals itself and its world. But at the same time they recall, as if against their will, a past (and a present) slate that will not be wiped clean. So as we stand before them, at one shoulder we have Milton Rogovin himself, the optometrist, the vision expert, as historical optimist, inviting us to look at the world through glasses of red rose. But at the other shoulder, a little farther back, we may sense the familiar presence of Walter Benjamin's "angel of history":

> His face is turned toward the past. Where we perceive a chain
> of events, he sees one single catastrophe which keeps piling
> wreckage upon wreckage and hurls it in front of his feet. The
> angel would like to stay, awaken the dead, and make whole what
> has been smashed. But a storm is blowing from Paradise; it has
> got caught in his wings with such violence that the angel can no
> longer close them. The storm irresistibly propels him into the
> future to which his back is turned, while the pile of debris before
> him grows skyward. This storm is what we call progress.[18]

Notes

1. Quoted in Melanie Anne Herzog, *Milton Rogovin: The Making of a Social Documentary Photographer* (Tucson: Center for Creative Photography, University of Arizona; Seattle: University of Washington Press, 2006), 28.

2. Quoted in Benjamin Genocchio, obituary for Milton Rogovin, *New York Times,* January 19, 2011.

3. For these biographical details, see Associated Press, "Late NY Photographer's FBI File Reveals Scrutiny," *newsOK,* January 7, 2012, at https://newsok.com/article/feed/333422/late-ny-photographers-fbi-file-reveals-scrutiny.

4. A notable exception is Janet Zandy, "Photography and the Work of Class and Race," *American Quarterly* 60, no. 1 (March 2008): 183–91. Zandy explicitly addresses "Rogovin's Marxist perspective" (190) and notes that "Rogovin brought his socialist political convictions to bear on his practices as a social photographer" (188).

5. Biography of Milton Rogovin, on the website Milton Rogovin: Social Documentary Photographer, n.d., http://www.miltonrogovin.com/biography.html.

6. See James M. Wood, Milton Rogovin, and Paul Strand, *Milton Rogovin: Lower West Side, Buffalo, New York* (Buffalo, N.Y.: Albright-Know Art Gallery, 1975).

7. Quoted in Anthony Cardinale, "Champion of the Poor: Milton Rogovin Reflects on the American Century," *Buffalo: Magazine of the Buffalo News,* March 25, 1990.

8. Judith Kellner, "Milton Rogovin and the Family of Miners," in Milton Rogovin, *Milton Rogovin: The Mining Photographs* (Los Angeles: Getty Publications, 2005), 7.

9. The Associated Press report on the photographer's FBI file says, "The Rogovins opted not to re-enroll in the party in 1958, according to the file." Interestingly, the report goes on, "Their children said the decision was more about protecting the family and Anne Rogovin's job as a teacher than politics" ("Late NY Photographer's FBI File Reveals Scrutiny"). The implication here is that the decision not to re-enroll was *not* based on a repudiation of the party itself.

10. Roland Barthes, "Myth Today," in *Mythologies,* trans. Annette Lavers (New York: Hill and Wang, 1972), 142.

11. Roland Barthes, *"The Great Family of Man,"* in *Mythologies,* 100.

12. John O'Brian, "The Nuclear Family of Man," *Asia-Pacific Journal: Japan Focus,* July 11, 2008, at https://apjjf.org/-John-O'Brian/2816/article.html, accessed November 20, 2018.

13. Karl Marx and Friedrich Engels, *The Communist Manifesto,* trans. Samuel Moore, in *Selected Works,* vol. 1 (Moscow: Progress, 1969), 98–137, at https://www.marxists.org/archive/marx/works/1848/communist-manifesto/ch01.htm.

14. Michael Frisch and Milton Rogovin, *Portraits in Steel,* foreword by Robert Doherty (Ithaca, N.Y.: Cornell University Press, 1993).

15. See the quotation from Rogovin given earlier from Cardinale, "Champion of the Poor."

16. Seymour Martin Lipset and Gary Marks, *It Didn't Happen Here: Why Socialism Failed in the United States* (New York: Norton, 2013), 15, 29, emphasis in the original.

17. Mel Rothenberg, "Michael Goldfield's *Color of Politics*," *Solidarity*, July–August 1998, at http://www.solidarity-us.org/atc/75/p1820/. See also Michael Goldfield, *The Color of Politics: Race and the Mainsprings of American Politics* (New York: New Press, 1997).

18. Walter Benjamin, "Theses on the Philosophy of History," *Illuminations*, trans. Harry Zohn (New York: Schocken, 1968), 257–58.

Working People Series, 1976–1987

Cynthia Negrey

DURING THE SECOND WORLD WAR, Buffalo, New York, was "the Seattle of its day" (Goldman 1983, 267). Employment in central Buffalo peaked during the war at 460,000, with nearly half of workers employed in heavy manufacturing (Perry 1987, 119). Buffalo's aircraft industry was integral to the war effort. Curtiss-Wright Corporation alone employed 40,000 workers in 1943, although employment there declined to 5,500 soon after the war's end, and in 1946 the company shut down most of its operations in Buffalo to consolidate in Columbus, Ohio (Goldman 1983, 267).

Buffalo had been known as "the Lion of the West" because of its position at the mouth of the Great Lakes and the Erie Canal. By 1850, it was the largest inland port in the United States and a major mercantile break-and-bulk point for the transport of raw materials extracted in the northern Midwest. Food processing, tanneries, furniture factories, iron workshops, and the nation's largest and most productive flour industry grew up around this commercial base (Perry 1987, 118).

By the turn of the twentieth century, Buffalo had emerged as a growing industrial region, although it remained the nation's third-largest port and was the second-largest rail terminus (Perry 1987, 119). By the end of the First World War, Buffalo had become an industrial giant in steel, railroad cars and engines, airplanes, and automobiles, led by the Lackawanna Iron and Steel Company (subsequently Bethlehem Steel) and later in combination with General Motors (Perry 1987, 119). Industrial growth throughout the Northeast and Midwest fueled population growth during the first half of the

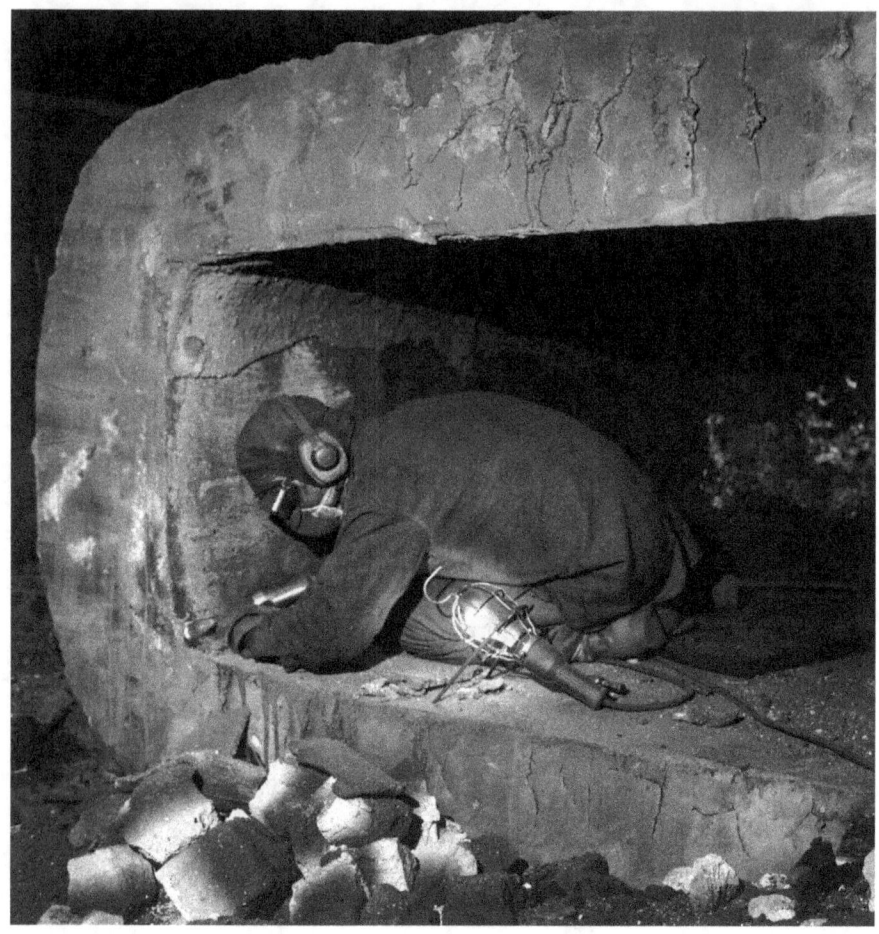

Untitled (Shenango, Inc., Steel Ingot Molds Division), *Working People,* 1978–1981. Photographic Archives, University of Louisville. Copyright © Milton Rogovin. Courtesy, Center for Creative Photography, University of Arizona Foundation.

twentieth century, drawing European immigrants and African Americans from the agricultural South.

By the 1970s and 1980s, however, Buffalo's industrial base was "shattered" (Perry 1987, 113), the result of socioeconomic changes after the Second World War that transformed America's manufacturing base and, disproportionately, cities such as Buffalo. During the 1950s, companies in the chemical industry, such as DuPont and National Aniline, closed plants in Buffalo, and

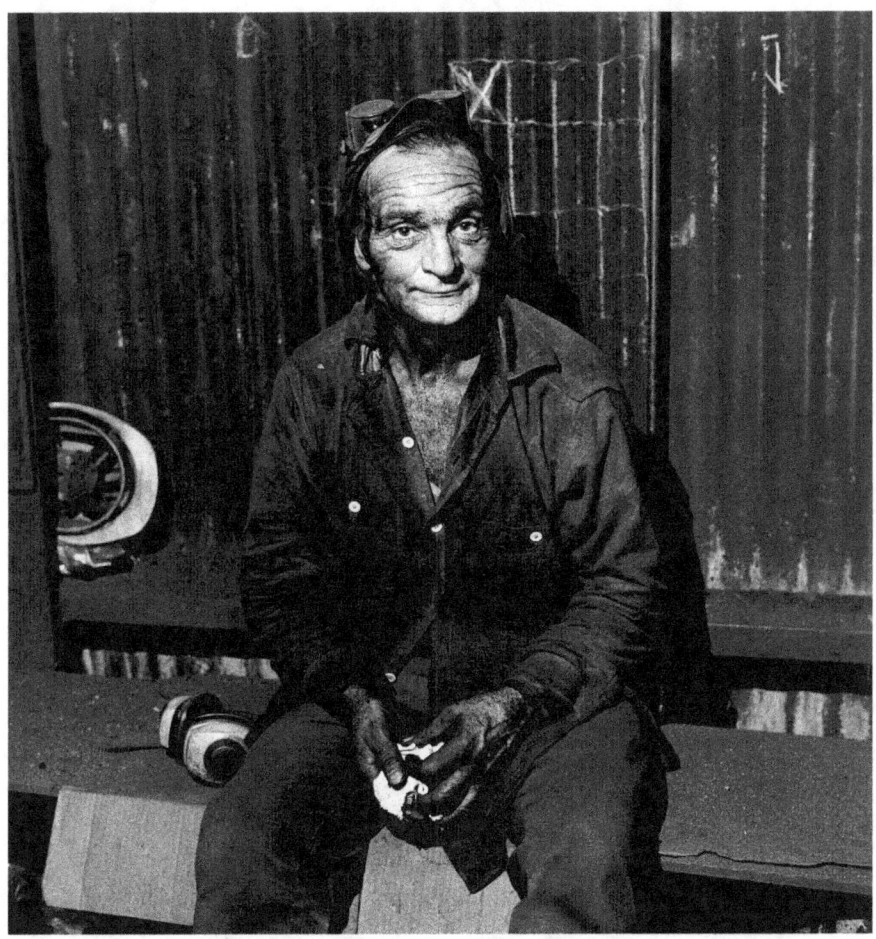

Untitled (Shenango, Inc., Steel Ingot Molds Division), *Working People*, 1978–1981.
The Rogovin Collection, Chicago. Copyright © Milton Rogovin. Courtesy, Center
for Creative Photography, University of Arizona Foundation.

locally owned breweries closed by the early 1970s (Goldman 1983, 268–70).
Buffalo lost its historic port function after the St. Lawrence Seaway opened in
1959 and bypassed Buffalo. As a consequence, waterfront industries closed,
and grain storage and flour milling declined (Goldman 1983, 269–71).

There was a steady decline of manufacturing employment in the Buffalo area after the Second World War (Perry 1987, 120–21). By 1975, Buffalo's unemployment rate was 12 percent, in part the result of mass layoffs at

Bethlehem Steel. In 1971, Bethlehem Steel permanently laid off half of its workforce of 18,000 (Goldman 1983, 273).

By early 1982, Bethlehem Steel employed only a skeleton crew in Buffalo, which was also the case at the General Motors and Ford facilities in Buffalo. These mass layoffs had ripple effects throughout the local economy, shuttering shops, stores, and restaurants and diminishing support for local arts, cultural events, and organizations (Goldman 1983, 275).

If industry had become the source of Buffalo's pride early in the twentieth century, by the late 1970s it was the source of its pain. Departing industry left Buffalo's workers jobless, and if that weren't bad enough, toxic wastes disposed at Love Canal from the Hooker Chemical Company near its Niagara Falls plant seeped into nearby residential basements in the late 1970s, leading to a federal declaration of a state of emergency and the evacuation of 710 families still living there. At least 153 contaminated sites were subsequently identified in the Buffalo area (Goldman 1983, 289–90).

Deindustrialization wasn't unique to Buffalo. The entire Great Lakes region was hit hard by the twin recessions of 1979 and 1982. Analysis of a slightly longer period, specifically 1979–1985, allowing for brief recovery, shows that the states in the Great Lakes region (Minnesota, Wisconsin, Illinois, Indiana, Michigan, Ohio, Pennsylvania, and New York) lost 16 percent of their manufacturing jobs, compared to 8 percent in the United States overall. The losses were especially pronounced in the cities. Among eleven lakefront cities, Buffalo among them (the others are Duluth-Superior, Green Bay, Milwaukee, Chicago, Gary, Detroit, Toledo, Cleveland, Erie, and Rochester), 25 percent of manufacturing jobs were lost from 1979 to 1985. The losses in manufacturing were not offset by growth in other sectors in the lakefront cities. Whereas the United States experienced growth of 9 percent in overall nonagricultural employment from 1979 to 1985, nonagricultural employment declined in the lakefront cities by 6 percent during the same period.[1]

The losses during the 1979–1985 period may be compared to a 4 percent *loss* in the lakefront cities in the prior decade, 1970–1979, and to a 9 percent *gain* in the United States overall from 1970 to 1979. The contrasting trends of the United States overall and the lakefront cities during the 1970s and the magnitude of decline in the Great Lakes region and the lakefront cities in the

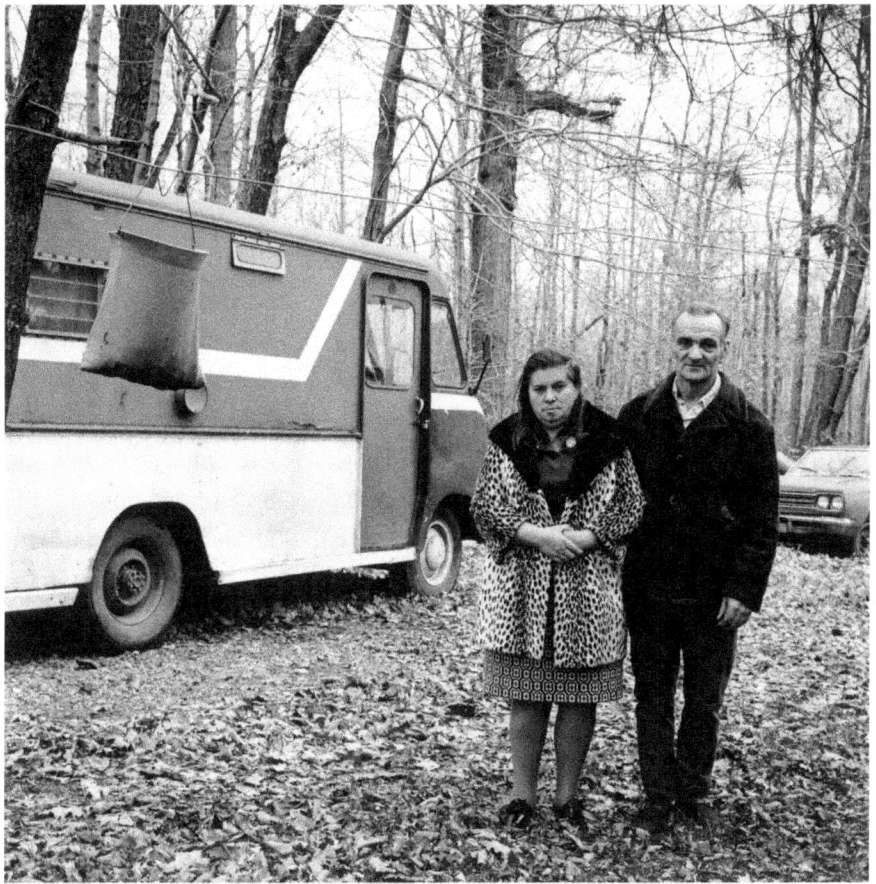

Untitled (Shenango, Inc., Steel Ingot Molds Division), *Working People*, 1978–1981. The Rogovin Collection, Chicago. Copyright © Milton Rogovin. Courtesy, Center for Creative Photography, University of Arizona Foundation.

first half of the 1980s represented significant structural economic changes disproportionately affecting cities such as Buffalo (Hill and Negrey 1987).

A longer-range view from the early 1970s to the late 1980s shows just how distinctive Buffalo and the eighteen other "classic deindustrializing centers" were (Negrey and Zickel 1994).[2] They were the only metropolitan areas in the country that lost both manufacturing jobs and population during the two decades. And the losses were not small—an average 29 percent decline in manufacturing employment and 5 percent decline in population. Nonagricultural employment in these metropolitan areas grew just 8 percent during the period, compared to 47 percent in the United States as a whole. The service sector doubled (or more) in many places in the United States over the course of the 1970s and 1980s, but that was not the case in the classic deindustrializing places (Negrey and Zickel 1994). While some of the deindustrializing places showed evidence of restructuring—Pittsburgh and New York City, for example—others, such as Buffalo, Flint, and Gary, were "destructuring" (Koritz 1991).

The 1970s and 1980s were pivotal decades in economic changes associated with oil-price inflation, increased foreign competition, globalization, the shift to a more service-, information-, and technology-oriented economy, and the declining influence of labor unions. The Detroit-based monopolistic "Big Three" (General Motors, Ford, and Chrysler) had dominated world automobile markets, but in the 1980s they faced mounting pressure, especially from Japanese producers of economical, fuel-efficient vehicles. Heightened foreign competition in manufacturing led US-based producers to look for markets and cost savings outside the United States. The search for lower costs created employment opportunities in manufacturing for workers offshore, particularly in countries such as Mexico, where wages were lower than in the United States, but at the same time this search meant declining opportunities and declining wages for American workers, who now had to compete with those lower-wage workers offshore. American workers displaced from manufacturing as well as those who couldn't obtain jobs in manufacturing turned to whatever opportunities could be found in the growing service sector. For workers with average educational attainment, this meant service and retail jobs paying lower wages than manufacturing and often with part-time rather than full-time hours. High-quality jobs emerging in new information and technology industries would require aspirants to obtain additional training and education beyond that which had been customary in manufacturing. Manufacturing had been the base of labor union strength in the Northeast and Midwest, and labor unions had fought for the high wages that characterized the industry. But as manufacturing declined, so too did union membership and power. The 1980s saw waves of concessionary bargaining during which unions and their members agreed to wage and benefit cuts to avoid plant closings.[3]

Production workers in durable-goods ("heavy") manufacturing were disproportionately male and disproportionately African American, and they were disproportionately displaced when the twin recessions occurred in the late 1970s and early 1980s. Nearly a third of all African American men working in durable-goods manufacturing in the United States lost their jobs (Hill and Negrey 1989). Although women were employed in certain types of jobs in heavy manufacturing, their numbers were few, and they were more likely to be employed in "light" (non-durable-goods) manufacturing, such as textiles, garments, and electrical goods. However, those industries were also affected by foreign competition and globalization, which further displaced women workers from manufacturing jobs in the United States.

Rogovin's photographs in the series *Working People* (1976–1987) reflect these racial and gender patterns in manufacturing employment, showing male workers, many of them African American, at Atlas, Bethlehem Steel, Republic Steel, Ford, and Chevy, as well as women, some of them African American, at Chevy, Ford, Westinghouse, and Buffalo China. The dates of the photographs, from the late 1970s into the 1980s, make me curious about the photographer's motives. Did the economic calamity unfolding around him in Buffalo inspire him to make a photographic record of workers in these types of jobs before the jobs completely disappeared?

Works Cited

Bluestone, Barry, and Bennett Harrison. 1982. *The Deindustrialization of America.* New York: Basic Books.

Goldman, Mark. 1983. *High Hopes: The Rise and Decline of Buffalo, New York.* Albany, N.Y.: State University of New York Press.

Hill, Richard Child, and Cynthia Negrey. 1987. "Deindustrialization in the Great Lakes." *Urban Affairs Quarterly* 22, no. 4: 580–97.

———. 1989. "Deindustrialization and Racial Minorities in the Great Lakes Region." In *The Reshaping of America: Social Consequences of the Changing Economy,* edited by D. Stanley Eitzen and Maxine Baca Zinn, 168–77. Englewood Cliffs, N.J.: Prentice-Hall.

Koritz, Douglas. 1991. "*Restructuring* or *Destructuring*: Deindustrialization in Two Industrial Heartland Cities." *Urban Affairs Quarterly* 26, no. 4: 497–511.

Negrey, Cynthia. 2012. *Work Time: Conflict, Control, and Change.* Cambridge: Polity.

Negrey, Cynthia, and Mary Beth Zickel. 1994. "Industrial Shifts and Uneven Development: Patterns of Growth and Decline in U.S. Metropolitan Areas." *Urban Affairs Quarterly* 30, no. 1: 27–47.

Perry, David C. 1987. "The Politics of Dependency in Deindustrializing America: The Case of Buffalo, New York." In *The Capitalist City: Global Restructuring and Community Politics,* edited by Michael Peter Smith and Joe R. Feagin, 113–37. Oxford: Basil Blackwell.

Notes

1. All data in this paragraph are from Hill and Negrey 1987.

2. These centers were: Akron, Ohio; Binghamton, New York; Bridgeport-Milford, Connecticut; Cleveland; Dayton-Springfield, Ohio; Detroit; Flint, Michigan; Gary-Hammond, Indiana; Jersey City, New Jersey; Johnstown, Pennsylvania; Milwaukee; New York; Newark, New Jersey; Peoria, Illinois; Pittsburgh; Springfield, Massachusetts; Utica-Rome, New York; and Youngstown-Warren, Ohio.

3. For a general overview of deindustrialization, see Bluestone and Harrison 1982, and regarding work hours and the transition from manufacturing to services, see Negrey 2012.

Photography and Oral History

Social Documentation to Social Change

Tracy E. K'Meyer

AS A SOCIAL HISTORIAN AND an oral historian, I view Milton Rogov-in's photographs through two lenses. As a historian concerned about race, urban life, deindustrialization, housing, and poverty, I read the images for evidence of past conditions and change over time. As an oral historian, I am intrigued by the affinity between Rogovin's creative process and oral history interviews because both seek to give the subject some "author-ity" (to use Michael Frisch's phrase[1]) to present his or her own self or story. Rogovin also shares with many oral historians roots in the social documentary tradition and the goal of recording and presenting the experiences of marginalized peoples in order to contribute to changing their conditions. This essay ex-plores the similarities between Rogovin's photographs and oral history and raises questions about the possibilities for translating their shared social doc-umentary impulse into action for change.

Although Rogovin's photographs are beautiful works of art, they are also historic "documents"—windows into the past, so to speak. As such, they contain information about work, urban conditions, social relations, recre-ation, material culture, race, gender, and poverty (some of which is discussed in detail in other essays in this volume). Like any trace of the past, however, photographs have limits as evidence of reality, past or present. As a snap-shot of one constructed moment, a photograph captures only what stood in the frame at a particular instant. There exists an inherent inequality in the relationship between the photographer and the subject in that the former for the most part chooses what goes in that frame, when to snap the photo, and ultimately what to do with the product. Although the subject may have his or her own reasons for agreeing to be photographed and expectations for the content of the product, the image is removed from "real life" in that the subject becomes conscious that this moment is being recorded for posterity and for an unseen audience. As the historian John Carter Steele puts it, "You are saying something when you allow yourself to be photographed"; in the shot, we are transformed as "we stiffen, we posture, we pose, and we become something that we are not."[2] The viewing of photographs can also obscure the authentic understanding of the subjects' experience. As cultural studies scholars have noted, when people see photographs, they connect them to preconceived images and understandings of what certain experiences and people are supposed to look like. In encountering social documentary photographs, viewers expect smudged faces, loose-fitting shifts, rickety and unpainted shacks. Can they see past those expectations? Do photographers consciously or unconsciously reproduce those expectations?[3]

Rogovin's modus operandi mitigated some of the limitations of photography in telling a story about people's lives. He photographed only with permission, and in most of his projects he asked his subjects to choose how to pose. People arranged their families, possessions, and clothing to reveal something about themselves to Rogovin and his audience. The relationship between photographer and subject never fully equalized—after all, Rogovin usually still chose what images made it into books and exhibits—but they collaborated on, even coauthored, the content of the image and thus the story told. Rogovin's work also broke out of the limit of the single frame. Over the course of his career, he developed the practice of shooting series and paired images and producing triptychs. In the paired images, he complicates our understanding of people's lives. They are not only steelworkers and miners but also husbands, wives, parents, music lovers, pet owners, and more. The skilled laborers who work in dangerous conditions also have homes that express their creativity and reflect an investment of their time and energy. The depiction of work and home environments in paired photographs produces a more robust picture of the working class at a particular moment. With the triptychs, Rogovin's images take viewers past a moment's snapshot and introduce them to minihistories of the families and communities that he pho-

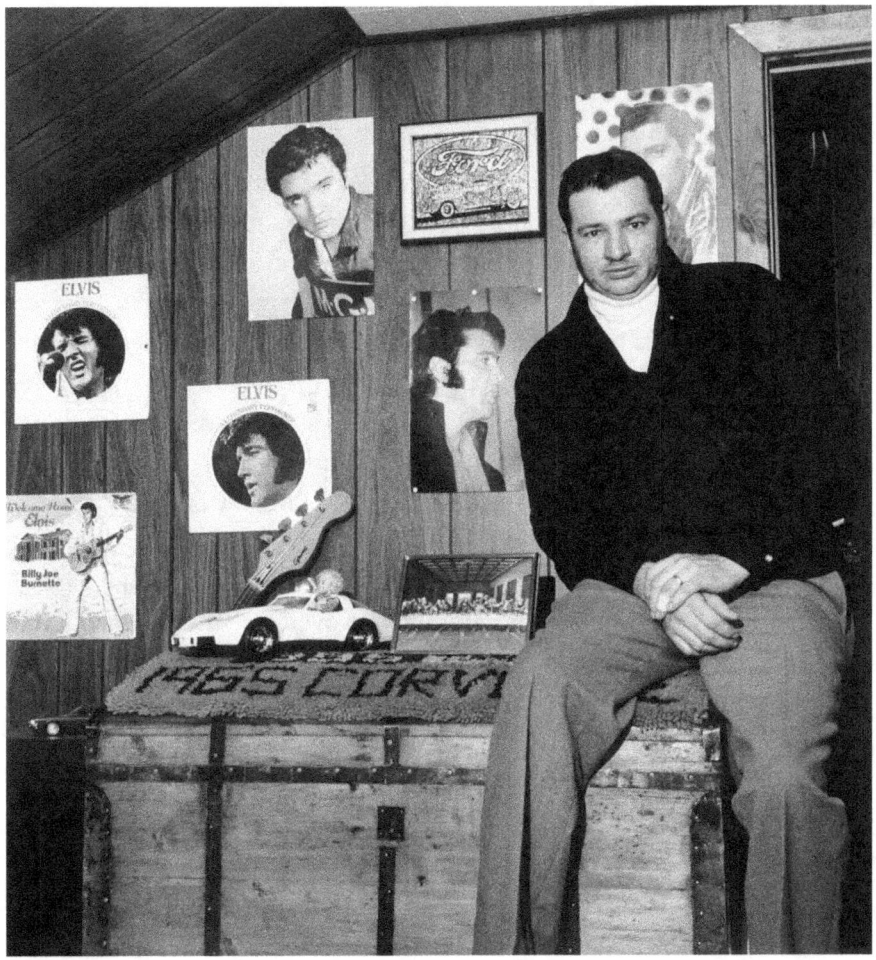

Untitled (Shenango, Inc., Steel Ingot Molds Division), *Working People,* 1976–1977.
Photographic Archives, University of Louisville. Copyright © Milton Rogovin.
Courtesy, Center for Creative Photography, University of Arizona Foundation.

tographed over many years. Perhaps the most "historical" of his work—in its
revealing documentation of change over time—is the *Appalachia* series, tak-
en between 1962 and 1987, in which the families' home life literally evolves
before the viewers' eyes. The threadbare porches and rusted wash pans that
evoke stereotypical images of Appalachians as primitive "others" give way
to posed families in dens indiscernible from those of northern, urban fami-

lies. Because of Rogovin's sensitivity to the complexity of people's lives and change over time, his images give the social historian evidence of the nature and merging of working-class lives across region and race.

Rogovin's creative process and historic sensitivity give his photography a kinship with the work of oral historians. Past social documentary efforts have paired photographs and interviews; the Foxfire project, an oral history and folklife program launched in 1966 to document daily life in the mountains of Northeast Georgia, is perhaps the best American example. In recent years, oral historians have joined a "visual turn" in the humanities, using the two mediums to draw meaning from each other. The connection has proved fruitful because photographs and oral histories share so much in common. Both are complex pieces of historical evidence that involve "memory and storytelling." Both are subjective and collaborative.[4] Both are products of a relationship. The historian/photographer approaches subjects/narrators seeking to document their lives. Although the relationship remains unequal, historian/photographer and subject/narrator work to overcome the distance and to collaborate in the production of the "story." Just as Rogovin had people pose themselves, oral historians allow narrators to tell their own story in their own way. Thus, in both photographs and oral histories, people have a chance to participate in shaping how they are viewed, remembered, and understood.

Both Rogovin and many oral historians share roots in the social documentary tradition and the goal of sparking social change. Rogovin worked in the tradition of Lewis Hines, Roy Stryker, and the Farm Security Administration photographers. Like them, he set out to record the lives of the poor, the working class, and the "downtrodden." As an activist, he saw his camera as a tool for making "people conscious of social and economic inequalities."[5] He specifically sought out Appalachian miners in the early 1960s, for example, because he saw them as the face of poverty among plenty. Notwithstanding its earlier roots, modern oral history grew out of the new social history of the 1960s and 1970s and had the goals of preserving the experiences of people missing from the archives—the poor, the marginalized, women, and minorities—giving them voice, and documenting their agency. By incorporating these voices into historical narratives, oral historians and their social history allies seek to democratize the understanding of the past. Some oral historians go further and explicitly employ interviewing as a way to change the present. In recent years, such individuals have organized Groundswell, a "network of oral historians, activists, cultural workers, community organizers, and documentary artists" who seek to "support movement building." They believe that stories are the "source of power" in struggles for social justice because stories can "build empathy," inspire, and motivate. To forward this goal, Groundswell's members meet annually, sponsor online dialogue, provide intellectual resources, and share strategies.[6]

Some historians have raised questions about the possibility and appropriateness of a true collaboration between the photographer/historian and the subject as well as the photographer/historian's activist goals. In a relationship in which there is such a difference in class, education, and cultural power, can trust be engendered, and if not, how does that lack of trust distort the image or story collected? In overtly activist documentary projects, the threat to "objectivity" almost inevitably arises. Is there exploitation of the marginalized person's story or image for the activist's purposes? What happens, as one contributor to Groundswell puts it, "when our interviews don't support our cause?"[7] Participants in change-oriented oral history concede the intellectually and emotionally difficult effort to value all voices and to yield control over the outcome of their projects. But their work, they argue, brings new evidence to light from perspectives that have been left out of too many histories, contributing to a more fully rounded picture than that produced by a professional "objective" approach. Moreover, the beauty of oral history is that it allows the opportunity not only for the subjects to share their stories but for the historian to probe for contradictions, disagreements, and the roots of conflicting views. In the end, a project will often yield different products (professional scholarship and public action, for example) or present varying interpretations within one product. New digital platforms likely will abet these outcomes because they allow a flexible form for presenting multiple perspectives.[8]

Considering Rogovin's career and photographs provokes more pertinent questions: Does social documentary photography or oral history necessarily spark social struggle? What limits the move from viewing to acting, and what can be done to tip the scales in the direction of action? Looking at

Rogovin's photographs, I often wonder if the beauty of the images—the light, the composition, the subjects' direct gaze—might veil the ugliness of the social forces that shaped these persons' lives. Oral histories often have a nostalgic element as narrators recall the warm embrace of family and community that sustained them through hard times. Like the art in Rogovin's and other social documentary photographers' work, do such stories keep our attention distracted? In a recent essay, Al Bersch and Leslie Grant critique the photography of those working in the Farm Security Administration tradition, including Sebastião Salgado, saying that "documentary projects operating in this vein, even those attempting to bring awareness to oppression, do more to maintain existing conditions than they do to promote social change."[9] Photographs like Rogovin's that focus on individual "others" and seek to elicit sympathy or even identification, like oral histories that center on one person's story, can mask systemic problems and hide the processes that caused the difference in the first place. Moreover, in my own work in oral history I have encountered narrators' resistance to portraying themselves as victims. In their stories, they emphasize their own agency and control of their destiny. Do Rogovin's photographs, in which people stand proudly, displaying themselves as skilled laborers with beautiful homes and children, accomplish a similar end? These photographs say, "I am not oppressed." Do they invite the casual viewer in the art gallery to conclude that no intervention is necessary?

Oral historians like those in Groundswell have been experimenting with ways to go beyond recording and sharing stories that help people understand and sympathize with the lives and conditions of the marginalized. The oral historian Dan Kerr interviewed homeless men in downtown Cleveland as part of an effort to understand the cause of homelessness from the perspective of those experiencing it. To bring the interviews to the public square, Kerr first played videos in places where homeless men gathered and then arranged to have the interviews broadcast on the radio. This effort publicized problems that were shared by the homeless and working-class residents of the inner city and, by shaping the local dialogue, led to policy changes.[10] In North Carolina, the Heirs to a Fighting Tradition project employs oral histories with longtime activists in workshops for grassroots community organizers. Workshop attendees learn about the intersection of race, gender, and poverty; how activists were radicalized; and how they acted to bring about change.[11] These projects do not set out to produce a book for a library shelf (though Kerr has published a scholarly monograph on the history of homelessness in Cleveland[12]). In these and many other cases, activists instead remove stories from the recording, book, and classroom and take them into the public arena to use them as a tool for organizing. In short, oral historians and the narrators themselves have tipped the scale to action by using the interviews in new ways.

Rogovin was aware of some of these questions about social documentation. But as his biographer Melanie Herzog notes, "Though he realized that photography alone could not bring about social change, he felt that by visually documenting the problems of the poor he could make people think about these issues of social justice."[13] That step was accomplished in his work, as in oral history, by reducing the distance between artist/historian and the subject/narrator. He brought us into peoples' homes, helped us to see them as rounded, complete individuals and not as stereotypes. While Rogovin lived, he encouraged a participatory production of exhibits of his Buffalo photographs in grassroots community venues. Since his passing, his family has developed a website with educational materials about using the photographs and collaborates with Syracuse Cultural Workers to produce low-cost traveling exhibits that local organizations that can't afford "Art" can mount.[14] Rogovin's work broke the narrow frame of photography by picturing people in the multidimensional realities of their lives. His process broke the frozen moment-in-time limits of a snapshot by documenting families and communities over decades. The next step in moving from social documentation to social action requires breaking out of the art gallery and bringing his work into communities and, like the oral historians in Groundswell, using the photographs to move past just engendering empathy to organizing.

Notes

1. Michael Frisch, *A Shared Authority: Essays in the Craft and Meaning of Oral and Public History* (Albany: State University of New York Press, 1990), xxi.

2. John Carter Steele, "Photography and the Difficulty of Context," *Heritage of the Great Plains* 42 (2009): 27.

3. On these questions, see Barbara Allen, "Digitizing Women's History: New

Approaches to Evidence and Interpretation in Museum Exhibits," *Radical History Review* 68 (1997): 103–20, and Carol J. Williams, "Beyond Illustration: Illuminations of the Photographic 'Frontier,'" *Journal of the West* 46 (2007): 29–40.

4. See Alexander Freund and Alistair Thomson, eds., *Oral History and Photography* (New York: Palgrave, 2011).

5. Melanie Anne Herzog, *Milton Rogovin: The Making of a Social Documentary Photographer* (Tucson: Center for Creative Photography, University of Arizona; Seattle: University of Washington Press, 2006), 43.

6. See the Groundswell website Oral History for Social Change at http://www.oralhistoryforsocialchange.org/, accessed July 29, 2014.

7. Groundswell, "Reportback: What to Do When Our Interviews Don't Support Our Cause?" Oral History for Social Change, January 27, 2014, at http://www.oralhistoryforsocialchange.org/blog/2014/5/13/reportback-what-to-do-when-our-interviews-dont-support-our-cause.

8. For a discussion of the challenges in sharing authority in oral history projects and of some of the proposed solutions, see "Special Section: Shared Authority," *Oral History Review* 30 (2003): 23–113.

9. Al Bersch and Leslie Grant, "From Witness to Participant: Making Subversive Documentary," in *Oral History and Photography*, ed. Freund and Thomson, 190.

10. Dan Kerr, "'We Know What the Problem Is': Using Oral History to Develop a Collaborative Analysis of Homelessness from the Bottom Up," *Oral History Review* 30 (2003): 27–45.

11. Luke Hirst, "Using Stories of Change-Makers to Make Change," Groundswell, Oral History for Social Change, September 19, 2013, at http://www.oralhistoryforsocialchange.org/blog/2014/5/13/using-stories-of-change-makers-to-make-change.

12. Dan Kerr, *Derelict Paradise: Homelessness and Urban Development in Cleveland, Ohio* (Amherst: University of Massachusetts Press, 2011).

13. Herzog, *Milton Rogovin*, 43.

14. "The Milton Rogovin Traveling Photography Exhibit," Milton Rogovin: Social Documentary Photographer, at http://miltonrogovin.com/travelingexhibit.html, accessed July 29, 2014.

Milton Rogovin and the Popular Front

The Legacy of American Communism

Catherine Fosl and Peter S. Fosl

THE COMMUNIST PARTY (CP) HAD a far deeper and more complicated impact on Milton Rogovin's life and work than the one most Buffalo residents realized when they saw him maligned as the city's "top Red" in the headlines of their daily newspaper on October 4, 1957.[1]

Although Rogovin's interest in vision and the visual might have led him to take up photography in any case, unpacking the broad cultural currents that whirled around the CP in the twentieth-century United States is crucial, we argue here, to situating his corpus of work and the life choices that drove it. This essay explores Rogovin's life and work in relation to the vibrant Popular Front social and cultural movement. Emerging in the 1930s, the Popular Front motivated Rogovin and many others, leftists and liberals alike, to work together, despite historic hostilities, in order to combat oppression, injustice, and the widespread suffering of the Depression using both political and artistic tools. His work, in fact, cannot be properly understood outside of that movement. We also examine briefly here the costs and consequences of the post–Second World War anti-Communist climate that one historian has called "the culture of the Cold War"[2] for Rogovin and his family because of their radical social commitments. One of those consequences, ironically, is that the repression Rogovin endured by having been publicly branded a Communist drove him to embrace photography more deeply and, through doing so, helped to forge the insightful and influential cultural figure he became.

When Rogovin joined the CP and when he left it remain, according to his son, Mark, "vague in the family history."[3] The young Milton, graduating from New York City's Columbia University in 1931 with an optometry degree, seems to have been introduced to "the Party" sometime in the year or two thereafter, when he and his brother attended evening classes through one of the many CP-led programs set up to promote worker education and organizing as the Depression tightened its grip on American families. Combining such political and economic education with social and cultural activities was not confined to Communists but was by the Depression era a long-standing core principle of the American labor movement—Marxist study classes, picket lines, and marches intersected in dynamic cultural streams with dances, parades, and drinking halls. This kind of left-wing cultural politics came to be characterized through the slogan "bread and roses," a phrase radical Socialist Party trade unionist Rose Schneiderman (1882–1972) had coined in a speech amid a major women's garment workers' strike in 1911. They were words Rogovin later embraced and employed for the rest of his life to describe his own approach to social change.

The radical milieu of cultural labor that Rogovin entered in the early to mid-1930s was broader than the CP, yet the party was in many respects at its vital center, especially in New York City, home to more than half of the CP's national membership of about seventy-five thousand. Rogovin's early experiences with the CP during its period of greatest influence in American history "completely changed" his "way of thinking," he reflected much later in a memoir, recalling both bread lines and the demonstrations and marches they provoked.[4] The first years of his involvement coincided with the coalescing of social dissenters of various stripes who had previously been at odds with one another but now, propelled by the deepening Depression, built coalitions of labor unionists, liberals, and general leftists that gave working people's culture as well as the dissenters' critique of capitalism wider visibility, especially in major centers of industry, such as New York City, Chicago, and Buffalo. These currents were already evident in the early 1930s, especially after President Franklin D. Roosevelt's New Deal in 1933 began putting people to work in ways that rebuilt the nation. With the establishment of the Works Progress Administration in 1935, those new government programs distributed expansive federal investment not only in infrastructural reforms such as parks and roads but also in cultural and artistic productions such as the Federal Writers' Project and the Federal Theatre Project.

The year 1935 also saw two other major political developments that spurred the new forms of cultural and social activism that were to frame Milton Rogovin's life work. Amid the worsening threat of fascism in Europe, the Communist International (Comintern), led by the Soviet Union and meeting in Moscow, set a major new direction by instructing national parties to build a "Popular Front" against fascism. That Popular Front directive inspired wider coalition politics to challenge unemployment, racism, and the rise of fascism, but it also instructed American CP branches to deepen their involvement in cultural labor: they would no longer establish their own cultural institutions but would join others in collaborative cultural projects. Soon afterward, the boost of industrial-labor organizing in response to the crisis of the Depression resulted in the formation in late 1935 of the Congress of Industrial Organizations, or CIO, an umbrella that united industrial workers as never before and included the United Optical Workers, which Rogovin joined as a charter member later in the decade (1938). CIO workers, influenced by the Comintern's directive as well as by the larger radical milieu out of which it took shape, both contributed to and employed the explosion of proletarian art and literature surrounding them.

The result was an unparalleled flowering of left-wing and liberal culture that did not lead to a revolution in the United States but had a profound impact on subsequent national direction. As even the anti-Communist, liberal critic Lionel Trilling acknowledged much later, "The radical movement of the Thirties . . . created the American intellectual class as we now know it in its great size and influence."[5]

Throughout the 1930s and 1940s (and, to a lesser extent, even before that), Marxist criticism of American fascination with individuals and their subjective experiences produced in rejoinder an explosion in proletarian literature and art that stressed instead the experience of collectives involved in revolutionary struggle or sowing the seeds of the revolution to come. While *Soviet Photo* magazine showcased the realization of socialist society and the talent of its photographers, social realist artists in the capitalist societies of the West documented the working classes and explored a proletarian aes-

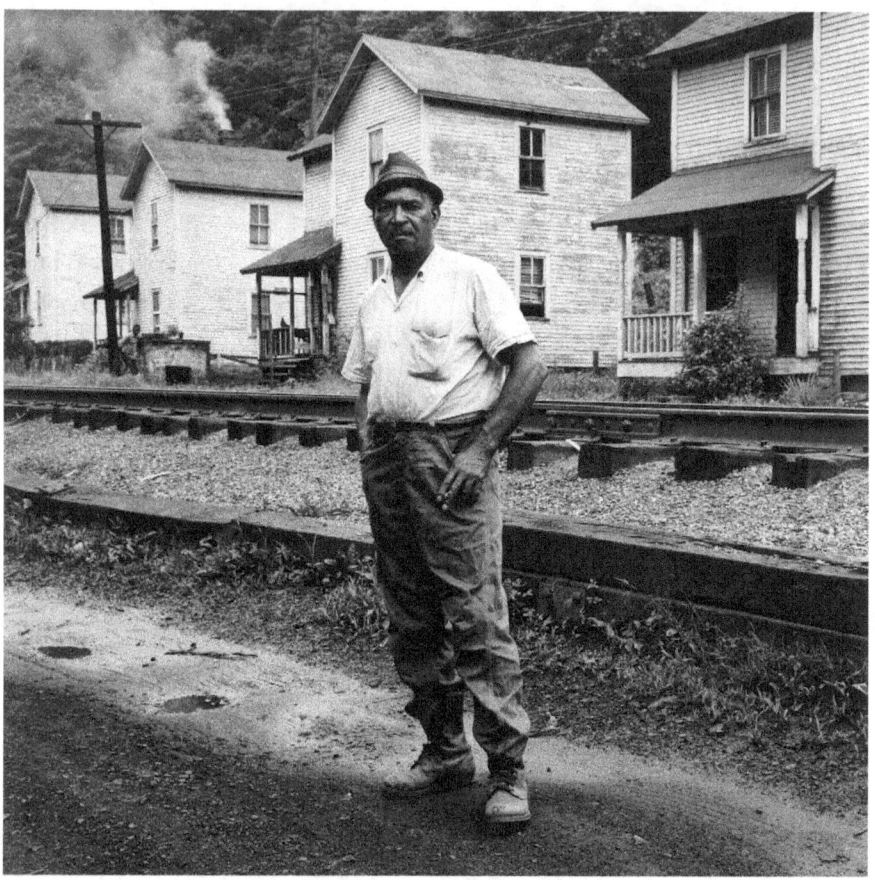

Untitled, *Appalachia*, 1964. The Rogovin Collection, Chicago. Copyright © Milton Rogovin. Courtesy, Center for Creative Photography, University of Arizona Foundation.

thetic in their own fashion. They typically depicted people of the working class at work, laboring in frightful conditions. Rogovin would have been familiar with many of these photographers and artists.

As a young man, Rogovin may have read proletarian novels by Mike Gold (1894–1967) and by the early feminist Meridel Le Sueur (1900–1996) and may even have personally known these writers. He certainly read the poetry of African American writer Langston Hughes (1902–1967), who was drawn to the CP for its staunch antiracist politics. There were documentary photographers who preceded Rogovin, such as Lewis Hine (1874–1940), whom Rogovin admired throughout his life. The visual artist Käthe Kollwitz (1867–1945), another of his acknowledged sources of inspiration, captured in her drawings and prints the heavy grief of the many losses to which the working class seemed condemned—except for the sudden retributive up- surge she captured in her revolutionary piece *Outbreak* (1921), wrought in the throes of the Soviet Revolution and Civil War. That image echoes the raised fists of defiant, angry, and sometimes victorious workers popular among left- wing artists all the way back to the French Revolution.

There is something of all these influences in Rogovin—their visions and their politico-aesthetic principles—but he is also an artist of a subse- quent time and a different vision. Although Rogovin purchased his first cam- era in 1942, he was more of a trade unionist than a photographer or cultural activist until the mid-1950s. Indeed, he might have stayed that way had it not been for the coming of the Cold War and with it the cultural hysteria that after 1950 became known as "McCarthyism," named after one of its most excessive proponents, Republican Senator Joseph McCarthy of Wisconsin.

It is hard to imagine how thoroughly left-wing politics and culture per- meated US society in those years. It is also hard to imagine how punishing and difficult it was for those on the Left when the vibrant cultural and polit- ical experimentation in which Rogovin's social and artistic convictions had gestated gave way to the fearful, suspicious, anti-Communist climate that cast a pall on so much dissent after 1950—throughout the world but with special domestic fury in the United States.

The subsequent "Red Scare" effectively demonized people such as Rogovin, his wife, Anne (who shared fully his social and political commit- ments), their children, and the sociopolitical networks they inhabited. Called before the House Committee on Un-American Activities (HUAC) in 1957, Rogovin asserted his Fifth Amendment rights in response to the common HUAC inquiry—"Are you or have you ever been a member of the Commu- nist Party?" But in doing so, he effectively discredited himself in the eyes of a public primed by "Red hunting" in popular television shows such as *Dragnet* (1951–1959). Rogovin subsequently lost about half of his optometry clientele; Anne's teaching choices were narrowed; and his children faced ostracism in their neighborhood as well as FBI harassment at school. "Close friends turned out to be undercover agents," and neighbors "would literally go to the other side of the street" in Buffalo when they saw the Rogovins coming, Mark Rogovin has recalled.

The CP never fully recovered from what its adherents knew as the "witch hunts" of the 1950s. By the time Rogovin testified before HUAC, estimates place US CP membership at anywhere from around thirty thousand (less than half of its peak in 1942) to as low as perhaps five thousand.[6] Unlike many who were called out publicly as Communists in this era, Milton Rogovin, who was supported fully by his wife, showed remarkable resiliency. The couple "worked hard to keep it together," Mark Rogovin remembers, pulling together as a family and immersing their children in the broad currents of culture that had informed their own coming of age in the 1930s. They toured the children through an array of cultural and natural sites, from museums to parks to Charlie Chaplain films, which they had to drive to Canada to see because Chaplain was allegedly too communistic to be shown in Buffalo in those years.

It seems, in fact, that one of the values of the left-wing subculture of which Milton and Anne Rogovin had long been a part that most impressed them was resiliency. In the years after 1957, when Rogovin began a photographic series of the storefront black churches in Buffalo, he increasingly immersed himself in a genre of photography that would define his vision, one he always characterized as "social documentary." He was typically accompanied in his work by Anne, who was equally socially committed and now became a work as well as life partner by providing the social glue that gained them entrée into the lives and later the homes of working-class people in Buffalo and soon beyond it. Mark Rogovin remembers vividly the doggedness, the "imperative," his parents brought to these many photographic endeavors. After 1978, Rogovin gave up his optometry practice entirely, and Anne's teaching supported the family, leaving them free to travel and photograph in the summers as he found wider acclaim as a photographer.

Amid the attacks on Communists and more moderate leftists, and in no small way because of the groundwork laid by the Popular Front, left-wing criticism also proved resilient, surviving and even expanding its lenses. The Frankfurt School of philosophy and social criticism (Theodor Adorno

[1903–1969], Herbert Marcuse [1898–1979], and others) established that the struggle against oppression must be waged not only in categories defined by factories, fields, and halls of government but also in the most ordinary elements of popular culture and domestic life. Theorists such as Antonio Gramsci (1891–1937) came to understand that the broader life of culture operates according to dynamics much more complex than the superstructure-substructure model that sometimes blinkered more orthodox Marxists. The blossoming struggle for the rights of people of African descent demanded that critics honor the power of racial identity and racism on their own terms; postcolonial movements carried the frameworks for change outside of European and American society; and feminists successfully argued that sex, gender, and the domestic sphere warrant distinctive analyses of their own. Rogovin remained a Marxist even after leaving the CP, probably sometime in the late 1950s or early 1960s, and he remained true to his brand of social documentary photography for the rest of his life. Yet his body of work increasingly reflected this same widening of the lens, this more expansive understanding of human life and in particular the life of workers.

True to a classical Marxist vision, Rogovin's photos capture the working life of laborers and the internationalism that socialism cultivates. His *Family of Miners* series takes viewers to diverse sites of work and exploitation—Mexico, Zimbabwe, China, Cuba, Scotland, and Appalachia—but they also expose us to women and workers of color. Perhaps most characteristic of Rogovin's vision are his photo series starting with the *Storefront Churches*, which give us access to neighborhoods, homes, front stoops, and private spaces. His photographs move beyond the worksite to illuminate working families at home, at worship, and with friends. Such series are increasingly attentive to the broad, plural sweep of subjects' gendered, racialized, and personal existence as well as of the lived universality they share as workers.

Rogovin typically asked his subjects to pose themselves, and in doing so he defied the demand of ideology that would reduce workers to a mere means for a political end. He preferred to see his work as educational, emphasizing its use in schools over museum exhibits, yet his compositional power fits all such venues. Viewers do become aware through his photographs of the relative material limits of workers' lives, but Rogovin evokes a much more complex and egalitarian range of responses than the pity or even the outrage raised so commonly by other political artists and social documentarians. Rogovin's subjects express pride in themselves and their lives.

Like the earlier photographers Lewis Hine or Jacob Riis, Rogovin educates us about working-class life, but he engages his subjects as more than representatives of the poor and working classes. We see the people he photographs as whole, as complete beings, as persons. Like Diane Arbus's photography, though without its prurient indulgence in the strange, Rogovin's work conveys a frank, direct, and honest face-to-face encounter. Like a more political Willy Ronis or a more neighborly Robert Capa, Rogovin understands people in a way that today might be thought of as intersectional—as individuals stuck in place and time, yes, but as more than tokens of their moment in the march of history.

In our view, the characteristic play between individuals and their sociopolitical positions as shown through Rogovin's complex photography—its humane, ecumenical, and historically sensitive sophistication—perhaps more than any other dimension of his work, manifests its rootedness in the ideology and cultural practices of the Popular Front. Rogovin's body of work is political and visibly socialist, but it is not reducible to agitprop or journalism or simple documentary. In Rogovin, viewers do not confront the working class and the conditions of its life. We join hands with this reality, with working people. Rogovin's photography is not the work of sympathy or fury but rather of knowing solidarity, just like the Popular Front on the best of its days.

Notes

1. "Rogovin, Named as Top Red in Buffalo, Balks at Nearly All Queries," *Buffalo Evening News*, October 4, 1957.

2. Stephen J. Whitfield, *The Culture of the Cold War* (Baltimore: Johns Hopkins University Press, 1991).

3. Mark Rogovin, telephone interview by Catherine Fosl, May 22, 2015, recording and permission to quote are in authors' possession. All subsequent quotations from Rogovin come from this source.

4. The point about CP influence is from Michael Denning, *The Cultural Front*:

The Laboring of American Culture in the Twentieth Century (New York: Verso, 1996), 4. "Completely changed" is from Melanie Anne Herzog, *Milton Rogovin: The Making of a Social Documentary Photographer* (Tucson: Center for Creative Photography, University of Arizona; Seattle: University of Washington Press, 2006), 28.

5. Quoted in Denning, *Cultural Front,* 3.

6. The thirty thousand figure is from Steve Nelson, James R. Barrett, and Rob Ruck, *Steve Nelson, American Radical* (Pittsburgh: University of Pittsburgh Press, 1981), 319. The five thousand figure is from Stephen J. Whitfield, "Civil Liberties and the Culture of the Cold War," in *Crucible of Liberty: Two Hundred Years of the Bill of Rights,* ed. Raymond Arsenault (New York: Free Press, 1991), 60.

Rogovin and the "Forgotten Women"

Karen Christopher

MILTON ROGOVIN PHOTOGRAPHED the "forgotten ones"—everyday working people, many engaged in physically demanding jobs in factories and construction sites. In this essay, I explore how Rogovin's photographs documented the existence of women in these jobs and bucked common stereotypes about all women, in particular women of color. In these ways, Rogovin was far ahead of his time.

Rogovin's depictions of women of color—African American women and Latinas—are among his most striking. In his prints of working people in various factory and construction jobs (at the Ford, Janna, Market, and Republic factories), Rogovin features many female workers: they wear dirt-smudged jumpsuits, boots, safety glasses, goggles, and hard hats, and some hold welding torches. Many of these women look directly into the camera with slight smiles, appearing to take pride in their work.

In one sense, Rogovin did "discover" these "forgotten" women: these women are not typical women workers. In 1980, around when these prints were taken, very few women worked in factories or on construction sites; most women of color worked in clerical and professional or managerial jobs (Dubeck and Borman 1996). Rogovin's photographs remind us of the existence of women of color in these typically male workplaces during this time.

But Rogovin's photographs do more than document the presence of women in these jobs; they also humanize these women by challenging pernicious stereotypes about women of color, many of which survive today. Patricia Hill Collins (2009) writes extensively on stereotypes or "controlling

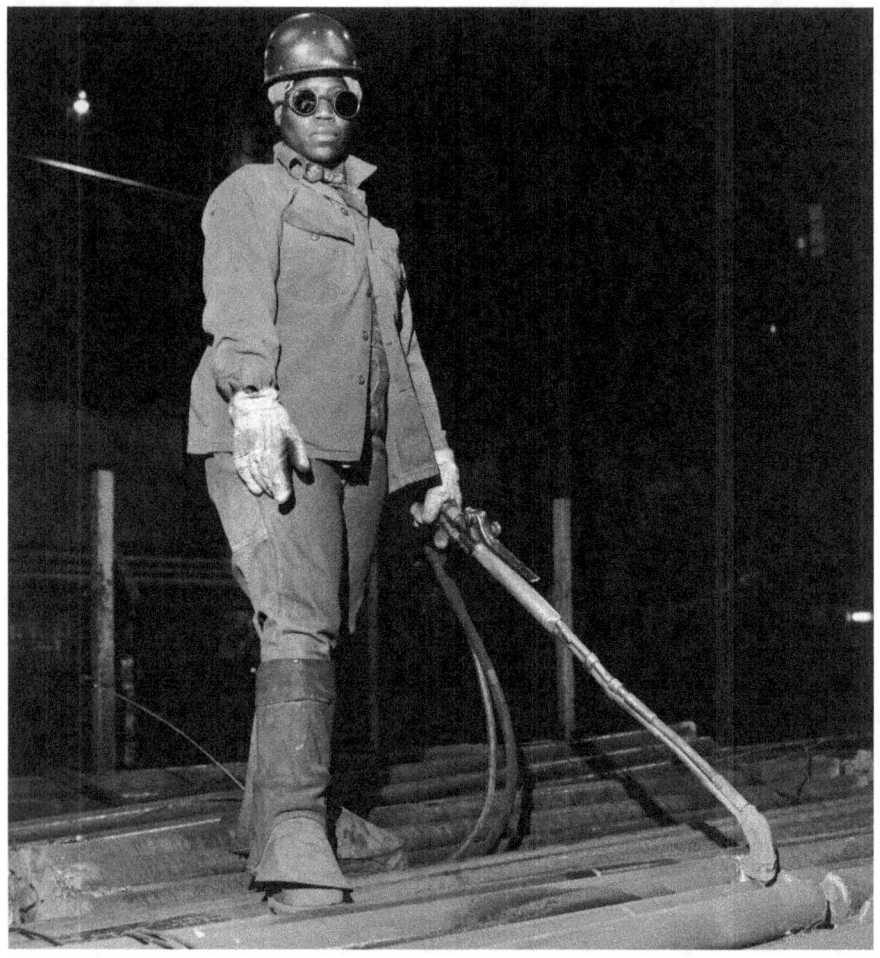

Untitled (Republic Steel), *Working People,* 1978–1979. Photographic Archives, University of Louisville. Copyright © Milton Rogovin. Courtesy, Center for Creative Photography, University of Arizona Foundation.

images" of women of color common in the mid- to late twentieth century: the "mammy" or faithful, obedient servant; the overly aggressive "matriarch" vilified in the Moynihan Report (Moynihan 1965) for not properly supervising her children and for emasculating the fathers of their children; the "welfare mother" who does not work for pay and depends on government handouts; and the "Jezebel" or sexually aggressive female.

Rogovin's photographs of African American women, in particular those that show them in their work and home contexts, belie *all* of these stereotypes. These women do physically demanding work in factories—they are not "mammies" in the domestic sphere or "welfare mothers" who are presumed to be unemployed. With his photographs of women of color in factory settings, Rogovin also accurately documents the progression of these women out of domestic work: whereas more than half of black women worked in domestic-service jobs in the 1940s, fewer than 5 percent of African Americans worked in these jobs in 2011 (Marks 1993; U.S. Bureau of Labor Statistics 2011). Showing women at home with children, and with what appear to be romantic partners, suggests that these women are not "matriarchs" who damage their children and partners. Furthermore, these women are in no way portrayed as sexually aggressive "Jezebels."

Rogovin's photographs that show women on the job and at home with their children and with male partners break down all of these stereotypes simultaneously; these women engage in hard work on the job—and they work hard for their families. Their "dirty" work pays off: the family photographs show nicely dressed women—often in silk blouses and skirts and with well-dressed children, in homes that are decorated with plants, pictures, and statues on coffee tables. More importantly, the women seem content in their family pictures—they typically smile and embrace their children (see, for example, the photographs of Dorothy McKinney with her sons in Christopher Fulton's essay, p. 000). These mothers are neither mammies nor overly aggressive, emasculating mothers nor sexually suggestive in any way. These photographs portray typical American families—and this in itself challenges pervasive negative stereotypes about African American mothers.

Rogovin's photographs also challenge a common gender stereotype—that women cannot or should not perform typically masculine, "dirty" work in factories or on construction sites. Here again Rogovin bucks social convention. Women workers are common in his photographs, and many work in factories and mines. Some of these women smile openly at the photographer, suggesting they take pride in doing their job. And in the photographs of them at home, many of the women are cleaned up, often in feminine clothes—skirts, silk dresses, and blouses—and often in a maternal role. Showing these women thriving in both work and home spheres helps break down the "separate spheres" ideology—that the workplace (in particular the mine or construction site) is only for men and the home is only for women. In family photographs, the children are smiling and well dressed; the children seem not to suffer from their mothers' "dirty" work; in fact, they seem to thrive. These images show that when women work outside of the home, they and their children can prosper.

Rogovin's photographs also suggest that gender is not something static or fixed but something we perform; as Candace West and Don Zimmerman (1987) suggest with their "doing gender" theory, we often perform gender in different ways, based on how accountable we feel to gendered expectations in different contexts. The women workers in the factories and mines look decidedly less feminine than they do at home—they look like workers engaged in strenuous jobs. Women's performance of gender varies according to their work or home contexts. Although research on gender did not explore different performances of gender based on social context until later in the 1980s, Rogovin's photographs provide much earlier illustrations of the performativity—and fluidity—of gender.

In sum, Rogovin allows women a far richer existence than other media depictions of women in the 1960s, 1970s, and 1980s. His portrayals of women of color are more humane than most other depictions of his time. His female subjects cross boundaries—they get dirty at a typically male job—and seem pleased to do so. Their children appear to benefit financially from their mothers' work and seem to have close relationships with their mothers. Rogovin was far ahead of this time—women's employment would continue to climb into the 1990s and 2000s, during which time they also slowly filled more jobs in the typically male occupations of factory and construction work. In the twenty-first century, more and more women's lives have come to resemble those beautifully captured by Rogovin several decades earlier.

Works Cited

Collins, Patricia Hill. 2009. *Black Feminist Thought: Knowledge, Consciousness, and the Politics of Empowerment*. New York: Routledge.

Dubeck, Paula, and Kathryn Borman, eds. 1996. *Women and Work: A Handbook*. New York: Routledge, 1996.

Marks, Carol. 1993. "The Bone and Sinew of Race: Black Women, Domestic Service, and Labor Migration." *Marriage and Family Review* 19, nos. 1–2: 149–73.

Moynihan, Daniel Patrick. 1965. *The Negro Family: The Case for National Action*. Washington, DC: U.S. Department of Labor.

U.S. Bureau of Labor Statistics. 2011. "Labor Force Characteristics by Race and Ethnicity." At https://www.bls.gov/opub/reports/race-and-ethnicity/archive/race_ethnicity_2011.pdf.

West, Candace, and Don Zimmerman. 1987. "Doing Gender." *Gender & Society* 1, no. 2: 121–55.

Rogovin

The People's Ambassador

Joy Gleason Carew

I ORIGINALLY LEARNED OF Milton Rogovin's work through his son, peace activist and artist Mark Rogovin. In the 1980s, I had worked with Mark on a number of projects back in my home town, Chicago, including celebrating the many peoples' murals that had begun to decorate neglected neighborhoods. But now, knowing about Milton Rogovin and studying samples of his extensive photographic work, I understand where Mark got his nobility and commitment to making the world a more peaceful and humane place.

Milton Rogovin's sensitive focus draws us into an "interaction" with people who are often left in the shadows. People whose "stories," although acknowledged at some basic, footnoted level, have been more often offered up as part of an out-of-focus social commentary. But Rogovin, who famously said, "The rich have their own photographers,"[1] makes us stop. He compels us to look and recognize the humanity of working people. It was this zeal for social justice that helped him turn the traumatic stripping of his livelihood by the McCarthyite tribunals into a new means of speaking out. This Red Scare climate of intolerance and fear made it hard to organize other optometrists into unions or to help register African American voters. And it severely diminished his optometry practice—just as it tried to choke the professional work of the great African American artist Paul Robeson and the sociologist and civil rights activist W. E. B. Du Bois. But also, like them, Rogovin found ways to circumvent this intolerance. Now wielding his camera lens, his avocation became his vocation: that of a "people's ambassador." And this passion would keep him—and his wife, Anne—actively engaged well into his senior years.

As a sociolinguist working in various black studies departments over the past forty years, now in the Department of Pan-African Studies at the University of Louisville, I have made it a point to craft courses that induct students into an appreciation of the multiple manifestations of human interaction. Whether in the context of social protest ("Language, Protest, and Identity in the Global Community") or of the impact of the global spread of the African Diaspora ("African Languages in the Diaspora"), I have encouraged them to be more mindful of the dangers of "knowing" without having "seen." As much as the Internet and social media have been convenient, they have also brought about the danger of intellectual "laziness," wherein we rely on what our friends tell us about the world rather than trying to experience and learn about it ourselves firsthand. This laziness is particularly worrisome in the case of human relations and the need to bridge the gap between the haves and the have-nots.

This is where Milton Rogovin's work comes in so brilliantly. With his embrace extending out in ever-widening circles, from the African American storefront churches in Buffalo to the poor and neglected communities in Buffalo and stretching down into Appalachia and families of miners around the world, Rogovin introduces us to people. As we gaze into their eyes and see aspects of their daily lives around them, we begin to see them in relation to ourselves. It is a dialogue of discovery.

In an interview at the Heartland Café in Chicago in June 2011, his son, Mark, said that a request to photograph one of Buffalo's African American storefront churches in East Side section of Buffalo not only thrilled Rogovin but also set him on a path to use photography to cross traditional boundaries and speak out against injustice. "A man had asked my father to photograph the cover for a Folkways [record]. . . . My father was so thrilled to get back out in the community. . . . [After the initial project] was done, . . . my father, being a progressive, was so intrigued by what he had witnessed in these churches that he continued on for three years every Sunday."[2] As the churches project exploded into a multiyear photographic recording, Rogovin was led to consult with W. E. B. Du Bois, who confirmed that Rogovin's chronicle of these churches would be important not only for the current day but also for posterity. In a commentary on a selection of Rogovin photographs from the *Storefront Churches* series, Du Bois wrote, "[These images] are astonishingly human and appealing. . . . [The activities within these churches] remain the most original and beautiful expression of human life and longing yet born on American soil."[3]

Rogovin documented the level of destitution suffered by people forced to live in Buffalo's East Side tenements and devoted many years to depicting the Puerto Rican community in the Lower West Side. His unadulterated work opened a window into communities of Buffalo into which few people—other than those who lived there—ventured. In recording the lives of working people, Rogovin understood that many of these communities, with their lifeways and the jobs that supported them, were under threat and that his photographs would serve as a testament to their roles in building the cities around them. Particularly for those working in heavy industry in Buffalo and neighboring Lackawanna, Rogovin's photos have served not only as a formal recognition of the individuals captured in the frame but also as a chronicle of certain kinds of livelihood, many of which no longer exist in the United States.

It is no accident that Rogovin often chose as his subjects miners and foundry workers, people whose livelihoods tied them to the very foundations of building societies, because their work was essential to the extraction and fabrication of basic industrial materials. As his photographs demonstrate, these workers crossed racial, ethnic, gender, and national boundaries. Their jobs often left them covered with a dark dust that obscured their individuality but at the same time confirmed their commonality as workers. Rogovin chose to document other aspects of their lives, too, though. These features were often not seen by outsiders but were vital components of their identities. Indeed, even as the larger society casually glances at them and rushes on, pigeon-holing them into small, discrete categories, Rogovin makes the viewer stop and look. Here the viewer sees these working men and women not only in their workplace but also in dramatically different places, shown in companion photographs. By insisting on these double views of his subjects, Rogovin challenges the viewer's assumptions and prizes open narrow prejudgments.

Milton Rogovin liked to do what he termed "diptychs" and "triptychs": sets of two or three photos of the same person in different settings taken in a relatively short span of time or over a longer period of time when he would return to photograph the person many years later. He would often depict working men and women in their workplace and later portray them at home or in a pub. This is a brilliant technique for expanding the image and identity of the worker beyond the simplistic template of the workplace. The photographs show not only the helmet, the overalls, and the dirty skin but also the person revealed after the bath, wearing specially selected clothes, and standing near significant family artifacts and beside family members.

Taking the liberty of this essay, I would like to propose a new triptych consisting of pictures from two of Rogovin's series. The first image comes from the *Working People* series and shows an African American foundry worker at the Atlas Steel Casting plant in Buffalo, taken in 1978. Next to this photograph, I would place two images of men from other countries found in Rogovin's *Family of Miners* series: one from Zimbabwe taken in 1989 and a second from Scotland taken in 1982. For this series, Rogovin had initially photographed miners primarily in the United States. But after he won the W. Eugene Smith Memorial Fund Award for Documentary Photography in 1983, he decided to broaden this "family" with members from several oth-

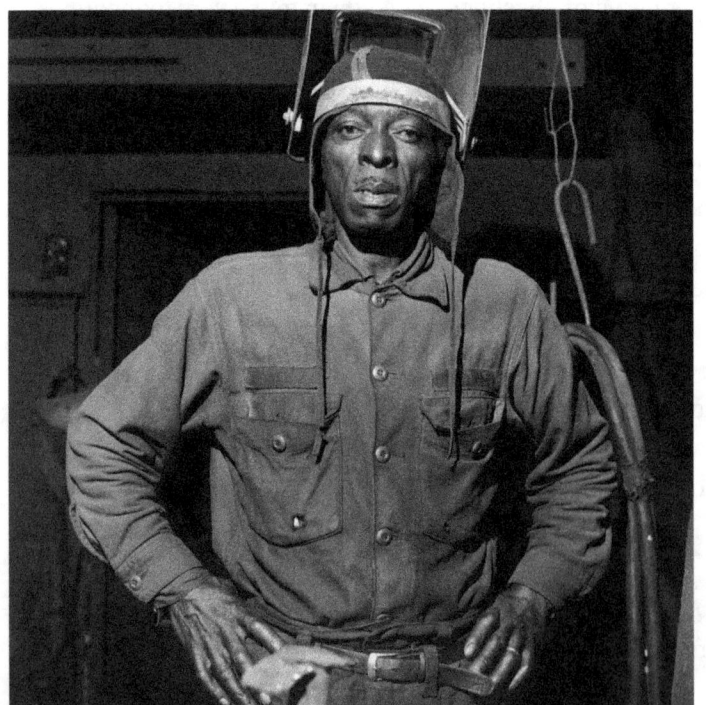

Untitled, *Working People*, 1976–1978. Photographic Archives, University of Louisville. Copyright © Milton Rogovin. Courtesy, Center for Creative Photography, University of Arizona Foundation.

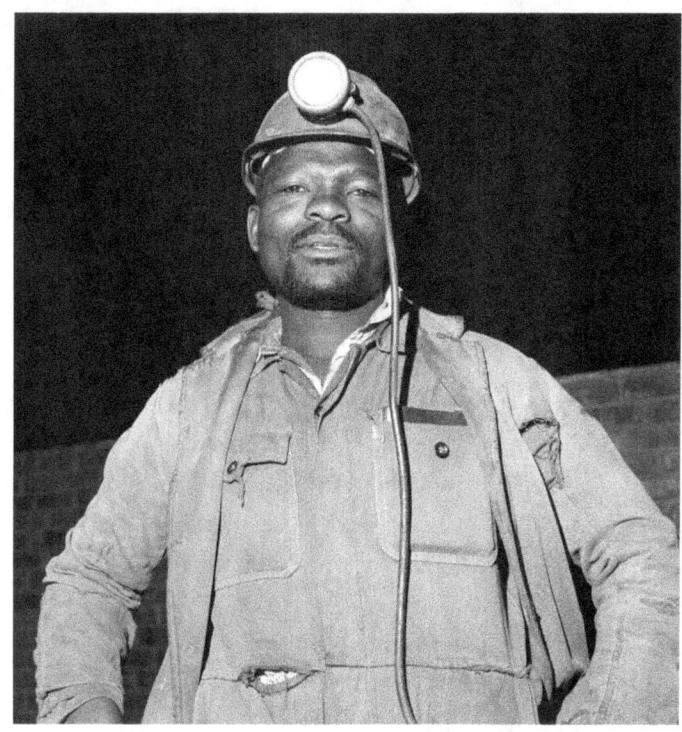

Untitled (Zimbabwe), *Family of Miners*, 1989. Photographic Archives, University of Louisville. Copyright © Milton Rogovin.. Courtesy, Center for Creative Photography, University of Arizona Foundation.

Untitled (Scotland), *Family of Miners*, 1982. Photographic Archives, University of Louisville. Copyright © Milton Rogovin. Courtesy, Center for Creative Photography, University of Arizona Foundation.

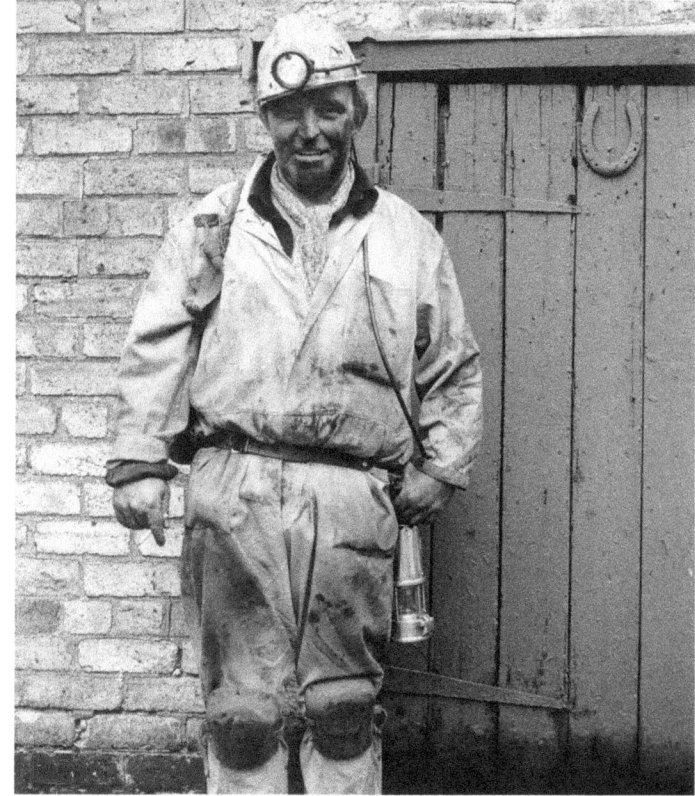

er countries. Over the next seven years, he expanded his work so that the full collection would include studies of miners from Appalachia (1962–1987), France (1981), Scotland (1982), Spain (1983), Cuba (1984–1989), Germany (1984), China (1986), Mexico (1988), Zimbabwe (1989), and Czechoslovakia (today's Czechia and Slovakia, 1990).[4]

These three men of my triptych—the African American foundry worker at the Atlas plant, the miner in Zimbabwe, and the miner in Scotland—are prime examples of Rogovin's social commentary. When we see them at their workplace, it is as if they have only just turned briefly from their duties to face the lens. Indeed, in a second photo of the African American foundry worker, he has turned back to his work, and the sparks are flying. But in the initial portrait we see him clearly, front and center. He is dark-skinned and dressed in his work clothes. He is also wearing his helmet, which protects him from the fire, although the visor is up so that we can see his face. There is no companion photo where we can see him in a context outside of his workplace, but other pictures in the Atlas Steel Casting series, which was done initially from 1976 to 1979, show workers both at the foundry and in their homes. These workers are not only African American but also white and Puerto Rican. Rogovin's point is clear: these people may share their work lives at Atlas, but they are also complex individuals who have multiple relationships beyond the plant. Rogovin underscored these latter points when he returned in 1987 to rephotograph many of those whom he had previously depicted. These follow-up photos introduce a temporal element into the series. Some ten years had passed, and the later photos taken in or near the subjects' homes documented how the individuals and their families had fared.

The next picture in my triptych is an image of a Zimbabwean miner. He, too, looks directly at us as he stands outside his workplace. He is wearing his work overalls, and on his head is a helmet with a light attached to the front. As in the case of the African American worker at Atlas, we do not see this particular worker in his home setting. But Rogovin has a number of pictures of other global mine workers at home or elsewhere in their communities. A special significance of this worker and of the series in Zimbabwe is that we get to see an alternate view of Africa and its people. These images contrast dramatically with the news headlines and stories that constantly intone accounts of backwardness, poverty, wars, and illness. Here are workers operating on the same level as their brothers and sisters in mines elsewhere around the globe.[5]

The third photo, the shot of a Scottish miner, looks remarkably like those of the Zimbabwean and the African American. Mining is dirty and dangerous work. He, too, is in his work overalls and has a helmet with a light on his head. The coal dust and soot show easily on his light face. Though the dirt is not so easily seen on the faces of the others, the fact of their workplace, which is easily seen in their clothing and surroundings, indicate it. Though these three men are divided by thousands of miles, cultures, and even dialects of English, it is clear that they share a basic humanity. Here, they are willing to work, hidden by dust and soot, breathing air that is injurious to their health and pushing their bodies to the point of pain and exhaustion, so that they can provide for their families.

Rogovin also shows us this Scottish miner in nonwork settings, as he does with a number of others in the Scotland series. Again, here is the importance of the community reference, for the subject is seen with family and friends and with cultural artifacts that are significant to him. Here, too, as observed with the Zimbabwean miners, we see the importance of music and dance as part of their social life once the work day is over.

The Zimbabwean series and Scottish series provide a striking reminder of the fact that these miners of the European and African continents are locked into a global system of mine workers, as are those of Appalachia, Cuba, China, and the many other countries of Rogovin's *Family of Miners* series not discussed specifically here. Their specific locations may be different, but their relationships to their employers and coworkers, on the one hand, and to their families and communities, on the other, have clear similarities.

These and many other images on exhibit in the Photographic Archives at the University of Louisville as well as those found on the Rogovin Collection website (www.miltonrogovin.com) mean that visitors have the opportunity to appreciate what Milton Rogovin knew—that people, despite their various and diverse personal lives, share the need for dignity and the ability to provide for themselves and their families. That this website provides the same information in various languages, such as Spanish and Mandarin, demonstrates his and his family's commitment to see that his work should serve as a global portal for human relations. In a world fraught with miscommunication and misunderstanding that fan the flames of racism, class bias, and xenophobia, Ambassador Rogovin boldly crosses boundaries, both domestic and international. He fosters new dialogues and opportunities for engagement. We may not be able to travel physically to the many places he visited, but by bringing us, even briefly, to these places and into this "conversation" with his sitters, his photographs allow us to see each other in new ways and grant us the opportunity to form new opinions about our fellow man and woman. As Jimmy Webster, one of the miners he photographed, commented, "Whenever you look at his photographs, you just see people for who they are. And we're all people: rich, poor, black, white. That's what you can learn from it."[6]

Notes

1. See the documentary *The Rich Have Their Own Photographers*, directed by Ezra Bookstein (Muse Films & Television, 2007), and Eileen Reardon, "'The Rich Have Their Own Photographers, I Photograph the Poor, the Forgotten Ones': Milton Rogovin," *People's World*, February 10, 2006.

2. Mark Rogovin, interviewed in "Live from the Heartland Radio Show," WLUV, Chicago, June 4, 2011, YouTube video at https://www.youtube.com/watch?v=Tgyc_owg9pA, accessed September 3, 2014.

3. W. E. B. Du Bois, commentary on Milton Rogovin, *Store-Front Churches— Buffalo, Aperture* 10, no. 2 (1962), at http://www.miltonrogovin.com/education.html #resources.

4. "About Milton: Biography," Milton Rogovin: Social Documentary Photographer, n.d., at http://www.miltonrogovin.com/biography.html, accessed September 3, 2014.

5. The *Family of Miners* series represents women miners only in the United States because women very rarely held mining jobs in other countries during this period. See the *Family of Miners* series at Milton Rogovin: Social Documentary Photographer, http://www.miltonrogovin.com/photoseries/familyminers.html, accessed September 3, 2014.

6. Quoted in Nate Burgos, "Underground and Unforgotten: Milton Rogovin's Mining Photographs," *MetalMiner*, January 28, 2011, at http://agmetalminer.com/2011/01/28/underground-and-unforgotten-milton-rogovins-mining-photographs/.

Acknowledgments

THE CONTRIBUTORS TO THIS BOOK wish to thank those who helped bring the Rogovin photographs to Louisville and those who made possible this celebratory volume. Our special gratitude is extended to David Knaus, who arranged the Rogovin gift by soliciting donations from several collectors, and to Mark Rogovin, who encouraged the gift, contributed additional material to the Photographic Archives, and provided support for our research. We are, of course, immensely grateful to the donors and their generosity to our university: Mr. and Mrs. William Braunstein, Dr. Philip Grider, Dr. John and Laura Knaus, Mr. and Mrs. Steve Spile, and Jon and Ellen Vein. Working with David Knaus in facilitating the donations were Tiffany Phelan and Amanda Doenitz, whom we also thank. From the University of Louisville, Denise Nuehring, director of Major Gifts, University Libraries, and Amy Purcell, associate registrar, University Archives, also assisted with the gift. Instrumental in the mounting of the inaugural exhibition of the gifted photographs in the autumn of 2015 were Ying Kit Chan, former chair of the Department of Fine Arts and director of the Hite Art Institute; Chris Reitz, gallery director of the Hite Art Institute; Peter Morrin, former director of the Center for Arts and Cultural Partnerships; and John Hale, director of the Liberal Studies Program. Support was also received from the Anne Braden Institute for Social Justice Research and the Program of Jewish Studies. We would further like to acknowledge the special contributions of photo historian Steve Plattner and Michael Frisch, professor emeritus of the University at Buffalo, who wrote the preface to this book. For aiding our research, we thank Gabriela Zoller of the Albright-Knox Gallery, Buffalo, and the friendly staff of the Library of Congress, Washington, D.C.

This publication would not have been possible without the capable direction of Ashley Runyon, formerly of the University Press of Kentucky, and Patrick O'Dowd, the acquisitions editor at the press who brought the book to completion.

List of Contributors

Thomas B. Byers is professor emeritus in the Department of English at the University of Louisville. Professor Byers publishes on contemporary American literature and film, particularly on postmodernism in theory and practice. Until his recent retirement, he served as director of the Commonwealth Center for the Humanities and Society.

Joy Gleason Carew is professor in the Department of Pan-African Studies at the University of Louisville. Professor Carew works on issues of diversity and African American intellectual history. She is the author of *Blacks, Reds, and Russians: Sojourners in Search of the Soviet Promise* (2008).

Karen Christopher is associate professor in the Department of Sociology at the University of Louisville. Professor Christopher's research explores the intersections of gender, race, and class in the family, labor market, and welfare state. Her recent projects focus on North American mothers and their negotiation of paid and unpaid work.

Catherine Fosl is professor of Women's, Gender, and Sexuality Studies at the University of Louisville, where she also directs the Anne Braden Institute for Social Justice Research. A historian by training, she is the author of three books, including the award-winning *Subversive Southerner: Anne Braden and the Struggle for Racial Justice in the Cold War South* (University Press of Kentucky, revised ed. 2006).

Peter S. Fosl is professor of Philosophy and founding director of the Philosophy, Politics, and Economics Program at Transylvania University. He is the author of numerous books and essays on topics ranging from the history of philosophy to military suicide. As the 2013–14 David Hume Fellow at the Institute for Advanced Studies in the Humanities at the University of Edinburgh, he began a major work on Hume's skepticism (University of Edinburgh Press, forthcoming). www.PeterFosl.com.

Michael Frisch is professor of history and American studies and Senior Research Scholar, emeritus at the University at Buffalo, SUNY. He is an American social and urban historian involved for many years in oral and public history projects, often in collaboration with community history organizations, museums, and documentary filmmakers. He is the author of *A Shared Authority: Essays on the Craft and Meaning of Oral and Public History* (1990) and the prizewinning *Portraits in Steel* (1993), in collaboration with Milton Rogovin. He has served as editor of the *Oral History Review* (1986–96), as President of the American Studies Association (2000–2001), and as President of the Oral History Association (2009–10).

Christopher Fulton is associate professor in the Department of Fine Arts at the University of Louisville. Professor Fulton works in the social history of art and the art of political engagement. He is author of *An Earthly Paradise: The Medici, Their Art, and the Foundations of Modern Art* (2006). He has more recently investigated Mexican art, with articles on modern and contemporary practice and concerning the work of muralist David Alfaro Siqueiros.

Tracy E. K'Meyer is professor of History at the University of Louisville. Her work focuses on modern US social movements and the role of progressive faith-based activism. She was previously public history director at New Mexico State University. She is the author of *Civil Rights in the Gateway to the South: Louisville, Kentucky, 1945–80* (University Press of Kentucky, 2009), *Freedom on the Border: An Oral History of the Civil Rights Movement in Kentucky* (coauthored by Catherine Fosl; University Press of Kentucky, 2009), and

From Brown to Meredith: The Long Struggle for School Desegregation in Louisville, Kentucky, 1954–2007 (2013). Her most recent work is a study of the American Friends Service Committee's housing activism.

Cynthia Negrey is professor in the Sociology Department and is affiliated with the doctoral program in urban and public affairs at the University of Louisville. Her areas of specialization are political economy, urban labor markets, and gender. She is author of *Work Time: Conflict, Control, and Change* and coauthor of *Working First but Working Poor: The Need for Education and Training Following Welfare Reform* (2001).

Elizabeth E. Reilly is curator of and associate professor in the Photographic Archives of the University of Louisville. Professor Reilly curates exhibitions drawn principally from the collection. She is also an archivist for the Louisville Underground Music Archive. She publishes on the history of photography and on the management of archival resources.

Index

Index

www.ingramcontent.com/pod-product-compliance
Lightning Source LLC
Chambersburg PA
CBHW070420290526
45791CB00005B/1767